# Discover True Faith

# Discover True Faith

## Faith Concepts, First Principles, Blessings & Curses, Practical

## Dr. Adolf Jonker Ph.D

Order this book online at www.trafford.com
or email orders@trafford.com

Most Trafford titles are also available at major online book retailers.

Printed in the United States of America.

ISBN: 978-1-4907-0730-3 (sc)
ISBN: 978-1-4907-0729-7 (hc)
ISBN: 978-1-4907-0731-0 (e)

Library of Congress Control Number: 2013912180

*Trafford rev. 08/03/2013*

 www.trafford.com

**North America & international**
toll-free: 1 888 232 4444 (USA & Canada)
fax: 812 355 4082

# dedication

I dedicate this book, with every fibre of my being, to God the Father, Son and Holy Spirit. "Most High God **(YHWH)**; as a mere mortal, I do not know how to thank You. Thank you sounds so extremely insufficient! My gratitude extends all borders of my linguistic abilities. May my spirit convey the humanly impossible as I say: 'Now unto the King eternal, immortal, invisible, the only wise God, be honour and glory for ever and ever.' Amen" (1 TIMOTHY 1:17 KJV)

# acknowledgements

Thank you Lord for all our predecessors, scholars, those who committed and dedicated themselves in putting together dictionaries, commentaries, concordances and all the different Bible translations. This makes our own study of the Bible and who You are so much more beneficial, way easier attainable, and all are to advance us in our walk with You.

**THE STAFF AT TRAFFORD** and all those who have been involved; thank you for your commitment, and your truly professional approach and execution!

**ALL MY OPPOSERS AND ADVERSARIES** your persecution and rejection truly drove me into the embrace of God. Indeed, you were instrumental in my spiritual growth, and what was intended for my downfall, launched me into building a strong faith in God, and let me to embrace a lifestyle of thinking, acting, walking and living by faith. May God truly bless you within the borders of His perfect will.

**TO EVERY PERSON** during my lifetime, for whatever contribution you have made, especially prayer, I sincerely thank you.

**TO THE EDITING TEAM** Jean, Jose, Karin, Sibongile and Serelda. Without your competency, skill, efficacy but mainly your willingness to be serving with endurance as unto God, it would have been impossible for me to complete this book. You are so blessed!

**ALL THE PEOPLE OF RIVER OF LIFE CHURCH, KROONSTAD** partners of God's vision: "You are simply the best. God's hand of favour rests heavily on you!"

**TO ALL THE AUTHORS OUT THERE**: We may be paying a few dollars for the books you release but most people have no idea as to the amount of work, time and energy that went into it, the mixture of frustration and joy, the loneliness, your perseverance and motivation to complete that which have been started. Thank you so much. We appreciate you and may God bless you to continue your good work.

# table of contents

# preface

Jacob wrestled with God. His name meant fraud, indicative of a future of failure, lies, and mishaps. He was quite aware of his fraudulent identity. His wrestling was indicative of his inner turmoil, drive and motivation to reach out to God and alter a cursed life to usher in the true identity of God. In his wrestling with God, as a human being, he didn't want to let go of the transcendent God. He wanted God to change his identity and to primarily bless him. The content of this book puts your name in the place of Jacob's, and will lead you to wrestle with God in positioning you into the true identity of God. Once you finish the last page of the book you will be able to say that you have struggled with God as to not leave you until He has blessed you.

The book is not about the author trying to convey spiritual knowledge. The purpose behind the book is for the reader to gain insight understanding and knowledge in discovering true faith to think, act, live and walk by faith. Inescapably your life will be revolutionized and transformed and will give you a new perspective in God, about God and His Word. The core of the content is to reverse the event of the Garden of Eden and to boldly and unashamedly accept and believe in God and His Word. You will inescapably become an agent of God expressing and exhibiting His glory, which will radiate to people, but will also be as an offering of worship to Him. The concept of you honouring God excites me!

In the coming pages, I will not flood you with scriptural references but just lay an adequate foundation to support my line of teaching. There are sufficient study material; concordances, dictionaries, commentaries and other Bible translations that the reader can refer to in further studying the concept of faith. This book is divided into four parts; concepts, principles, rules and practical. The books order is Faith, First Principles and Blessings and Curses and ending with a fourth part which is the Practical. However, the correct biblical order should be: first principles, faith concepts, and rules relating to blessings and curses and lastly the practical application of the above. The specific order in which I set it out is to introduce you to faith and then to let you know, by enlarge and throughout history, the church was negligent and ignorant regarding the first principles. There is one order that has a guarantee of success, even before you apply it: it is the order of God. Anything contrary guarantees us of repetitive 'dark ages' in the existence of the church. Simply said: our ways are turning things upside down. I have also added, here and there, testimonies of what happened in my own life. My purpose for doing this is to let the reader know that outside of Moses and David and all other biblical figures, God still today, in a 21$^{st}$ century rational, pre-modernistic society, performs miracles. It is to encourage the reader that if He has done it for me, He will certainly do it for you.

The writing contains some controversial issues that became institutional constants, but are merely human inventions, culturally and traditionally embraced in the church. These incorrect interpretations, erroneous teachings and false doctrines are addressed not with the purpose to attack or judge anybody, but to address and reveal the truth. The book is therefore not written to oppose anyone or to be in competition, or to debate specific issues, but its purpose is to state biblical truth in a concise, fresh and new perspective.

The inclusion of First Principles and Blessings and Curses were inevitable and were done unapologetically. Revelation 22:3 KJV says: "And there shall be no more curse . . ." The interpretation is self explanatory. John elucidates the scenario surrounding the End Time church, thus biblically promoting that the curse will be till the end; the end spelling out the 'Parousia' (Second coming of Jesus). Simplistically said, that till the end, the church will face and have to deal with the curse. The curse is in direct opposition to the blessing. It is an either or situation. God's intention for us to live in His image points directly to the fact that every part of His existence is blessed beyond human comprehension! Restoring the image in us, as born-again children of God, falls nothing short from being blessed holistically.

I am entirely convicted that God is currently positioning the church to regain true identity; to rediscover biblical truths crossing the line from the natural into the spirit with a day to day interaction between the natural and the supernatural. Humanly speaking; to live the supernatural life of God in the physical realm as natural, thus, erasing the divide between the over-emphasized natural and the ignored spirit. This means raising up of a generation, a new breed, of the five wise virgins who are more interested in what is on the inside of the lamp (the anointing of God) than the outward appearance of the lamp (aesthetic approach), moving from an aesthetic approach to inner quality, which is the divine deposit of Holy Spirit within the believer. The believer's dependence turns back from relying on a natural ability to God our helper. It is a lifestyle singing a new song: I lift up my eyes, where shall my help come from? My help comes from my maker! (PSALM 121 KJV) The focus is not only on one individual of the Trinity, but understanding the unity, economy and protocol of God the Father, God the Son and God the Holy Spirit: all three equally God.

I am certainly excited about you as reader and will strongly advise you to read this book more than once. The information put before you is not something that you can grasp overnight. I have included a glossary at the end on pg. 275 to assist those who do not have English as their first language.

As you read this book, I urge you to lay aside all your preconceived ideas and allow Holy Spirit to walk you through and be by your side in this journey. Bible translators had their own prescribed strategies and agendas in achieving their goals and objectives. However, much of what has been translated is not always completely reflective of the true meaning of the Greek and Hebrew words. One of such cases points to the interpretation of 'Khristos' (Greek) 'Mashiach' (Hebrew). There was no English word available for these two words and instead of interpreting the actual meaning of the word; translators took it upon themselves to anglicize it to the word 'Christ'. Here and there, in the Bible, the word is correctly interpreted as the Anointed One with His anointing. (PSALM 2:2 AMP) During my writing, I felt lead by God and preferred to use only the correct translation to create awareness of who He really is. In chapter one I have used both words: Christ and the Anointed One, to help the readers familiarize themselves with the true meaning of the concept. In the rest of the chapters I preferred to use the Anointed One, in the place of Christ. Albeit, when quoting scriptures, I have not altered what was written in the specific translation and stuck to Christ.

The journey in discovering true faith will become much more efficacious if you pray the prayer in Ephesians 1:17 NIV which is that God will truly by Holy Spirit enlighten your heart and transform you.

> **Ephesians 1:17-19 NIV** *"I keep asking that the God of our Lord Jesus Christ, the glorious Father, may give you the Spirit of wisdom and revelation, so that you may know him better. (18) I pray also that the eyes of your heart may be enlightened in order that you may know the hope to which he has called you, the riches of his glorious inheritance in the saints (19) and his incomparably great power for us who believe.*

**Concept 1** INDISPENSIBLE

**KEY SCRIPTURE:** **Romans 1:17**(KJV), "*. . . The just shall live by faith.*"

**KEYWORDS:**

    *Assumptions*
    *Transformational*
    *Fundamental*

**KEY CONCEPT:** Contact with God equates faith as primary entity.

# WHAT FAITH IS – the journey

When first reading the title 'What faith is'; the common perception is to mentally interpret it as a question. However, that is quite the opposite. When one asks 'what is faith?' it is a question that can be answered a multitude of ways. The question is now reversed to a statement "What faith is". This pronounces that in reading this book, you will journey with God and not only discover but have true godly revelation of "What faith is."

Scriptures, keywords and specific concepts will be the framework and road markers on this journey. Why do we speak about journey? Isn't it interesting that during a journey you travel from one place to another? We have all been on vacation. Some families prefer to go to a specific place every year, or every so often. They know the exact road they will be travelling and GPS brought a lot of ease to our lives. However, although you may have a mental picture of where you are going, you will have new impressions every time you travel that road. There will always be something different; something new that will draw your attention. Isn't this true, especially when you travel through nature? Doesn't matter how many times you've seen it, you will get to appreciate it as if it is the first time. The waves of the sea are another excellent example. The beauty of the rolling waves can fascinate one for hours. They may all appear similar but have the ability to capture one's attention in such a way that you appreciate every rolling wave as if you have seen it for the first time.

This journey on what faith is can be likened to the above examples. Every single individual will then have an understanding of, and answer to what faith is. Why then write about it? Is there more to faith? More to the understanding of what faith is? I am convicted.

This book will not present you with a religious be all and end all of faith. It is and never will be the author's intention. The purpose is to have you embark on discovering, that although what we have and

Dr. Adolf Jonker Ph.D

believe is true, biblical and solid, there is not only more to faith, but also an almost inexplicable desire from God to have His people live in true faith. Yes, He did say that only faith pleases Him, but that is not the only reason He wants us to walk in its fullness. He wants us to have the joy of a fully satisfied supernatural life in Him; the best of the best! This is the exact reason why this book's title focuses on discovering true faith.

## THE CHALLENGE: TO ASSUME OR NOT

This made me think of my grandson, Jadon, who recently turned one. He visited us and during his stay he became sick with a bad bout of flu. I had to take him to see a physiotherapist. Melissa, our eldest daughter, phoned the physiotherapist, gave all the details and made the arrangements for us to take him. However, the morning of his appointment my wife couldn't accompany me. We arranged with a lady from church to look after Jadon when my wife wasn't available. That morning this lady, Sibongile, accompanied me to the physiotherapist at the local hospital. It snowed for the first time in many years in Kroonstad, and because of the freezing cold Jadon needed to be wrapped in a couple of blankets and kept warm.

The time of the appointment came and I took him in. The friendly physiotherapist started working on his tight chest and every now and then handed him to me when she wanted to do something different. What struck me was what she said every time: "There Papa, hold your child." I thought "Well let's leave it at that for now. I wasn't in the mood to have a long explanatory discussion about it'. I knew my eldest daughter had made arrangements about the payment, and at the end of the session I asked her about such as I wanted to settle the account. Her response was another surprise, because she informed me that my wife had phoned and already taken care of such arrangements. I realised then that the understanding of this lady was that my eldest daughter was my wife, and my grandchild my son! The truth is that Melissa is my eldest daughter and Jadon the firstborn grandchild.

Why am I sharing this incident with you? The fact of the matter is that wherever this lady goes, and even when she sees me again, she will think of me as the husband of Melissa and the father of Jadon. She simply made the assumptions based on the facts she had available. However, it doesn't matter how convicted she was, her assumptions were untrue and false. The purpose of me making this point is to lead you, later in the book, to challenge your own convictions and assumptions.

Then I realised what could have happened! If the lady who looked after Jadon, went in with the two of us, and mentioned to the physiotherapist that we had phoned the previous day, the physiotherapist would have assumed that the lady accompanying me was the mother. She would have been in for a major surprise, because she could not initially see Jadon, wrapped in a lot of blankets, because of the cold weather and flu. Upon opening the blankets she would have thought, 'Well this baby surely has a very light skin, especially taking into consideration the huge colour difference between mother and father!'

Isn't the above experience a clear example of what we do in life? We see situations, gather so-called facts with what we hear and see, and then make assumptions based on it. Isn't it true that we all have things we believe in life, based on what we have been presented with, which are assumptions? Do the ill-informative facts mean an assumption is correct? No, not by far! Yet, how many times do we believe something as if it is true, when it is not?

Ever since childhood I always knew that eating the marrow, especially of pork was forbidden. Why? My grandmother completely assured us that if we were to eat the marrow, it would surely cause madness and we would become crazy and mentally unstable. Then, years and years of believing this I met with a friend who is a medical doctor. I do not remember how we came to this subject, but we discussed the theory of not eating the marrow. He explained to me that they scientifically tested the marrow at a well-known university and that the specific marrow theory was hogwash and had no truth to it whatsoever! However, that was what we were been taught, believed and lived by all the years. It just so happened that I was presented with a piece of pork the very next day. I looked at the marrow and said to myself: "It was a hogwash story . . . just open your mouth and eat it!" Did I? No, I just could not get myself to do it. I had this inner battle with 'Well, maybe they made a mistake'. The mental stronghold of what was in actual fact completely untrue stopped me from having what I could have enjoyed.

I've challenged the people in our congregation once by asking them what they would think and do if they saw me walking into a Liquor Store early in the morning. We had interesting responses. However, I want to share this one. What if some of them react with fright and think: "No way! He has started drinking! Why else would he be going to the liquor store this early?" Then they might even contact some intercessors to please pray for me, because seeing me walking into a Liquor Store surely suggested the fact that I was an alcoholic? The liquor store is around the corner from our gym. What if I ran out of water and I was just so desperately thirsty? This happens many times after training. What if I only needed a bottle of water? The liquor store is the closest and one of few shops open at that time of morning. Wouldn't that be the quickest way to get water?

Allow me to share another true life example. We have a single, handsome and sold-out to God young man in church. One morning, a young lady accompanied him to the Sunday worship service. Everybody took note because he had received a prophetic word on marriage a couple of weeks back and now everybody was excited for him because now he had a girlfriend. But then, two Sundays later, another young lady accompanied him. Do I need to say he had all eyes on him? Was she now the new girlfriend? However, then it only got real interesting because the following Sunday both accompanied him, together with a new one. What was the assumption now? Did he want to follow in the footsteps of King Solomon and have many wives? No, he didn't! Truth is he owns a lion farm and the young ladies accompanying him were volunteers from other countries. They volunteer to work with the lions, but in the process he brought them to church to also receive ministry. The young man's motive for inviting them to the worship celebrations was to give them an opportunity to be in the presence of the Lord and experience His love and grace, which is life-changing.

Kroonstad, in the broader sense, can be described as a typical small town where many people still have racist mindsets and lifestyles. It cuts both ways. I live on a smallholding outside town and have to fetch the people working for me in town. It happened on several occasions that I needed our church secretary to help me in my office at home. Wherever we drove and stopped in town, people looked wide-eyed and surely made assumptions. Although it is wiped under the town carpet, prostitution is active and there are affluent men who make use of the services of young black ladies. Does driving with this lady indicate the above? Never! Yet, that is sure enough the cause of the wide-eyed response. The saddest truth is that we make assumptions in life; then put all of our energy into believing them and thereby making them 'our truths'. The question I pose is this: How many of our 'truths' are really truth and true?

## ARE OUR TRUTHS REALLY TRUE?

We will start from scratch, giving a thorough teaching on what the Bible says faith is. In general assumptions are also part and parcel of what we believe faith is. For this reason it is of utmost importance for us to come to the place of understanding that not all assumptions are truth. Many of our understandings are also not truth but mere assumptions based on what is presented. What then will be the starting point in this journey? We can and will never learn or change unless we are willing to completely surrender, not in fact, but in act,

Dr. Adolf Jonker Ph.D

to Holy Spirit. I encourage you to take a bold step and pray about it first and foremost saying: "God, I submit to You whatever I believed about faith before, whether it had little or a whole lot of assumptions. I want to let go of anything that is not 100% truth, and for Holy Spirit to help me to move away from assumption to truth regarding faith."

Assumptions can best be described as a system of beliefs which we embrace as truth and then build our understanding as well as lifestyle on them as a foundation. This is not only limited to situations we perceive wrongly but can very well be doctrinal errors or improper knowledge of the Bible, and we can then be influenced with what we are taught from childhood. My earliest understanding of church was that it was a time of torture and receiving hidings afterwards for not sitting still! My Dad ensured that we were there an hour before the starting time of the service. Can you imagine the temptations a young lad like myself suffered? I was not allowed to move at all, and as one can expect, as a young boy I fell asleep even before church started! Whenever I opened my eyes after a nap and saw my Dad's look, I knew what was waiting at home: a big hiding for embarrassing my parents and disrespecting the house of the Lord. This happened week in and week out. What understanding did I form about church? Going to church simply and clearly spelt punishment. The other perception was that God Himself was a 'punisher', taking note of each and every thing I did and always ready to chastise and punish me. That is a lot of guilt on a child! Can you see the power this assumption had on my life and how it influenced me into believing something that was far from truth? However, how sad that many of us experience this in one form or another and the most hurtful is that we do not change our perception about God when we grow out of childhood. We will not be magically able to now see God as loving, caring, forgiving (which is totally who He is!). God by Holy Spirit needs to help us to change erroneous assumptions that became truths!

Let me bring it back to faith. Without revelation knowledge from Holy Spirit about faith, we are likely to live by assumptions. We need

God's intervention in removing assumptions from us and revealing to us truth about faith. We need God to come and transform us: our ideas, doctrines, belief systems and perceptions so that we can arrange our lives accordingly. I can elaborate on many situations that I've shared with people in our congregation, but at this moment it is you reading this book. Hear my heart when I ask you to take a moment, even if it is just one, and let Holy Spirit minister to you about assumptions you might have. You see it is not about the initial intent of what caused the outcome, but the outcome: where and how it affects your life and steals true life and joy from you. My Dad's intention was not to punish me; he wanted to teach me to respect God and obey the Word of God. However, the assumptions I formed caused me to run from God instead of to God.

## CONDUCT BASED ON ASSUMPTIONS

Do we ever really think about the impact assumptions have in life? People have assumptions and base their conduct according to their assumptions. Isn't this what we do with the Word of God and more so God Himself? We have our ideas of how to serve the Lord, how to have a relationship with Him and worship Him. Then we come into situations where people's ideas and perceptions differ from our own and we immediately feel resistant because their way is wrong. This occurrence in the Church has caused much strife, and mostly, in the end, led to ungodly actions and reactions. One subject that often causes problems is the debate on how we should or should not worship God in song and dance. We have an elderly lady in church, of British descent, who will often feel the worship is too loud and the dance too wild. She doesn't have a problem per se but always articulates how that is not the way she feels comfortable. I've asked her once what she would have done in the time of Nehemiah. The Bible makes it clear that some were weeping, some were laughing, and it was such a commotion that one could not even hear oneself think. What would have been her comment about them? Maybe she would have felt that they are not people of God and that they are way too noisy? Why would she react this way? This is exactly the way she grew up; the perceptions she had formed from a very young age, and the assumptions she made even regarding her own life, of what she could and couldn't do. Isn't it obvious that she missed out on change because of the influence of the assumptions she had and maybe also on blessings God wanted to share with her? Now the question I pose is this: "Do we operate any differently with faith?"

I want to single out two very important scriptures that speak about faith. The first one is **Hebrews 11:1** and the other **Hebrews 11:6.** When faith comes to play you cannot exclude these two scriptures because it is vital to your life, and without understanding and living it, you will experience misery. Let us look at what these scriptures say: *". . . But without faith it is impossible to please him: for he that cometh to God must believe that he is, and that he is a rewarder of them that diligently seek him."* (HEBREWS 11:6 KJV) *"Now faith is being sure of what we hope for and certain of what we do not see."* (HEBREWS 11:1 NIV) The correct translation should read that 'faith is the substance of things that we hope for, and the evidence of the things we do not see.' The concept of being certain of what we do not see is surely different from it being the evidence, which in itself is a strong word. When you have evidence you cannot be proven wrong. Being certain? Well, something or someone might influence you to have doubts or even think differently.

Habakkuk 2:4; Galatians 3:11 and Romans 1:17 KJV, clearly indicate who faith is applicable to: the just. All three speak in one accord that the just shall live by faith. Therefore, friends, we can compare faith to oxygen. Without oxygen there would be no life on earth. Faith is as important! We need it as a living necessity. It is of paramount importance and is not a point of discussion of whatever nature, however religious it may sound or not. At best, faith has been abused, or neglected and ignored. The importance is evident! John 8:24 NIV tells us about the devastating effect and consequences a lack of faith has. *"I told you that you would die in your sins; if you do not believe that I am the one I claim to be, you will indeed die in your sins."* Let us meditate on this point. Imagine you are walking along a beach, enjoying yourself and the surroundings. Then out of the blue a man walks up to you and tells you to "drop whatever you are doing because I am the Son of God." Can you even remotely think what will go through your mind? You will think 'but who is this person to tell me to let go of all I was doing and follow Him and then He proceeds to tell you that if you do not believe that He is who He claims to be, you will die in your sins. Hasn't the church realm, at large, made an intellectual academic concept of the Bible and removed it from the nitty-gritty of our everyday lives and the things we experience? Isn't that why. the Bible does not say or mean too much to too many people? Isn't this the outcome of the Word of God being separated from our lives? At times we in the church want to make out of the Bible a 'school-business'. The reason why we are to teach people is so that they can apply it to their lives. If you minister (in whatever depth or area) but you do not apply the Word of God to your life, it will mean nothing to you in ministering or the person or people to whom you are ministering.

> **Revelations 21:8 NIV** *"But the cowardly, the unbelieving, the vile, the murderers, the sexually immoral, those who practice magic arts, the idolaters and all liars—their place will be in the fiery lake of burning sulfur. This is the second death."*

It indicates that the absence of faith can cause a person to end in hell. Hebrews 4:2 says that unless you mix faith with your hearing of the Word, it doesn't profit you. So, if you do not apply faith in your life you will not profit in whatever you do. Apply faith in every single thing you do. The following is not an uncommon phrase heard in church: "We pray for you; it is the only thing we can do; it's the only thing left to do." Doesn't this look as though we, as children of God, placed prayer and prayer in faith, in the backroom of our storehouses? It almost creates the idea then that when we have depleted other resources we will pray as a last resort. Prayer should never be the last resort. Instead it should be the starting block from which we depart. The moment people are thrown into a crisis, they resort to prayer. Shouldn't we also pray before the crisis and exert faith? Prayer without faith is a rhetoric circus with no life-effect!

I am passionate about God above every other thing in my entire life. I am as passionate about prayer and walking in a living faith relationship with God. Added to these, I just simply love sport because I've been trained, and trained most of my life. I also participated in many championships as a sprinter. With that said, it is quite normal for me to have a great interest in sport and specifically the Olympics. I enjoyed watching the 2012 Olympic Games but there was one incident that made a huge impact on me. As I watched the high jump, I was drawn to a specific American lady, Brigetta Barret, and without knowing her; I could discern in the spirit that she was a born-again child of God. Later as I read her Twitter profile status: 'To God be all the GLORY!' it confirmed my first impression. She was placed second, but what seemed unnatural was that there were other athletes that showed stronger skill and potential than she did. However, she jumped higher than the others. After she conquered the highest height she walked back with the television cameras fixed on her. When she sat down and the cameras zoomed in on her, one could see her lips moving. It was evident to me that she wasn't speaking in a natural language, but that she prayed in tongues. It hit me! This woman relies 100% on God and she is mixing her faith with what she attempts to achieve with the high jump. She asked God to enable her, and focused on Him and not only on her own abilities. The moment she slid over the high bar the announcer's words were that this lady had jumped higher than what she was in fact able to do, which was a fact. Yet, the truth was that she completely trusted God to enable her, and executed faith in every jump.

In this incident faith was not a mere mental concept but a true life example of the efficacy and ability it gives when we include it in whatever we do as a central part of operation. This athlete is a pure example of someone living in faith and mixing it with her daily activities. Faith should be part of every facet of our lives and every single minute in whatever we do. We should not only extend our faith towards God when we're in need, but do so regardless. Extending faith should be part of our lifestyle! What was the purpose of extensively elaborating on the importance of assumptions and the role it plays in our lives? We now have a foundation from where we can move on to exploring and understanding that we cannot live without faith and the revelation thereof. Its importance in actuality exceeds human comprehension.

## FAITH INDISPENSIBLE

The Biblical clarification on the importance of faith is evident! Without faith we will not please God. That is what the Bible clearly states and I believe this scripture is of incredible importance. However, the true meaning of pleasing God with faith has been thwarted with human perceptions. Many people in the church think that if they live good lives, they are pleasing God. The understanding of 'good lives' usually centres on 'not looking lustfully at either men or women', and because of this, we abstain from sin in this regard. God will always be delighted when we abstain from sin, but to please God with faith is not to have a list of religious do's and don'ts that we can tick off. Abstaining from sin is part and parcel of our character building.

Think about this illustration of a 40 day fast. It is saddening, at times, that children of God can think that when they've done a 40 day fast, they are included in an elite group who are truly committed to God, pouring out their very lives in surrender and suffering for God. Does fasting 40 days make you part of an elite group? God's perspective on this is that we should not boast about it or let our left hand know what the right hand is doing. God tells His people not to pronounce it on the street corners because it is not pleasing to Him. Fasting is to benefit you in your walk with God. There are many other examples. Going to church is also a well-known 'God-pleasing activity'. People in general think that if they attend church regularly they are pleasing

Dr. Adolf Jonker Ph.D

God. I was one of those people, at one point in my life. This was before I was truly born-again. I did not miss out on any meeting at church. I went every Sunday morning and evening, to Wednesday prayer meeting, Friday youth meeting, Saturday young adults meeting, and any other special meeting. If they had a meeting they could count on my attendance and I did all of this because I thought that it was pleasing to God. Wrong assumption! I thought I was a true Christian whereas in fact I was a good church-goer. Then we should also understand that we have no leeway to now drop attending church and the meetings. Changing to the opposite behaviour will also not please God and no, you will not feel better. I've tested that too. Whatever meeting we attend, we should do because we love God and not because we seek approval and have a multitude of other assumptions about it.

Pre-eminence of faith and its superiority is very clear in the Bible. I understand that many will come and question this with 1 Corinthians 13 which says that of all of these love is the greatest. My question is this: does the Bible say that you will be saved by love? You can have as much love as you want, but you will still end in hell if you do not have faith. In saying this, I am in no way belittling love but am just pointing to the clear indication of the superiority of faith in its function, in the Bible. God uses a very strong Greek word 'adonatos', (G102, STRONGS) which means impossible. He says it is impossible to please God without faith. 'No faith' leads to 'no pleasing God'. According to the Word of God we are incapable of pleasing God without faith and a sure way to touch God is by FAITH.

Many years ago I attended a Friday night signs, wonders and miracles meeting of a mighty preacher, and one for whom I had a great deal of respect, and still do. I looked up to this guy in a major way and was extremely encouraged and motivated by what was happening in and through his ministry. I will never forget that night because it was the very first time that I saw children of different ages, 7, 8 and 10 years of age, who were born dumb and deaf and never spoke a single word . . . that was until that night when God healed them. Before that night they could not hear or speak and I clearly remember the first words of one young lad: "Where is my Mommy?" She wasn't on stage with him but it took her seconds to get there. Deaf ears were opened and people who had never heard one word in their entire lives were now able to even hear a whisper. It was so powerful! There was such an incredible anointing, and we saw miracle after miracle taking place. This was the very first time in my entire life that I saw miracles happening the way they did that night and I was simply overwhelmed. I am not talking about one, two or even 5 miracles . . . but certainly above 50. That night, at the end of the meeting, the preacher announced that he would be leaving for a conference at a coastal city, which was more or less a 9-hour drive. On Sunday morning I attended the regular church meeting and on my way to church discovered that this preacher was on the front page of one of the leading Sunday newspapers in the nation. The shocking news was that they weren't reporting on the miracles or the conference but that he was found staying over in a hotel with a woman who was not his wife. This sent shockwaves through my being and had the same effect on many people who truly loved and supported him. He eventually divorced and married the other woman. Many years later he confessed his sins and repented. Two weeks after his repentance he died in a vehicle accident.

Why am I sharing this story with you? After the big revelation of the love affair I pondered on it, but also on that Friday evening and all the major miracles, not forgetting the incredible power, presence of the Lord and anointing that were undeniable. The fact of the matter is this, that he had already made all the arrangements with that lady before the Friday evening that he left because they were caught the very next morning.

How is it then possible that we experienced what we did? And all the amazing miracles? How is it possible that all those miracles manifested, because according to human perception it should not have happened. The problem in our understanding lies in the fact that we look up to the ministers of God's Word and think signs, wonders

Dr. Adolf Jonker Ph.D

and miracles manifest because of their spirituality and high standard of living. It does not. It is by faith. Does it mean we condone sin? Certainly not! We also clarify sin not only as 'sexual immorality' but lying, stealing God's tithe, not offering, racism, prejudice . . . the list is endless. You understand what I am saying? When we apply faith God takes note and He draws it toward Him. He accepts all kinds of faith: small faith, little faith, almost no faith, and draws it toward Himself and we can touch God. We can never touch God without faith. NEVER! It doesn't matter what you do, how you conduct yourself, your life, your relationships and family and your business; you will only touch God one way and that way is by faith. There is no escape route and no Plan B as a last resort.

## PLEASING UNTO GOD ONLY

How do we understand the word 'pleasing'? Pleasing God is completely linked with faith and inseparable. The Greek word for the above is 'euaresteo' (STRONGS, G2100) which means to gratify entirely. The word 'entirely' struck me. You see, extending faith towards God gratifies Him entirely. We all have our hiccups and do wrong things from time to time. We allowed religion to speak to us in a negative way, saying that when we have sinned we have to stand back from God a meter or two. And if we dare sin more, we think we have separated ourselves from God eternally. This is far from the truth. What is true is that when you extend your faith to God an in God, no matter what circumstances you find yourself to be in, you entirely gratify Him. I'm reminded of a man who once attended our worship meetings. He was a chain smoker. This was an incredible burden to him. He cried his heart out, went for prayer week after week, but nonetheless he couldn't stop smoking. He eventually left the church because of his smoking habits. He reasoned that God could not forgive him because he was struggling to quit. His understanding was that he could only touch and please God by overcoming his problem.

What he refused to embrace was that he had already touched God the moment he reached out in faith, desperately praying: "God I cannot quit this habit on my own. Please help me." It did not mean that the next incident of smoking removed him from God because he was still in the process of trusting God. Let me just make this clear: I am not saying that we have a right to sin. Never! I am saying that the focus is the faith we have and its release in God is what is touching Him, and there will surely come a day where He will remove from us that which is hindering us in less than a split second.

God worked such a miracle for me many years ago. I worked as a farm manager and foul language and cursing were part and parcel of every conversation I had; cussing words left my mouth left, right and centre and anyone listening to me had to focus real hard to actually get what I was saying in between the curse words. This was an integral part of my life and the way I communicated. I knew no other way until the day I got saved. God entered my life and without me even thinking to pray about it, every curse word and all foul language left me immediately: the cul-de-sac of foul language in my life! However, with aggression it worked differently. It took me more than eighteen years to have victory over my own aggression and the lifestyle of having to always defend myself in all situations. These situations are those where I still feel aggression occurs, but I can totally control it in God.

Why did God remove the swearing immediately and not the aggression also? Because He is God and He knows perfectly well who I am and for the last eighteen years He allowed me to continually seek His face in this regard. Recently I encountered a very challenging and unfair situation. If I had allowed it, my aggression would have boiled over. But I didn't. Instead I spoke to the Lord and told Him about my aggressive turmoil and that I was coming to Him and reaching out to Him in faith, trusting that He will in return reach out and touch me and anoint me with freedom. My going to God in this situation, completely acknowledging my crying out for Him, entirely gratifies Him. Paul had a similar problem and described it as 'some thorn in his flesh'. Nobody knows what it was, many speculated over the ages, but only Paul and God knew what he so desperately wanted God to remove from him, yet God did not do so. His simple reply to Paul was: "My grace is sufficient for thee." (2 CORINTHIANS 12:9 KJV) And then on another occasion he said that he knew what he had to do right, yet he still did wrong. (ROMANS 7:15 KJV)

Romans 8:1 clearly state that there is no condemnation for those who are in the Anointed One with His anointing (Christ). According to God, zero condemnation! I questioned myself whether I, and so many children of God, really understood the magnitude of this message. If we truly did why would we walk around with condemnation? How does condemnation get an inroad? Isn't it simply because we take it on ourselves that we disqualify ourselves? Do we not think at times that we do not meet the standards of God or the standards of the Bible, or the Church, or religious leaders and people? The evidence of this lies in how we operate as children of God. We would not want to pray when we have a smoking and drinking problem, or swear a lot (to mention only a few), because although we mentally grasp that there is no condemnation, we still follow the Old Testament path of 'saved by works', and think God will judge our prayers based on what we are involved in or even struggling with. I've experienced this sad habit throughout my time in ministry. Leaders who judge a specific individual because of the evident sin in their lives, send out the message that their sins separate them from God.

The truth is that no matter who we are, and what we are struggling with, when we reach out to God with a prayer of faith it pleases Him entirely. This does not mean freedom to sin as much as you like. It simply indicates that we have a new covenant in Jesus the Anointed One. It is a covenant of grace and not law, and we have freedom to approach His throne with boldness because we are in Him and therefore condemnation should not be part of our relationship with Him. What should be part is faith; faith extended to Him with the absolute decision and conviction that it pleases Him and He will surely work out all the small details of our lives because He already attained the complete perfection for that on the Cross. He said: "I,

God, did it all for you and it is finished!" (JOHN 19:30 KJV) When you sin, you look at the definition of what you have just done and the consequences you might experience. When God looks at your sin He only sees the blood of Jesus. I've also had to deal with this religious lie. Many times I would be on my knees desperately wanting to pray. Just to see the baggage of what I've done doing a salsa before me and then getting tripped into not praying. My focus is then misdirected towards the details of the sins I've committed and allowing them to hinder me from embracing God's viewpoint. When God looks at these sins, He truly only sees His Son, gruesomely hanging on that Cross, taking all the sins on Him so that I can say 'no' to sin and condemnation and also live without condemnation. He does this with all of our sins.

There is one thing God asks of us regarding sin. It is written in 1 John 1:8-10 ". . . if you confess . . ." He asks of us to acknowledge and confess. He does not say: "Now because you have committed this huge sin you have to take 3 days weeping, crying and fasting", or rituals like even going to the Pope, Priest, Minister, or Pastor to get absolution, in the hope to be forgiven. God does not require those things and certainly nothing from human inventions. Those are part of our manmade plans. He only says that we need to confess; telling Him that we acknowledge that we have sinned. Confessing to God will primarily be incredibly beneficial to you and when you do it in faith you are pleasing Him also. Just remember that I am not saying we should not go and pray with someone because we can and should when God leads us to do so. We see yet another perfect example in the real life experience of Achan in the book of Joshua. Achan sinned and was exposed. Joshua simply said to him: "Son, confess and tell us what you have done, don't hide anything and give God the glory. (JOSHUA 7:19 KJV) The confession of sin brings glory to God and never condemnation or the pointing of fingers of ignorant people. The key is in our hands to decide whether we are willing to lay down our pride and submit to God, or like Achan refuse the opportunity of God's grace.

1 Thessalonians 2:4 says that we should please God more than we please men. Sad but so true is that the modern day church mostly functions in more pleasing men and conducting most of what we do in church to satisfy and please people, and doctrinal religious concepts. Why would we try to please people more than we please God? Is it because we want them to stay in our congregation and not leave to go to another, and certainly not allow them to take their finances with? We need to reverse the order. God's requirement is that we please Him and He promises to look after the rest Himself. The reversed order of pleasing man instead of God will harm us and will certainly numb our faith in the process. However, when we please God, we do what He asks of us whether it is pleasing or very displeasing and uncomfortable to man. We please God knowing and trusting Him and His Word.

There are so many true life examples of this. Mahatma Ghandi was one leader who truly wanted to please man. Yet pleasing man is not a good-work-gateway to heaven. The same rings true for Nelson Mandela. He truly is a remarkable man with an incredible testimony. Both these men are acknowledged as true heroes in society, truly iconic, and history will applaud them with accolades of praise across all forms of media. The bare truth is this: if they have not confessed that Jesus is the Son of God and accepted Him as their only Lord and Saviour before they die, they will spend eternity in hell. Take note, pleasing man instead of God is a dangerous thing to do. It should always, in every situation, be: God first and man second. Faith in God is indispensible.

## LIFE TRANSFORMATIONAL

Faith is a life-transformational concept and a key to life. "I have been crucified with Christ [in Him I have shared His crucifixion]; it is no longer I who live, but Christ (the Messiah) lives in me; and the life I now live in the body I live by faith in (by adherence to and reliance on and complete trust in) the Son of God, Who loved me and gave Himself for me." (GALATIANS 2:20 AMP) This scripture says that you have been crucified with the Anointed One with His anointing (Christ). My first question is, when have you been crucified? Did anyone see you hanging on that cross? Isn't it true that you have no physical evidence? This leaves us with a problem; however, in asking how it happened, we will get the answer. We have been crucified with the Anointed One with His Anointing (Christ). When God the Father looked at the Cross and saw His Son paying the price, He saw us hanging with Him, also paying the price. The scripture continues to say that the life we live in our bodies, we live by faith in Him who was crucified and paid the price for us all. 2 Corinthians 5:15 together with Galatians 2:20 speak of living one life at first and then changing and living a different one. 2 Corinthians 5:15 indicates clearly that the life I live now is a new life. Thus, in other words there are diverse levels of different lives. Paul says he lived a specific life, but then lived another, thus talking about different kinds of life.

Holy Spirit being deposited to live in our hearts adds a divine nature to the individual's life. (ROMANS 5:5 KJV) When we speak about the lives each and every one of us is living, in this present body, we should acknowledge that it cannot only be earthly. No wonder the Apostle Paul emphasises that "whatever you do, whatever you think, whatever you say, whatever you dream on earth, keep your eyes and your mind on the things above, (COLOSSIANS 3:1-2 KJV) because that is what really matters; we trust God not for this life only. (1 CORINTHIANS 15:19 KJV) Previously I lived a life of sin, now I live the life of the Anointed One with His anointing (Christ) by Holy Spirit and conquering all sin. Now another question: who did Jesus the Anointed One with His anointing (Christ) came to die for? Did He come for those striving to live in perfection or those who can produce the shortest list of sins? Or did He only come for those considered self-righteously holy? No, He did not! As a matter of fact He came and died for the ungodly, the adulterer, the alcoholic, drug addict, the thief and the murderer, the liar and the blasphemer! He came not only for those that religion disqualifies, but sometimes also those it qualifies as righteous. The

Dr. Adolf Jonker Ph.D

nature of God is that He died for those who least deserved it, even whilst knowing that many will resist and reject Him. No sin can ever extend beyond the limits of God's grace!

God doesn't come to us, pull us to the side and say: "We need to have a little discussion here! Let Me speak to you about all the wrongs you have done. You were stealing, swearing, and you were caught up in adultery. Now come on, don't lie to Me, is it truth or not?" Is this the way God operates? Not in a million years. He knows that He has already paid the ultimate price of dying on a cross. Sure, He knows your sins, your wrongs, failures and weaknesses as well as the sins of your parents. Yet in the midst of it all He never loses focus. His focus is fixed on the redemption He attained for us on the cross. Oh, how we need to truly become more like Him. Isn't it interesting how we, with our own faults and sins, can so easily discern and point out those of other people. How easy it is for mankind to shift blame, thinking that justifying ourselves will portray our holiness! Yes, it may be true that you were never involved in adultery, drinking, smoking and swearing. But this does not classify you as not 'ungodly'. The Bible clearly says that the Anointed One with His anointing (Christ) came for one group of people: the ungodly! This makes God more than a fantastic God and Father. He gave everything to those who rejects His everything. How many of us will do something good for someone who hurt and rejected us? We hurt and reject God in many ways, yet His reaction is not one of revenge or receding. He simply says: "I will give My very, very best for you!"

A friend of mine spoke to me about marriage problems. He said he and his wife had a long discussion about the subject and came to the realization that they were not having marital problems but personality clashes. That was a profound revelation, because it also speaks, in fact of 'who wants to be on the throne'. We shift blame to the institution of God, whereas we ourselves allow selfish behaviours and personality differences to cause problems. Jesus unselfishly laid down His perfect life for our imperfect ones. What a lesson to learn and live by! One can only do this when you have faith; faith where you first and foremost give yourself and all you have to Him. He Himself will give the rest to you, now, immediately, and it will be in due time. God says we should have faith then we shall truly live.

It is therefore an undeniable reality that the very moment you stretch out your hand in faith, your whole being is affected and transformed. Touching faith is the art of rewriting your complete spiritual DNA. No wonder the Bible speaks about becoming a new being. I want to add that every single day of reaching out in faith to God, is a day where your being is dimensionally renewed and settled, to be in a completely different state to what it was the previous day and all your 'yesterdays'. Faith in God is indispensable.

# FUNDAMENTAL FOUNDATIONAL ELEMENT ALLOWING ENTRANCE TO (a) Eternal life (b) Kingdom of God

The story of Matthew, the tax collector, paints for us a different angle of understanding concerning going to God and confessing our sins. Tax collectors were known for their greed, fraudulent deals and most probably stealing. How did it happen then that he became a disciple of Jesus? Did he go to him and confess all his sins? On the contrary! Jesus approached Matthew and said to him: "If you follow Me, you will be saved". Did Jesus tell him to first confess his sins and then follow Him? No, He did not. Looking at this incident we might even wonder whether we should confess or not. Yes, we should. What are we saying then? According to the Bible we have all sinned and fallen short of the glory of God <sup>(ROMANS 3:23 KJV)</sup> and that if we say we do not have sin we are liars. <sup>(1 JOHN 1:8-10 KJV)</sup> What is the emphasis then? Many of us get stuck with a specific method and also 'to do list' when we confess. Jesus said that outside of faith we cannot live, and by living in faith we can come to Him despite our sins, whether we confessed or not. Without faith, a person can never be born again and the focus of the sinner's prayer should be that by faith God establishes a right standing with Him by washing us with the precious blood of Jesus. Jesus did it all. We cannot add to what He has done, nor should we follow steps 1, 2, 3 of confession before we feel 'free' to communicate with Him. The Bible makes it irrefutable that the root of sin is unbelief! Where does one start when dealing with sin? At the root! With unbelief being the root it opens the way for other sins to follow. Thus, the entrance or gateway to moving away from sin and unbelief is to proclaim your faith in God.

Can one say that the very moment after you have accepted Jesus as Lord and Saviour that you know Him and love Him? We can certainly experience feelings of love, yet cannot already love God in the sense one loves someone after years and years of an intimate relationship, therefore our surrender and the commitment we make to give our lives to Him is done in faith. Then He pours Holy Spirit into our hearts and we begin an incredible journey of starting to love Him and also experience His love for us. We can only enter the Kingdom of God by faith and do not come to God and accept Him as Lord and Saviour because we love Him. Before our rebirth we rejected Him and we know it is different with different people, yet He still paved a way for us to eventually be able to come to Him in faith. In Revelations 1:18 ISV Jesus made this comment: *"I have the keys of death and Hades"*. Isn't it true, then, that faith is also a key to overcome death, because He says that when you release your faith you will certainly receive life? Releasing faith in God is to overcome every form of death.

It saddens me so many times to hear people questioning God and His purposes because of situations happening to Christians. Many question how come God allows a Christian to die in a horrible accident on the road, or sickness to attack them, or this thing or that thing. It doesn't matter how many unanswered questions we have about things like this, the truth is that we know and believe that Jesus took the keys of death and Hades. It is in His hands and certainly does not belong to satan. And the one holding these keys is saying that we should come to Him in faith and receive life. Amos 5:4 reads "Seek God and live." Let us reverse the scripture by saying that if we do not seek God, we will not live but die. If the Bible says we should seek God and live, and we can only live by standing in faith, then faith is a key we cannot go without! Without it, we will not see God. Won't you agree that this makes faith even more important than the very oxygen we need to inhale in order to live? Oxygen enables us to continue living a life in our physical body. However it doesn't matter how much we inhale oxygen; it cannot produce eternal life. The way to eternal life is by faith, and using faith to express faith in God continuously is a sure gateway to life in the realm of seeking God. Seeking God demands faith. You and I are going nowhere without faith. We have to grasp the intensely important role thereof and ensure that we re-adapt our lives to align and be a testimony of *"the just shall live by faith."* (ROMANS 1:17 KJV)

## LIFE POSTULATES FAITH

Life postulates faith; in other words, it demands faith. Everything in life is about faith. Think about this: you meet an atheist who boldly declares: "I do not believe there is a God!" Will you say that this atheist has faith? Unquestionably, the answer is yes, because although the atheist declared there is no God, in order to say that he had to believe in something. What the atheist exhibited was faith, but faith in believing something different from the Word of God. It is cognitively reasoned out, and although not divine faith, it is still faith. The conclusion is that every single thing we think or do is as a result of what we believe, and whether you believe in God or not, you do still believe something. I want to clarify this by saying that every single human being that has ever lived or will still live, practises a dimension of faith and it only differs in its specific nature.

If I announced that I'd won three Olympic gold medals, some would believe me, others would believe that I lied, and yet there will even be

Dr. Adolf Jonker Ph.D

those who may not even know what I am talking about. Fact is, whether you believe me or not, you are exerting faith. Do we understand that everything we do is by faith, and when we have a job we have to believe in what we're doing and not merely do it to receive a salary? If you allow fear about your tomorrows, thinking you might fail at this or that, then you yourself release faith into what you fear, and will most probably reap a harvest of failure. What you believe will be so. The Bible says that as a man believes in his heart, so shall it be. (PROVERBS 23:7 KJV)

God can let mysterious things happen if we only believe. Remember what happened with Moses when he stood before the sea? He said to God that he had the whole of the Egyptian army behind him and the sea before him, and his observation of the situation was that they were in deep trouble. Just think about it . . . what would you have done if you were standing in Moses' shoes? What would your reaction have been? The Lord gave Moses quite a surprising answer. God told him that it was not the time for prayer, but God wanted him to release his faith, speak to the water and command the water to open up. Moses did just that and God started to open the waters. What would have happened if he questioned the method and rather wanted to pray? Do we not also harm ourselves when there come times in our lives when God wants us to simply have faith and declare God's complete victory and help in achieving the impossible? It's high time that we realised that God wants to do the impossible for us, if only we are willing to believe. Faith will inevitably unlock, with God's key, the revelation and divine direction of His plans for our lives. Faith is indispensible in God!

## GOD HONORS THE USER

In Hebrews 11:2 and 39 the Bible speaks of a good report of those who lived by faith. There were uncountable people in the Bible who walked by faith and had a good report, so much so that the Apostle Paul commented that there was no space to talk about all these people and more so impossible to even list the names of all. Do you want to receive a good report over your life? Start expressing your faith in God and walk out and into whatever situation comes your way saying: "God I trust you only!"

Listen to this. Many of those who had very good reports about living lives of faith never received the promise and fulfilment of what they trusted God for on earth. God still honoured their faith with or without the manifestation of what they'd trusted God for. Receiving the answer or the manifestation is not 'proof' that you have trusted and believed. How many times do we allow feelings of failure when we trusted God for specific things and interventions and it seemingly never happens? Doesn't this cause many people to allow feelings and mindsets of failure, thinking that they either did not have enough faith or that their faith was worthless? These thoughts are nothing more than religious assumptions, because God clearly says that if you extend your faith in Him, you not only gratify Him entirely, but you bring Him pleasure with your faith and He will certainly give a good report over your life.

I want to pose a question as an example. Do you want to have fame on earth and be on television every day, whether it is on the news or magazine programs, and they all praise you for being one of the greatest achievers in history? Do you want to open magazines and newspapers and see your picture with all the great things you have accomplished, have multitudes applaud you and write articles and books about you? How would all the fame and approval of man on earth benefit you in hell? It would be a horrific shame and tragedy. Many iconic people are very outspoken about their beliefs and that they are not concerned about life after death and whether there is a heaven or hell, or even if they made it to heaven or not. What a sad stance!

What will you choose? I am sure no-one wants to willingly end in hell. Why not just say: "God I would by far rather put all my effort into releasing faith in You my God, and by doing that which pleases You. Whether I see the fulfilment of the promise and that which I've trusted You for in this lifetime or not, none of that matters. What does matter is that my hearts' cry is to give you pleasure by living a life of faith".

Have you ever been in a worship service where you could just feel God's anointing all over you? Does that bring pleasure to God? It certainly will when we say: "God, You are our King; we believe in You, we believe that You are a supernatural God and we believe that nothing, yes absolutely nothing, is impossible for You!" When we align our hearts, the worship and word we speak with faith in God; it is certain to please Him.

It isn't easy to stand up and say "by faith in God I believe" when you've been struggling with something for many, many years, and in the natural realm it seems like you are not able to overcome. I've been there more times than I can even count. Somehow God wants us to stand up from the muddy clay. He wants us to stand and declare that with His strength all that matters is: "I believe in God; this is what I decide to do and will never turn away from it". God encourages us not to gather for ourselves the millions and billions on earth, but rather to gather in heaven. Let me tell you in faith; that when this is your focus, He will prepare marvellous things for you.

## ONcept 2 — SEMANTICS

**KEY SCRIPTURE:** 1 Peter 2:6b ISV

"The one who believes in him will never be ashamed!"

Isaiah 28:16 ISV

". . . . therefore this is what the LORD God says: Look! I am laying a foundation stone in Zion, a tested stone, a precious cornerstone for a sure foundation: Whoever believes firmly will not act hastily."

**KEYWORDS:**

**Faith**

**Trust**

**Believe**

**KEY CONCEPT:** The purpose of addressing semantics is to clarify our understanding of keywords in the equation of faith.

# DIFFERENT WORDS MAKE A CLUSTER GROUPING BUT ALL HAVE THE SAME MEANING

These words are:

Reliance
Belief; believe; believers
Trustworthy
Trust
Faithful
Fidelity
Confidence
Conviction
Persuasion

We introduced the concept of assumptions, the reality thereof, and possible deceptions, in chapter one. These refer to human perception without actual proof, claim or any evidence to support it. I elaborated on basic human inferences on what our personal, cultural or traditional opinions are regarding specific situations, topics and much more. This chapter on semantics will help us discover true faith as we look into the meaning of specific words that are used in the equation of faith. It will also bring clarity, because the strategy of this chapter is to first elaborate on all, and then conclude with a single minded synoptic idea.

All of these words mentioned above, have basically almost the same meaning, yet they are used in different grammatical and syntax application. This is the result of word choice and preference, according to culture, nationality and denominational church relation. A silly example of word choice preference in South Africa is that we use the word 'car' and less often 'vehicle', whereas in the United States the word used is automobile. In South Africa we fill our cars with petrol to avoid an empty tank. In the United States they fill their vehicles with gas. Both speak of exactly the same objects, yet different word preferences are used. The same rings true with faith. Many folks love to use different expressions; however, the bottom line is that they don't really say anything different.

So, I will show a broader understanding through elaboration of these words; but we will end up with a concept stripped of presumption. The true understanding of faith will help everybody to think, act, talk, walk and live faith. Many people are oblivious and simply do not know what faith is. There are also those who have lived for years with an understanding of faith and will encounter a fresh, new and solid understanding, which will leave them saying: "Now I really know what faith is!" In looking at the different words many assumptions regarding them will fade.

## ROOT WORD

The root word for faith in Greek is 'pistis'. (STRONGS, G3982) The simplest way to define the translation is with two key words: persuasion and conviction. During the Old Testament times, the word faith (pistis) as described in the New Testament was only used twice in a 4000 year history. Isn't this strange? Again, I want to remind you to keep in mind the influence of national and ethnical preferences. There is absolutely no reason why the Jews could not have used this word. They used the word faith in Deuteronomy 32:20 as 'emun' (STRONGS, H529) and in Habakkuk 2:4 as 'emunah' (STRONGS, H530) (which correctly translated means faithfulness). In the Old Testament it is evident that they mainly spoke about 'belief', whereas faith is the primary word used in the New Testament. The book of James 2:19 speaks of 'faith' and 'believe' and continue that 'even the devils believe'! I would say that for this very reason we surely need clarity on the above. Simply said: the saving faith of Ephesians 2:7-8 differs from the faith of James 2:19. I put this to you:

Dr. Adolf Jonker Ph.D

✓ Godly faith (spiritual by nature and a gift from God, divine, pure and holy)
✓ Mental faith (pragmatic acquired faith, mostly as a result of particular knowledge, and natural in essence)
✓ Demonic faith (spiritual but evil)

Therefore, I declare unapologetically that when we talk about other religions and their faith, it is not godly faith but evil in nature. It is scripturally evident that it is different from the faith we have in God, YHWH; the one true God. The faith of other religions can be defined as either mental, demonic or both. I believe in most cases it is an intertwinement of both. The gods of other religions are not the same as our God, YHWH, and they are simply demons.

The word 'pistis' (STRONGS, G3982) (faith) has additional counterparts for example:

'pisteuo' (STRONGS, G4100)—believe;

With the grammatical additions to the word we have cluster groupings. Another example is

Pistikos—trust or trustworthy(STRONGS, G4101)
Pistos—believe, trust or trustworthy(STRONGS, G4103)

These words, and many more, are one related to the other and only differ due to the Greek grammatical style.

Jesus used the word 'pistis' more or less twenty times in the New Testament. In Matthew 23:23 He referred to a different interpretation: fidelity. Allow me to argue that all these words are like a mathematical equation. We all know $1+1=2$. The mathematical equation for faith would then be: Reliance + believe + believers + trust + trustworthiness + faithfulness + fidelity + confidence + conviction = faith. All these words combined equal one word, and this word is faith. The word and concept 'faith' encapsulates all these words.

# OPPOSITES

It will be irresponsible to neglect the fact that all these words have antonyms which are the exact opposite in meaning and function. I will direct my focus on three of those words: unbelief, doubt and fear. The very nature of these words is completely destructive and if there are three words that humanity, society and the church must press a final delete button on, and eradicate from our vocabulary, it is these three: unbelief, doubt and fear.

# UNBELIEF

The different Greek words for unbelief will help us to attain a clear understanding and not just settle for what we have been taught in our own language. Firstly, we look at the word 'apistia', (STRONGS G570) which is translated as distrust. If you have distrust, do you believe or have faith? No. You function with the opposite of faith. Secondly we have the word 'apeitheia, (STRONGS G543) which spells out disobedience, as we see in Romans 11:30-32 and also in Hebrews 4:6&11. The third word we look at is 'pisteuo'. (STRONGS G4100) John 16:9 explains the meaning, saying that sin is as a result of not believing in Jesus Christ the Anointed One with His anointing. With the above said, we can conclude that both the root and fruit of sin are narrowed down to unbelief. Jesus was rejected because of the fact that they refused to believe He is the Son of God. Does this not parallel a similar pattern and ways as those in the Garden of Eden? John 1:1 explicitly says that in the beginning was the Word and the Word was God; He became flesh and ascended to heaven and we have the written Word. The written Word spells out that we should daily eat from Him and live. If we refuse we will have to accept that if we do not eat and be one with Him daily we will slowly but surely die.

Sin is rejecting faith in the Son of God and His written Word. This rejection and unbelief creates doubt and distrust. This is exactly why satan used this deceitful statement: "Did God say?" Of course God said! He knew God said, yet still he arrogantly questioned it the same as he does today, with the sole purpose of creating doubt and causing distrust in the Word and God. If we succumb to this type of questioning, we will doubt and distrust and we will surely sin in the same way they did in the Garden of Eden.

## DOUBT

Isaiah 7:9 speaks on 'believe not'. The meaning of 'believe not' is doubt. James 1:6 highlights the fact of having two thoughts battling one another; where the one is committed to believe and the other thought to doubt. Doubt opposes belief, or in other words faith. It withstands the power of faith in order to understate and ultimately nullify it. Doubt can mainly be described as opposing thoughts, and at times it is accompanied with demonic power. The purpose of doubt is to get you confused instead of convinced and to be unsure instead of having a clear-cut conviction. It aims at getting you to be 'like a wave—driven with the wind and tossed back and forth'. (JAMES 1:6 KJV) Wherever faith is curbed by two opposing thoughts and where these thoughts are allowed to brood and we ponder on them, doubt is certainly present. It will use every opposing thought or situation to subtly creep in! 'Doubts' dress code is mostly pretty humane and religious arguments with the intent of being well camouflaged. Similar to any social meeting, doubt will call on friends for support. Many times people and friends will have good intentional ideas to support, yet they are ignorant of what they are in actual fact supporting. They may think they are supporting the person with the purpose of a positive outcome, however, supporting doubt will never lead to a godly outcome.

What do we do then when we are overcome with such thoughts? Jesus set the precise example. Peter could not see that the plan of God was for Jesus to go to the cross and when he addressed Jesus about it he had good intentions. However, he uttered words supporting satan's cause. Jesus immediately reacted and with authority rebuked the one speaking. Did He rebuke Peter? No, He addressed satan, rebuked him and told him to flee. We may think but it was Peter who spoke. Has the church world become so attached to what we see and hear that we have stopped 'seeing and hearing'? We need to see beyond the natural and understand that Peter allowed satan to speak to him, and he released the words of satan and not those of Peter, and certainly not the words of God. We need to follow Jesus' example, but at times it looks like some of Christianity wants to portray it as a club for the meek and mild to be walked over. This is a perverse form of worship. We have the example of Jesus rebuking satan harshly when Peter spoke, and again God says that 'the Kingdom of God shall be taken by force'. (MATTHEW 11:12 KJV)

Jesus was immediate in His actions and reactions towards any contradictions of God's Word. He rather offended the person than allowing and tolerating double-mindedness. He left no space for arguing or nurturing the negative. On the contrary, He saw it for what it was and always addressed it accordingly. In the same manner you and I should follow His example and live a victorious faith life. Rebuke the devil in anything he uses to come against your faith, cast out the negative thought and proclaim God's Word and will. When you reach the end of this book you will have been challenged in what you have believed previously, but take heart, your lifestyle will also be enlightened by Holy Spirit. You will be completely captivated in Him to decisively live positively and think, act, talk walk and live in faith. Nothing and no-one will be able to stop you in God; for greater is He that is in you than he that is in the world. (1 JOHN 4:4 KJV)

You see, faith establishes a person like nothing else. In Matthew 28:17 the disciples worshipped Him but some doubted. This means that His very own children, chosen ones, those who were part of Him, allowed doubt in their hearts. Unthinkable! However, in modern day society and in the church the picture does not look any different. Millions are worshipping the King of Glory but some doubt and do not live by faith. It looks as though we are not so different from Adam and Eve as we wanted to believe. However, if you have doubt, and do not live in faith, it can easily be corrected. All authority belongs to us in Jesus, and we can remove our names through repentance from the doubt-list. In many or most cases (please remember that I generalize), people want to see physical evidence before they believe. I call it the Thomas syndrome. Thomas also wanted to see the physical marks left by the crucifixion on Jesus' hands and feet before he believed. Only after he saw was he convinced and said: "My Lord and my God!" (John 20:28 KJV) Jesus' reaction was incredible. He said: "Because you have seen Me you have believed; blessed are those who have not seen yet have believed!"(John 20:29 KJV)

Folks, some people have become so accustomed to moving in pragmatic faith that they do not even realise that they are not walking in faith. Pragmatic faith is not walking in godly faith. It is based on what is seen and learnt. Pragmatic faith wants to see and demands evidence. However the Biblical definition focuses on what Jesus calls the 'blessed ones'; those who do not see but still they believe. Nobody on earth can 'see' God; you have to believe and make it your own. God does not need to prove Himself to anyone. Only in releasing pure faith, supported by Holy Spirit, will you know God and see Him in the spirit. How? Your faith will grow stronger and stronger each day that you decide and then act and walk in faith.

Doubt, of course, has a very nasty side-effect. What is this side-effect? Doubt creates fear. It's an evil cycle where the question is elaborated: "If God won't help, what then?" This evil cycle has a chain reaction. It is initially sparked by rejecting God's Word. Look what happened in the Garden of Eden. They questioned God's Word, and unbelief, which is the root of sin, entered, as they started to doubt God's Word. That was also the entryway for the fig leaf fashion, because they feared and were ashamed of being naked before God. Now, because we have rejected God's Word (like Adam and Eve), we have to look for our own solutions. The first thing humankind (we) ate from was unbelief and doubt, and then we attempted to solve our problems in 'fig leaves'. This is outrageously ridiculous. It has been a never-ending story throughout the history of mankind. We grabbed hold of the secular, humanistic ideas, developed our own gods and called it religion. From one era to another we moved from one fig leaf campaign to the next, all in varying degrees; and the heartbreak is that it is still ongoing in this current era. We have social norms, cultural institutions, scientific arguments and so much more,

In the process we have destroyed many lives and the world is unfortunately not a better place whatsoever. Life has proven itself to be a brutal arena. Outside faith it is inevitable that a person will live in fear.

## FEAR

Fear is the number one side-effect of doubt. It is deemed to be this monstrous enemy, but on the contrary, fear cannot stand in the presence of the truth of God's Word. Allow yourself to embrace this truth today, learn it by heart: Fear is a lie and it does not originate from God. The question then is where is its origin? If it does not come from God it will either come from man or evil. You decide. My belief is that the only power fear has is when a person believes the lie. Believing the lie empowers it. The lie can be explained as anything contrary to the Word of God. The lie is always camouflaged by religious mindsets, humanistic reasoning and incorrect doctrinal interpretation. You and I must settle in our hearts that God is a good God and one thing that He is truly incapable of is lying. God cannot lie! His Word is the truth. If a billion evolutionists endeavour over hundreds of billions of years to prove that God does not exist, I am telling you today, He is God and certainly not dependant on scientific, religious societal belief or proof of humanity. God is truth. Always!

Fear manifests itself primarily as an emotional concept supported by thoughts of suspicion and scepticism. Thoughts concerning circumstances, evoking distressing emotions, are part and parcel of the mechanism of fear, hence the accompanying concepts of stress, discouragement and feelings of failure. Thoughts are vital in the equation. If you take all negative, fearful thoughts away, the foundation of fear has to collapse. If you view your situation and circumstances according to the viewpoint of God, you will see

Dr. Adolf Jonker Ph.D

definite cracks increasing in fear's foundation, when you start to only focus on God's truth that says: "everything works together for the good for those who love the Lord." (ROMANS 8:28 KJV) You just need to answer this simple question: "Do I love God?" If you do, what can go wrong? Nothing! I can tell you that just by reading this book you will either love God or have an inclination towards becoming His child. So, NO MATTER WHAT happens around you, if you love God and hold onto Him and His Word, believing Him completely, everything will turn out for your good, I assure you! Believe God!

## DEFINITIONS

The next step involves looking at certain words which I call cluster words. We will determine the meaning in order to have a deeper understanding of faith. This is not a grammatical lesson by far, but simply an elaboration in the context of faith.

## RELIANCE

Reliance has a 'brother and sister' in 'rely' or 'reliable'. The focus of this word is on a confident dependence; in other words, when we rely on God, we are confidently dependent on Him. Reliance is the expression or exhibition of your trust in the integrity of God.

## BELIEVE

This is such a major word in our understanding of faith. Two vital concepts to understand believe are confidence and truth. This boils down to you having confidence in the truth of something or someone; this someone being GOD and His Word. This confidence is the truth that persuades you to solidify what you believe.

## TRUSTWORTHY

Trustworthy refers to something or somebody that is worthy of being trusted or we can say that are reliable. Psalm 121 says I lift my eyes, where shall my help come from, from the reliable One, One who is trustworthy: God! Think about it. Does it not spell out that God deserves the confidence we put in Him as He is ultimately trustworthy.

Naturally mankind suffers from a lack of trust. Trust, I will argue, is to set your mind confidently on the integrity of God. You rely on His honesty and this confidence leads you to be dependent on Him. This is a confidence that depends on God's integrity. Hence, your trust is set on Him, focused on the ". . . author and finisher of our faith . . ." (HEBREWS 12:2 KJV)

## FAITHFUL

Faithful touches on the same borders as reliance. It is trustworthiness because of the measure of truthfulness. God says 'let your yes be your yes' and your 'no' be your 'no'.(MATTHEW 5:37 KJV) There are few things as beautiful and admirable as people who are true to their word and who can be relied on. God is not human, and when He says that He promises, declares and proclaims, then you must know that heaven and earth will depart but not His Word—never! (MATTHEW 5:18 KJV) It is yes and amen. Fidelity is a word closely related to devotion—to wedded partners.

We have seen now that all the words discussed in the last couple of pages are intertwined. Not only are they intertwined but in a sense the one refers to the other and the grammatical context determined the use, but it doesn't alter the definition. They are all related to one and the same thing.

## FAITH EQUALS PERSUASION

Faith is a primary concept focusing on trust. Trust is the focus of reliance. Reliance is based on dependency, and on the integrity of God and His Word. God being faithful to Himself, and His Word, spells trustworthiness.

Knowledge becomes an equivalent of faith. However, knowledge is not faith and does not become faith either. It accompanies and supports faith. God says that without knowledge His people perish. (HOSEA 4:6 KJV) Be reminded of the following facts: first of all they were God's (His) people. The gaining of knowledge did not make them His people, but in order to walk this walk of faith, we as His people need to know and understand God and His Word. *"How then shall they call on him in whom they have not believed? and how shall they believe in him of whom they have not heard? and how shall they hear without a preacher?"* (ROMANS 10:14 KJV) Will you allow me to interpret the last part in saying that the author's intention is to get you to believe by telling you about Him, and faith in Him, and the absolute wonder it is to walk with Him.

Faith is also related to obedience. Obedience is the practical application involving your will, a dimension of your soulish being. In other words, you incorporate your mind to come into agreement with faith in God. Therefore, a decision always precedes the expression. This can only be the result of a deep conviction. It is compelling evidence you embrace in your spirit-man of the trustworthiness of the integrity and honesty of God. This conviction emphatically persuades you to believe. The persuasion I refer to is a spiritual force released in God in trusting in His faithfulness.

# CONCLUSION

Allow me to use an illustration which is grammatically incorrect but it correctly shows the meaning of the cluster words connecting to faith:

> I trust God
> I rely God
> I faith God
> I trustworthiness God
> I faithful God
> I believe God
> I reliance God

All the above sentences mean one and the same thing. Only two are grammatically correctly written and the others not. However, the expressions are similar and have the same meaning. The grammar doesn't alter their definition. Language has linguistic rules in order to make it practically understandable for humanity in interaction and communication. Language is a natural entity and can be conjoined by the spirit. Hence, God is saying that we should worship Him in spirit and in truth.

Faith is, then, irrespective of all cluster words, one concept:

> Defined
> Elaborated
> Elucidated
> And expressed in diverse manners

Thus, in moving forward we conclude that all other faith-related words are encapsulated in the one word: faith. So it is important then to know what faith is.

# Oncept 3 — TRANSMITTAL

**KEY SCRIPTURE:** **Acts 3:16(KJV)** "And his name through faith in his name hath made this man strong, whom ye see and know: yea, the faith which is by him hath given him this perfect soundness in the presence of you all."

**KEYWORDS:**

Movement

Interactive

Active

**KEY CONCEPT:** Transmittal indicates the movement of faith.

# IN HIS NAME

*"In His Name"* [(ACTS 3:16 KJV)] is indicative of the 'object' receiving faith. Faith, thus, is not a loosely hang-around idea of something airy-fairy, or a pie in the sky idea. It's substantial. The object is the Name of Jesus. However, it is not directed towards a name on its own. This name represents a person, the Person Jesus, the Anointed Son of God.

> **Acts 4:10 KJV** *"Be it known unto you all, and to all the people of Israel, that by the name of Jesus Christ of Nazareth . . ."*

This isn't just a religious name, or chosen by anybody. Faith is 'IN' the name of Jesus the Anointed One and His Anointing. The name then represents the person,

> **Acts 4:30 KJV** *"By stretching forth thine hand to heal; and that signs and wonders may be done by the name of thy holy child Jesus."*

Acts strongly focuses that faith is in the name and the name expresses who the person is. This name represents power (dunamis) and authority (eksousia). Thus power and authority belong to the holder of the name, which is Jesus, and also express who He is. The concept; the Son of God!

Friends, with the above it is clear that this name is not grammatical by nature or a church concept or doctrine, or some historical or philosophical idea. This name indicates real power and authority. This is not some magical name, or a quick-fix solution to our problems. It is not a name we research, or have free reign and the liberty to debate our way to an answer. Jesus is clear about His authority.

God has raised Him from the dead and set Him at His right hand in the heavens to be next to Him, above every power and force and every other name that is named. [(EPHESIANS 1: 20-21 KJV)]

Dr. Adolf Jonker Ph.D

**Ephesians 1:22 KJV** *"And hath put all things under his feet, and gave him to be head over all things to the church."*

There is no name like His, there is no identity in any other name, as his, there is ultimate, God-given eternal authority and power in this name (indicative of the title holder). This name, chosen and directed by God, carries with it authority and power. Whenever you mention the name of Jesus, you and I have got to realize this: Firstly we mention the greatest name that was ever given to anybody, secondly this name has eternal power and authority and therefore is not bound to a specific time frame, and thirdly, this name has more authority and power that has ever been given to anybody. If you look at iconic figures of history, we are astounded by their accomplishments, their leadership skills and characteristics, their spheres of influence, and so on. Look at the power and the authority that we have seen that the US president in modern history carries. But, even all the accolades and facts of the above people cannot be mentioned in the same breath as that which the name of Jesus entails. Jesus' status is not comparable to any earthly concept. His status is divine; He's not chosen for a specific term of presidency, but He has eternal dominion.

When you touch the name of Jesus, power and authority come into motion; you release power and authority beyond human comprehension or any imaginative thought. As far as humanity is concerned, Jesus' name has limitless power and authority. After the 1994 election in RSA, where Nelson Mandela became the president, I travelled to Turkey. At passport control the officer looked at my passport, saw I was South African, and immediately allowed me to go through. His comment was "oh you're Mandela's people, you can go through!" Mandela's name carried with it a measure of power and authority. Folks, this is what happens when a worldly name is used that carries power and authority. Jesus is on a totally different level altogether. Imagine what you can accomplish in life, in eternity, if you release your faith IN the name of this Holy Son of God.

There are flood waves of scriptures that clearly state faith is in the name of Jesus. In other words He is the recipient of your faith.

Divine faith is not a belief in yourself, or a belief in someone or a doctrine or institution or race group or some knowledge you have, and the list goes on. Divine faith is in Jesus' Name. Look at some KJV scriptures:

| | |
|---|---|
| **Acts 3:16** | "Faith in His name" |
| **Acts 20:21** | "Faith toward our Lord Jesus" |
| **Rom 3:26** | "him which believeth in Jesus" |
| **Phil 3:9** | "the faith of Christ" |
| **Rom 3:30** | "one God who will justify by faith . . ." |

Godly faith is directed toward God and God alone. Abraham, the father of faith, believed in God. (GENESIS 15:6 KJV)

## FOCUS ON GOD

This faith in God, what does it encompass? What is the focal point? What is the truth behind it? Let me answer with divine scriptural elucidation. Look again at Hebrews 11:6 KJV ". . . *he that cometh to God must believe that he is . . .*" Yours and my faith released in God focuses on His existence as God. God, the invisible or hidden God, wants humanity from within the natural realm of a life influenced by our five senses, to believe in His existence. It is clear; He will not make Himself known to us in the natural outside of what He has already shown with Jesus. In all of humanity's history, this revelation of God, of Jesus, in human form lasted only 33 years. Outside those 33 years we are known to the 'invisible God' concept. This is faith. We cannot see, touch, smell, taste, hear in the natural, and 'extremely important, God is not in the scientific 'proving of Himself' business. His very nature and mindset always were for humanity to extend the natural borders and go beyond it, to believe outside the natural evidences in the 'supernatural God'.

The grammatical use of 'He is' is vital in our understanding. He is "esti" in Greek, is present indicative (Strong's G2076). God is eternal. Personally, I don't think eternity really incorporates a past, present and future as we understand it. Thus God wants us to believe 'He is and now is', not as such yesterday or tomorrow. We believed yesterday, 'He is' and we will believe tomorrow 'He is'. But for today it is important to believe, He is living, existing today. He is involved in our current affairs as much as He was yesterday, today or will be. (HEBREWS 13:8 KJV) He is always the same God. If God is, then He exists. If He exists, He is the Creator. In His existence He alone is God, and God Triune. That is what Hebrews 11:6 spells out. If He is God, He is omniscient, omnipresent, omnipotent, eternal, transcended, supreme ruler, and sovereign in His being. All the above is encapsulated in Him saying to Moses: "I AM", the Hebrew translation **'Yod He Waw He'** abbreviated in English YHWH. All other translations of YHWH are all mere human inventions and have no Scriptural support.

The above faith takes an added faith substance when we then "believeth that Jesus is the Son of God . . ." (1 John 5:5 KJV) The same chapter extends more light to it. *"Whosoever believeth that Jesus is the Christ is born of God."* (1 JOHN 5:1 KJV) The identity of Jesus is that He is the Anointed One with His anointing, the Son of God. Jesus is our mediator between us (believers—humanity) and God. Believing that He exists entails then the belief of who Jesus is: the name, the identity, the person, a multi-concept interwoven as 'He is".

In believing Jesus the Anointed One we have encapsulated within this name what goes beyond human comprehension. We receive, by believing in this name, life, eternal salvation, justification, communion, grace, mercy, divine fellowship, forgiveness, joy peace, long suffering, kindness, goodness, power, healing, deliverance, restoration, escape hell and eternal punishment, eternal crowns and who knows what else! It is a complete package. Thus believing in Jesus the Anointed One opens a flood wave of receiving for the believer. Vital now, believing therefore enables receiving irreversibly.

The importance of this name lies in Jesus being the incarnate God and revealer of God.

## SOURCE OF FAITH

History has been flooded with debates about the origin of faith or the definition. Let's not argue with a secular humanistic approach, and compromise with our scientific methodology, but ask Holy Spirit to reveal the written Word.

> **Hebrews 12:2 KJV** *"Looking unto Jesus the author and the finisher of our faith . . ."*

Here we clearly see faith has been initiated by Jesus, He is the author. Hence our eyes are settled, established on Him. But my focus is that faith originates from God. Look at the following scriptures to verify:

| | |
|---|---|
| **Galatians 2:16** | "The Faith of Jesus Christ" (KJV) |
| **Galatians 3:22** | "Faith of Jesus Christ" (KJV) |
| **Revelation 2:13** | "My faith" (KJV) |

Jesus, according to the Bible, claims ownership of faith, indicative of God being the source of faith. The disciples knew it too well and asked Him to increase their faith. (LUKE 17:5 KJV) They understood that God was the source, they understood that if they needed more, they had to go to the One it belongs to. The best we, as humanity have ownership of, is 'unbelief'. (MARK 9:24 KJV) Our heavenly Father makes it clear that what He initiates He will also complete. (PHIL 1:6 KJV) We know we start off by faith in our entering the kingdom.(JOHN 3:5 KJV) Paul says that we refer to this entrance into the kingdom as being born again. The salvation plan of God is by faith and grace.

> **Ephesians 2:8 KJV** *"For by grace are ye saved through faith; and that not of yourselves: it is the gift of God . . ."*

Dr. Adolf Jonker Ph.D

Grace then is God freely giving us faith. Faith is necessary to believe in God and to receive salvation. Illuminated to the core; we don't own or have godly faith as humans. We received it from God, not as a result of what we have done, but by His grace. Other religions, in expressing the concept "faith" do not refer to divine godly faith, as been revealed in the Bible, God's final word on the topic. So when they profess their faith in a god, they refer to demons. (GALATIANS 4:8 KJV) Hence, other religions possess demonic faith.

In other words, most precious child of God, when the Bible speaks about 'our' faith,(HEBREWS 12:2 KJV) we need to understand our faith in the context of something received from God. God, in Jesus, is the author and finisher thereof; He is the first and the last. Hence my statement: 'our faith is sandwiched, or encapsulated in God', clearly saying: our faith outside of God does not exist, and it leaves multitudes with mental faith. This kind is faith in themselves alone, their talents gifts and skills; their own ability and some knowledge, soulish power; or faith in somebody, doctrines, or human ideologies. All mentioned are destructive in the end. The other concept of faith, demonic by nature, is explained in the above. It is imperative for us as Christians to know our faith comes from God, thus making God the source of faith.

## CONTENT

We have already established that faith comes from God; hence our statement that God is the source of divine faith. I refer to it as Jesus' Faith. If faith then comes from God we have to look deeper at its content. God is spirit, His life is spirit, and everything as a matter of fact about Him is spirit. His faith then is spirit, thus making faith a spiritual substance. Take note—not a spiritual religious idea. The substance of faith is spirit.

Our difficulty lies in our understanding of spiritual substance, as we are so naturally inclined. In the natural we discern its content easily as it's made up of time, matter and space. Contrary to the natural we don't really have a picture or reference of the spirit realm. It makes it 'hidden', not tangible, and therefore most people think of the spirit as subject to the natural, making the natural superior to the spirit. Friend, the truth is that eternity of eternities ago, immeasurable times of the spirit realm existed before the creation of the natural realm. This is problematic for humans as they can relate with ease, and like second nature to the natural realm. We can touch, smell, see, taste, hear and with our five senses therefore interact with the natural. The spirit realm, however, cannot be touched by the above natural senses, on the contrary, your five senses are of no use in discovering the spirit realm. You can only touch it by faith. Albeit, as we understand the substance of the natural we have to understand that the spirit has substance even as the natural has substance. It leaves us defining the substance of the spirit realm as spirit (invisible).

What we definitely know from scripture is that spirit has form, content and communication. If we look at God we discern personality. In other words, He can think, have emotions, thus feelings, can hear, can talk etc. (PSALM 2:4; JOHN 11:35, EPHESIANS 4:30 KJV). The Bible says that God created the angels; they have wings and can communicate. Let's think, angels are spiritual beings, hence their substance is spirit. If spirit has no substance, then God could not have created them, so even if they are spirit-created beings, their forms differentiate them from the spirit realm. Their personality is spiritual, their communication spiritual and their form is the make-up of spirit substance. We can also learn, from the instance when satan discussed Job with the Lord, that there was communication similar to what we as humans have. However, their communication is spiritual and our conversation natural, thus leaving evidence of the similitude between spirit and natural, where the difference then lies in the aspect of content. I trust you will have a more elucidated understanding of spirit.

The question that is frequently asked is: "Where is the spirit realm?" Let me explain analogously. If you take a sponge, squeeze it tightly in your hand, then put both your hand and sponge in a bowl of water.

Take out your hand. The sponge will still look the same, but is now filled with water and immersed completely. Let us then say that the sponge represents your natural being and the water the spirit realm. For the purpose of the book this will have to suffice.

The question that sequentially follows is: "What is the difference?" To expand the above, I will have to draw your attention then to the role players. The spirit realm consists of God and His holy angels; unfortunately it also accommodates the demonic, which are the fallen angels. The third group is us human beings. Let me now talk to you about the spiritual line. The problem relating to both spirit and natural realms is not with God or the diabolic, but we humans in our understanding of the spirit realm. Suffice to say we are acquainted with the natural realm. It is natural for us to move in the physical of time, matter and space. In John 4:24 AMP Jesus made a remarkable statement saying "God is a spirit (a spiritual Being) and those who worship Him must worship Him in spirit and in truth." So Jesus moves away from a natural approach, not abandoning the natural altogether; however, He urges people, human beings, and children of God to Worship God in spirit. Now we have drawn a line between the natural and the spiritual.

## THE LINE BETWEEN SPIRITUAL AND NATURAL

As a result of the above, I want to clarify the concept 'the line' between natural and spiritual. The first point I want to make is that if Jesus said this is a new generation to worship God in spirit and truth, then there was a reverse side prior to that and it entails people worshipping God in the natural. With the coming of Jesus: His crucifixion, resurrection, ascension and then outpouring of Holy Spirit, the children of God now move away from a natural approach to a spiritual one: worship in spirit. Therefore, friend, people choose to worship God either in the natural realm or in the spirit. If we, humans living in the natural realm want to worship God, we have to cross the line between natural and spirit.

Let me further elucidate. Jesus, after His resurrection, visited His disciples and decided not to use the door but walk through the wall. What happened? Briefly, let me say that the natural realm consists of three dimensions; we all know that. In order for Jesus to walk through the wall He had to move in another dimension. I want to argue that the close relation between the natural and spiritual as illustrated with the bowl, water and sponge analogy, suggests then that the 'spirit realm' is a fourth dimension. There are scientists who argue, due to mathematical equations, that God moves even in a tenth dimension; some even speculate up to a 27th dimension. I don't know how much truth there is in it, but it makes perfect sense to me as being probable. In light of the above, you and I function in three dimensions on planet earth, in the natural: when we worship God and have contact, or communion with Him; or we release our faith, we also 'walk like' Jesus through the wall; we cross the line between the natural and spirit realm. Differently said: we cross the border. The apostle John says *"I was in the Spirit on the Lord's day, and heard behind me a great voice, as of a trumpet."* (REV 1:10 KJV). Friends, he crossed the line of dimensions one, two and three and walked into dimension four. Differently and plainly, he moved into the spirit realm. Did his physical body move into the spirit? Absolutely not! His spirit conjoined with his soul, crossed the line. I would also like to say, according to the above scripture, that the spirit realm is not a "spooky" idea. There is real life, and John could hear voices as sounding similar to trumpets.

Let's explore the above further. In Rev 4:1 (KJV) John said a voice called him into heaven. Let's establish something: heaven is a spirit concept. He was called into heaven, but did his body accompany him? No. He continues this remarkable story and says in Rev 4:2 he was in the spirit; in other words, he crossed the line between natural and spirit. Then he continues and says he saw certain things. Question, did he see them with his natural physical eyes? No. Were the voices he heard, then, with his natural physical ears? No. Revelation 5:4 "I wept

Dr. Adolf Jonker Ph.D

much." Question: was it in his physical, natural condition? Absolutely not. Therefore, as spirit-beings, you and I can function in the spirit as we do in the natural. That's why Jesus said, "There will be worship in spirit and truth."

## FAITH

When we come to faith we have discovered: firstly, it comes from God, secondly, it has substance, and thirdly, the substance is spirit, and fourthly coming from God, faith is a godly spirit substance and not an intellectual concept, a linguistic rhetoric or even religious philosophy. We have also discovered, as a result of the above that humanity doesn't have ownership but is a recipient. God allows us then to grow as humans in this gift of faith.

Taking everything said thus far, relating to contents and the discoveries we have made, let's explore even further. God created the heavens and the earth and all of creation for that matter. Faith belongs to Him as He is the source. I will argue that God made use of His own faith in Himself to create as He did. That makes faith a creative force. That's why the Bible says: "Call those things which are not as though they are." (ROMANS 4:17 KJV) Faith is then the spirit substance we use to connect us with God and His creative power. That makes us also creators with God in whatever endeavors we are involved.

## TRANSMITTAL

Examining the source, the object and the content we can clearly see that faith has movement; it's transmittal. Faith, spirit substance, is sent by the source or owner of faith, God (spirit), from the spirit realm, crossing the borders, entering the natural and maintaining all its characteristics. Man becomes the first recipient. However, faith is not dormant by nature, therefore man in the natural becomes the releaser of this faith, crossing from the natural, to the spirit border and directing his faith to God (object) who now becomes a rewarder, due to being gratified by receiving man's trust in Him. The Rewarder answers in spirit, this connective creative force, and manifests its mandate. Mandate is then the content with which He was entrusted. Your faith becomes the mandate of the actualization of your request. The result: man in the natural receives what he/she trusted God for.

Thus the believer's request is processed and finalized in the spirit, through God's power, stating:

(a) Nothing is impossible for God (MATTHEW 17:20 KJV)
(b) Whatever you ask, ask in My name (MATTHEW 21:22 KJV)

This makes us the initiators of our faith and becomes extremely important in our faith arsenal and thus faith release. To sum up this transmittal concept, we see it has movement (action) and is directional, with man as the role players. Faith, a spiritual entity, moves from the supernatural to the natural. It is received in our spirits, where it is being processed by our biological faculties, becomes relevant in our soul (mind, will, emotions) and therefore ends in the natural. We can conclude by saying: it has action, and we interact between the supernatural realm and the natural. The only thing that remains the same is faith as spirit substance.

## SOUL

Bringing the spirit in context with who we are we have to examine the soulish realm. It becomes imperative to establish once and for all the makeup of man. Irrespective of historical events and debates, the Bible makes it clear that humanity is a triune being, meaning: spirit, soul and body. (1THESS. 5:23 KJV) The Spirit, the first part of our makeup has substance referring to spirit and contains the eternal life of God, the residing place of Holy Spirit (talking only about born-again believers, according to John 3:5). Our physical bodies accommodate our spirits and thus become the temple of Holy Spirit. (1 CORINTHIANS 6:17&19 KJV) The substance of our physical biological bodies, according to scripture, is 'dust'. (GENESIS 2:7 KJV) Paul shed some light on the substance of our soul (mind, will, emotions) *"be renewed in the spirit of your mind"*. (EPH. 4:23 KJV) Mind refers to our soulish realm and thus verifies the fact that our soul consists of spirit substance. So, currently we have a 'spirit' as spirit substance, our soul (our personality—our being) as spirit substance and our present bodies as natural substance: soil. However, when we are resurrected one day, we will have glorified, resurrected bodies with spirit as substance. Then it would read as follows:

| Spirit | – | spirit |
| Soul | – | spirit |
| Body | – | spirit, |

the culmination of creation, the final product of being created in the image of

| God the Father | – | Spirit |
| God the Son | – | Spirit |
| God the Holy Spirit | – | Spirit |

## BRAIN

The above necessitates the inquiry into the place of our human brain. Where does it fit in? What is its role and place? Our brain forms part of God's creative design and plan. God is spirit, but decided to create a physical domain and put man within this domain as natural, in context of our physical bodies. Our physical bodies are for this present dispensation, God's plan. We however have two components of man that are made up of spirit substance: spirit and soul. Your soul is the part of you that highlights you as an unique individual with your own personality and unequalled gifts and characteristics. Your soul is you! Living in the natural we need to communicate in the spirit. The brain becomes the processor or modem (if you wish) for your mind (spirit) to translate the spirit content in the natural. The human brain is an interactive component, translator between spirit and natural. Analogously, I can relate it to a television, the radio waves (representing spirit) moving through the air being picked up by the components within the television (representing brain), and the screen (natural) displaying the content of the radio waves.

> **John 1:1-4 NIV** *"In the beginning was the Word, and the Word was with God, and the Word was God. He was with God in the beginning. Through him all things were made; without him nothing was made that has been made. In him was life, and that life was the light of men."*

God was from the beginning. The Word of God is then the expression of God Himself. This is not intellectual academic words on paper but the revelation of God's expression of Himself, verbalized in the natural, for our brain to understand the spirit and have contact with it. The verbalization is in a heavenly language called 'revelation' (spirit), and expressed on earth in diverse languages (natural). In the interaction between spirit and natural, the human brain becomes pivotal. It is also pivotal within a biological framework.

A last but very important word: the capabilities of your brain, for example your IQ, have no bearing whatsoever on your spiritual status. The brain serves only within the parameters as pivotal to our physiological function and our interaction with the spirit realm. I am aware of a multitude of debates and opinions regarding the above. However, I am not debating with anyone. I therefore do not endeavor to give detailed explanations of mental faith or demonic faith. However, all my energy is spent in helping the believer to discover true faith as confirmed by the scripture and interpreted by Holy Spirit. (1 COR. 2:10-15KJV)

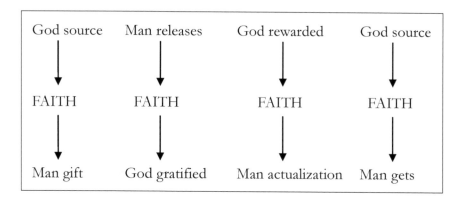

This concludes our examination of the concept 'transmittal':

> God—object of our faith
> God—source of our faith
> Faith—spirit and necessitates interaction

## Concept 4 — RECIPROCAL

**KEY SCRIPTURE:** 2 Corinthians 4:18 KJV "While we look not at the things which are seen, but at the things which are not seen: for the things which are seen are temporal; but the things which are not seen are eternal."

**KEYWORDS:**

Recipient

Sender

Interactive

Investment

**KEY CONCEPT:** Reciprocal is the demonstration of the interaction between God and man.

# MIND AND EYE

As we continue, let me once again remind you that faith is indispensible, meaning that you cannot live without it. Second to the above, you should apply faith to your life; in doing so nothing and nobody will be able to stop your personal transformation!

In the previous chapter we discussed the concept 'transmittal'. We move on now to investigate the idea 'reciprocal'. There are major similarities between reciprocal and transmittal; however, the difference lies with humanity in its capacity as sender-back to God.

Faith is a spiritual substance originating from God, and thus invisible by nature to mankind, in the natural. It cannot be seen with the natural eye. Therefore my statement, that faith is a presentation of a visualized image to the eye of the mind, and speaks of that which the eye of our biological body cannot see. It is of extreme, paramount importance to understand; the eyes of your physical body cannot see faith.

It becomes even more important to comprehend the following; there is nothing natural about faith! Nothing of the natural realm belongs to or can assist in the equation of faith. Your physicality cannot comprehend, grasp or embrace faith. The natural clashes and oppose every part of faith. Thus, please take careful note of the following: where and when you bring the natural realm into your faith release, you destroy the head start of your process. You thwart the flow of faith, and your beginning has a prophetic end; it will fail!

Transmittal portrays the image of movement, thus creating interaction between God and man. Reciprocal, though similar, speaks of the particular movement between God and man. In this chapter we will investigate faith as substance being reversed and sent by man to God. Prior to the above, God was owner, source and sender and man became the recipient of divine faith. The roles polarized in this transmittal process changed, and now man in his faith release, becomes sender and God-recipient.

# VISUALIZATION

Understanding man's reversed role necessitates that we examine visualization. Visualization is the formation of a picture, or image if you wish, that you formed in your mind's eye.

To understand the above I would like to recap quickly on what has been said previously regarding your mind. The Bible says that we are spirit, soul and body. On this we agree. However, it does not function in compartments and on its own, but holistically, as a unit. Therefore, we can say there is a constant interaction between spirit, soul and body. Thus, when referring to the eye of our minds it entails the following: Our brain has the capacity to produce a picture, relating to the natural in terms of visualization. The process in getting this picture is a mental one. Your mind's eye is your soulish realm. This is where the Bible says *"I will give you the desires of your heart"*. (PSALM 37:4 KJV) Friends, this is not rocket science. Nobody on earth's biological heart has the capacity to utter any premeditated desire. It is a clear work of your soul, isn't it? It speaks about a premeditated image that has been formed within your soul, and your personality, and this formation, as the result of an intertwined interaction, has been processed to your understanding. You thus formed a visualized concept in yourself and presented it in a processed picture to your mind's eye.

The above image, what you believe or trust God for becomes the object you present to God. The visualization is a process of formation of the final product; the picture of what you desire should manifest. It is the end product. This process cannot be successfully done or completed without a constant reliance, trust and help of Holy Spirit. 1 John 5:14 says that we will receive what we ask for if it is in accordance with God's will. Nobody can help you better in this regard than Holy Spirit. Jesus said with great clarity that His departure to heaven was for the explicit reason that another Helper would come. (JOHN 16:7 KJV) Holy Spirit's role is to assist us in whatever we do. Who better than our Helper to enable us to form the perfect

Dr. Adolf Jonker Ph.D

picture of what would become the image we have that we trust God for, or present to God?

Visualization is the beginning stage of your faith release. Simply said visualization is to systematically organize the formation of what we want. Therefore, we can say that part of the faith package is the important concept of visualization. There are multitudes of people who cannot define what they request from God. I want to say to you that without visualization and the presenting of your mind's eye's image, the request of your faith will not be successful. Years ago my wife came to my study one day to tell me our deep freezer was empty. At first, I thought she was overreacting, and went with her to make sure for myself. Well, when I looked inside the deep freezer it looked exactly the same as the day we bought it, clean and empty. I told her, "Close your eyes and we are going to lay hands on the deep freezer and call forth meat, good quality and different kinds." I started to picture what would fill the deep freezer. Folks, God be my witness, within two hours, we had somebody bringing us a slaughtered lamb, a pig and two cows! We couldn't fit it all into our deep freezer and had to give one animal away. Visualization forms an integral part of faith.

A pastor friend of mine, who went to be with the Lord, once told us that they were really battling financially. One particular day, when it was almost noon, they had no food. His wife asked him what they were going to do. He replied quickly and simply that they would put the plates on the table and then picture food on them. They sat down, held hands, and started to pray over the empty plates, as if they were filled with food! When he said "Amen" the doorbell rang. As they opened the front door a very well-mannered lady asked them politely if they would mind her bringing them lunch. She felt led earlier that morning to prepare it for them. I believe visualization is your gateway to releasing faith.

The visualized image becomes your prophetic declaration of the outcome of your faith. I partook in athletics as a sprinter. I once had to run a race against an excellent athlete and champion. I knew he was better than me. Two weeks prior to that specific meeting, I lay in bed every night, visualizing every part of the race, every stride, every breath; even exerting energy and winning. When I went down in the blocks that day of the race I knew I would win. I had pictured my victory and I won the race comfortably. Visualization is the formation of your desire / request and the image of the manifestation. The visualized image becomes your declaration throughout the process in your walk of faith. I cannot stress enough the importance of what I wrote here. Please allow it to permeate you and become part of how you live and think.

## FAITH WALK

Let me explore the dynamics of faith and break it up in three major parts for you. Dynamic number one encompasses the process of visualization and all it entails. We have discussed it in great length, yet there is still one point to discuss. After you have formed the picture of your request, you will only receive it by asking God for it. James 4:3 KJV says that 'you have not for you ask not.' You need to ask God. In other words, visualization is your gateway and verbalization of it becomes the initiation of your faith. Let me say then, that the above in itself isn't the walk of faith, but merely the beginning of the process.

Now, before we proceed to dynamic number two, we are first going to number three. Dynamic number three is the phase of your 'faith walk' which we talk about, as the manifestation of the request. In other words: you receiving what you have asked for. Hebrews says faith is what you don't see. Therefore the manifestation is a seeing, witnessing part and therefore, as a standalone dynamic, it is not faith as defined by the Bible. Before you misconstrue this statement, let me talk about dynamic number two. By way of illustration, suppose that dynamic one is the starting point; dynamic number two is the phase directly after your faith request, and prior to your receiving the manifestation of your request, and dynamic three is the finalization. I call dynamic two phase:

Dr. Adolf Jonker Ph.D

the 'faith-time-zone'. This is a period of which only God knows the duration. When the disciples asked Jesus about the End-Times, He said that only the Father knows the times, as determined by His authority. (ACTS 1:7 KJV) So as much as we can call this phase a 'faith-time-zone', we can infer, with great conviction, that faith is accompanied with patience and certainly inseparable from longanimity!

It is during this time zone that you and I, as children of God, really walk by faith—the time where we think, act and walk faith. This is a time where patience will test the durability of your faith. The manifestation is the verification thereof. This time zone is a process where a multitude of things take place. It is the testing of your patience, thus your persistence in walking by faith. Friends, we can therefore infer and say that patience tests your faith. During this phase of dynamic number two, the enemy will attack you in the primary focal point with: "Did God say?" Your belief in God, in His Word and in His promises will be attacked. This is the time where you see nothing coming into fruition. It is the time where adverse circumstances will aggressively sow seeds of doubt. It will be the order of the day. It is during these times where your persistence will be severely tested by family, friends, close ones, Christians; many will come and in effect say "Did God say?", or they will discourage you with natural facts as evidence. The purpose and focus of all that take place is to simply discourage you and change your focus from what is unseen to what is seen. And most of these people that you come in contact with during such times will have good intentions and no inclination to harm you. Some would, however, be differently inclined.

However, the time when Noah built the ark, it never-ever rained until the great flood. How outrageously ridiculous to build a boat / ship of such a humongous size in the desert! And best of all, nobody ever experienced the rain he was talking about! Can you imagine how much factual evidence, and correct statements regarding the geographical location were presented? The building part of the ark was the faith walk, and not God commanding him, nor the time when it started to rain. It was the in-between, faith-time-zone where you as individual will have to decide to allow the plan and purpose of God to grow in you, and to ensure you to do what's required to reach full term for it to manifest. This is where Noah's faith was tested by patience and endurance. Diverse attacks were launched against his patience in order to thwart

(a) Noah's faith
(b) God's plan

It is then also very important to remember the positive effect of walking with patience. It helps you become an overcomer. We can say that faith has two sides to the coin; it can trip you and be the cause of your downfall, but its primary and main focus is to strengthen you! During this time you should not open yourself to any form of negativity regarding your faith, no matter who these people are that have an influence on you. Jesus did it when Peter said he would not allow Jesus to die in Jerusalem. Jesus rebuked satan and made the remarkable statement by saying "You are not thinking God's thoughts but human thoughts." (MATTHEW 16:23 CEV)

You see, Jesus didn't take chances by allowing anybody to derail His faith walk. He didn't tolerate any form of negativity. He didn't allow anybody to tell Him what the natural entails, the scientific facts, historical testimonies, the political environment, or the social economical status. He knew that faith is supernatural and not natural. The whole humanity united against Noah, presenting valid facts. The truth is that they were all wrong in the end. Joshua and Caleb, two of the 12 spies returned from their spying expedition in Jericho. Caleb said, "Yes, I have witnessed all the facts that you have presented and they are factually correct. However, you talk about the natural, but our God, supernatural by nature, deals in a different manner and He will outdo all the natural facts and establish a supernatural event.

Listen very carefully now. During this phase you will be attacked by yourself, loved ones, humanity, the Babylonian system we live in

Dr. Adolf Jonker Ph.D

(spirit of this world and the diabolic). It has happened to all believers and will happen to you, be assured. NOW—VITAL: during this time, never allow anything natural to come out of your mouth; most definitely nothing negative. Remember—VITAL: faith is supernatural, and its greatest enemy is the involvement of natural statements. Never ask God when; never think how; never, never ever think "what if?"

The above paragraph is beyond important. You will be attacked. Your reaction to it all is to declare your visualization, your image to God and in the spirit realm present it as a done deal. When will it manifest? God is in control, leave it with Him. How will it happen? Only God can accomplish the supernatural; don't think on His behalf, with your limited brain cells that can function and comprehend only the natural. It is this poison which kills the very concept of faith.

During this time constantly verbalize your faith. In other words speak it out with your mouth. Release your prophetic power to declare in God the end result: the visualized picture!

> **Romans 10:9 KJV** *"That if thou shalt confess with thy mouth the Lord Jesus, and shalt believe in thine heart that God hath raised Him from the dead, thou shalt be saved."*

You can continue to read verse 10 also. God makes it easy for us to live the faith path. He says "Believe in your heart (soul) and confess; speak it out with your mouth." Faith is action, which is the physical proclamation, hence my statement; you continually prophesy God's promises and your request in the spirit. Your verbalization nullifies any other word, as the Word of God is the strongest. You keep your focus on your image, (the vision you have) and put your trust in God. Close your ears to any contradictory thought or word. Don't tolerate anything contradictory, but expel and replace it immediately with God's Word. In this manner you invest in God your belief, your trust, your patience, and your victory over adversities and this faith investment will reward you with divine dividends.

The more you are influenced by the 'seen', the visible, the more you reject it and live by the unseen, the invisible.

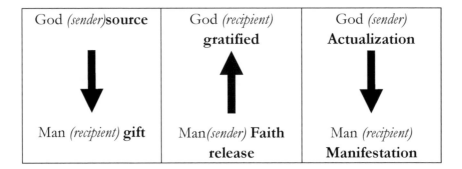

| God *(sender)*source | God *(recipient)* gratified | God *(sender)* Actualization |
|---|---|---|
| Man *(recipient)* gift | Man*(sender)* Faith release | Man *(recipient)* Manifestation |

Dr. Adolf Jonker Ph.D

# Concept 5 — MATURATION

**KEY SCRIPTURE:** 2 Thessalonians 1:3 ISV

> Brothers, at all times we are obligated to thank God for you. It is right to do this because your faith is growing all the time and the love every one of you has for each other is increasing.

**KEYWORDS:**

**Dimensional**

**Develop**

**Growth**

**Augmented**

**Measures**

**Increase**

**KEY CONCEPT:** Faith by nature is dimensional and develops and increases through application, therefore growth is inevitable.

# TIME ANATOMY

In discussing the concept maturation we have to evaluate our understanding of the time anatomy of faith, the growth component, the dynamics it functions with and lastly what increase entails.

Look at the following then we will discuss it in detail:

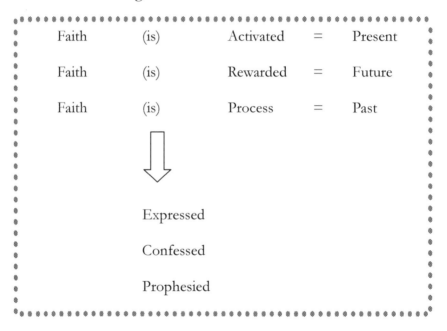

| Faith | (is) | Activated | = | Present |
| Faith | (is) | Rewarded | = | Future |
| Faith | (is) | Process | = | Past |

Expressed

Confessed

Prophesied

This is evident from the above that faith is dimensional and the dimensionality relates to specific time frames.

Albeit Hebrews 4:7 states that He again fixes a definite day—Today—saying long afterward David, as already quoted, "Today, if you hear his voice do not harden your hearts.

From the above, I want to make a few important declarations to clarify our understanding of time anatomy. Today is yesterday's tomorrow and tomorrow's yesterday. The importance is neither yesterday nor tomorrow but today. Thus faith is:

Dr. Adolf Jonker Ph.D

Not bound by time;

The Christian who releases his / her faith has a tendency to invoke God's power in his / her minds in accelerating the manifestation of the request. He / she expressing the value of what he / she put in the actualization of his / her faith. Thus putting more value in receiving the actualization then on expressing his / her faith in God to please Him. That is the reason why many Christians do not want to live in today because tomorrow's actualization is more important to them then today's faith release.

The important part for God is 'today'. Today is the faith—releasing section. We will become different human beings once we focus on the joy God has when He receives our faith. This speaks of 'Kingdom first' and secondary to the above is the actualization where faith alters and becomes praise. Faith is present. Faith will always fall in the 'today' time frame, which is the present tense. This is where you activate your faith by expressing your visualized picture; confessing out loud with your mouth, and where God will accomplish your request. You prophesy the will and Word of God over your life. Prophecy is not a spooky concept of only revealing dark or unknown facts about events or calamities or even things happening in people's lives. It is God's revelation in your mouth, spoken by you on God's behalf, the fulfilment of the request. When do you prophesy? Today! You understand the concept by now. It is a 'NOW THING'. What you did yesterday remains relevant but today become more important to you as you build layer by layer in the manifestation for tomorrow.

Faith released today is action taken that becomes the awaiting factor. The future of the above action will be the manifestation of yesterday's (today's) release of faith. This part represents the historical background of the process from the initiation up to the full potential being released and received. You can constantly see the 'movement' of faith. It is never stagnant, and thus postulates growth. We need to grasp that another dimension of the time anatomy of faith is growth which means it is not a once-off incident but something that involves continual development. Growth is a process and 1 John 2:14 NIV differentiates in dimensional status between child (infant), sons and fathers. This invokes the understanding that your faith growth levels are augmented day by day; phase by phase.

## GROWTH

Growth is beautifully depicted in Matthew 13:31-32 KJV "Another parable put he forth unto them, saying, The kingdom of heaven is like unto a grain of mustard seed, which a man took, and sowed in his field: Which indeed is the least of all seeds: but when it is grown, it is the greatest among herbs, and becometh a tree, so that the birds of the air come and lodge in the branches thereof."

We see, as with everything in life, a small insignificant beginning is representative of the beginning of the process of growth. Growth is always the process of development until the final product is accomplished. This is why faith can easily be put figuratively in the place of a mustard seed. It starts of minutely small, however, it is not stagnant, and inhabits marvellous growing factors. The end result in every situation will be something phenomenal and our God will receive all the glory.

## DYNAMICS

Faith is not stagnant. Stagnant faith is no faith and is indicative of complacency. The word 'augmented' gives colour to my concept. The development of your faith means faith becomes a more visible, tangible part of your lifestyle.

To develop you need to expand, and expanding necessitates the enlargement of your territory. It involves authority and anointing. You have to learn to trust God more and more. Each individual's life is different and not really comparable with any other. Thus faith is an

Dr. Adolf Jonker Ph.D

individual matter. Let's argue that a particular church trusts God for something specific. Their particular request in trusting God, portrays their unique individuality so you cannot compare yourself to them, and then also copy their request in equivalence. Faith is personal, it's individual, and you as individual make it unique. It's between you and God and not a compare-me-to-you scenario where we are influenced to want to have what others have, yet we never asked the Lord whether that is what He has for us. No one can help you with faith. They can support you but the sole activator is one—YOU!

Paul writes about the people's faith that has grown exceedingly. (2 THES 1:3 KJV) In other words, even the measures of growth can differ. What I want you to understand is that faith has an inherent growth factor. The determining factor of growth is determined by none other than you personally. Nobody can grow your faith—again it's personal and you determine the activation. You determine the level of development. You determine whether it becomes a lifestyle or not! The Bible emphatically promises that the growth measures are limitless, therefore the dimension you walk in, is as a result of personal choice. If you want to live in limitless dimensions the responsibility is solely on you, in either preference of contentment with where you are, or for a hunger for more of God wanting increase.

## INCREASE

In your growth you will need more faith tomorrow than today. So you might start off insignificantly or, even having been complacent all together, this means nothing. Our today and tomorrow need not be defined by yesterdays' wrongs, failures, mistakes, sins, wrongs, weaknesses, incompetencies and inability. We just need to start somewhere, and the scripture encourages us to do it in the time frame of 'today'. It is common knowledge that you cannot decide today to start yesterday. I encourage you to leave yesterday and its irrelevances as historical reminders only of tomorrow's victories. Thus start now; start small and praise God. Everything, such as in everything in the universe, starts small by God's unique design. Maybe we should take note and question whether things that just appear with a bang, and are big, are 'all God'. He can do that, but throughout His Word we see small insignificant beginnings, and by itself it almost always give reason to mock the vision's validity, yet God turned it around into a marvellous testimony when His children called on His Name.

Look at you; you started as a sperm and egg—microscopically small and look at you now: increase, expansion, enlargement, multiplication, augmented and developed. There was undisputed growth. The evidence of growth is found not in the manifestation but in the seed. It sounds wrong. No listen: Faith is something not seen. Think of the sperm and egg during conception. It was unseen. It existed but was not visible; almost as if it wasn't there.

It is the same with faith; it is unseen but existent. That's where the growth starts to take place. The final product lies in the start—the seed, not the end product. The full potential of the end product is encoded within the DNA of the seed. The seed refers to 'image' or the actual 'product of your visualization'.

Increase is mandatory. It's part of Gods original plan for mankind. Genesis 1 speaks of being fruitful and of increase . . . . In Gods fivefold plan for humanity, the second thing He commanded us to do was to increase. It's a God given command. Our faith, our love, our anointing, our character building, sanctification, deliverance, healing, every part of who we are, are under the direct command of God to increase, and to even increase in stature.

Hence my statements that increase come from God. No wonder the disciples said "increase our faith." (LUKE 17:5 KJV) Therefore we say faith comes from God, increase comes from God, and we interact in the Kingdom of God with the source.

The disciples were in a predicament, running short of adequate faith. They asked Jesus to increase their faith. And if you look at the Greek word, you can understand it clearer, by them asking God to add more faith to their existing faith.

It is, however, similar to the problem the father faced in Mark 9:24 ISV in crying out: "Help my unbelief." It could have been differently said: "God, please add to, or increase my faith, as I acknowledge my present faith is inadequate." Many people feel ashamed of their faith for diverse reasons. Some, on the other hand, feel superior and have a boasting, haughty attitude regarding it. Both are dead wrong, as faith is not a spiritual accomplishment but a divine gift. The wrong attitude will result in suffering, which is exactly the outcome for both groups. The one is too ashamed to walk by faith and the other walks in presumption and superficialness. Acknowledgement is a vital component in getting your faith on track. We have already stated with great clarity that God is the source. Faith is a gift and it is personal.

Sometimes I get the idea that certain individuals perceive faith as either some form of entertainment and / or some competitive concept that will put their name on the map. In other words, to make them feel important.

Thus my original statement; not discussing what is faith, but stating what faith is. Both the groups I have described earlier do not understand that firstly faith is a gift. However, many have a misconception in this regard. Secondly, faith, the anointing, love and any other gift are not to promote our social status or spiritual importance. The glory is focused on only one in all scenarios: GOD!!!! The gift is directly related to the exact benefit of God's Kingdom, pending the demand.

If you fall into any of these categories this is revival time: Acknowledge, or let me put it differently, confess and repent and yesterday will have lost its power. You have a clean slate to start again. Ask God, embrace His forgiveness and restoration to perfection, and move on. Let the records in heaven then read over your life that you have acknowledged and have asked God to increase and add to your faith. 'Today' is the relevant time concept and of paramount importance. Allow 'today' to determine your tomorrow, as yesterday cannot be repeated. You can only correct yesterday in the divine 'today' time framework.

Dr. Adolf Jonker Ph.D

## Concept 6 SUBSTANCE

**KEY SCRIPTURE:** **Hebrews 11:1 KJV** "Now faith is the substance of things hoped for, the evidence of things not seen."

**KEYWORDS:**

Hypostasis

Content

Confidence

Assurance

**KEY CONCEPT:** Faith has spiritual content.

# FOCUS ON FAITH

Hebrews 11:1 states that faith is the substance of what you hope for. The focus is not the things hoped for but the faith released. The Hebrew word for faith is 'pistis'. We will look further into the meaning of this word as we continue. Many people evaluate the 'hoped for things' in relation to the possibility of achievement. This will inevitably shift focus from faith to the possibility and probability of self-accomplishment regarding what they hope for. Their evaluations are based on the ability and possibility of humanity according to assumptions, perceptions and even what they consider possible or not. I trust to help you tremendously with the following section because the emphasis is on the truth of the Bible, which very clearly places all focus on faith.

The following analogy serves as an example of what I have said. Let us assume that a particular individual has a headache and has the perception (belief) that it is easy for God to heal him / her. Let's take it a step further: the same individual is diagnosed with cancer and all of a sudden the perception 'God can easily heal' changes, because of the perceived degree of the sickness. Now the perception is that it is more difficult to be healed from cancer than it is to be healed from a headache.

The truth is 'all things hoped for' by whatever definition, descriptions or levels are equally **EASILY** attainable for God. I have prayed for people who were instantly healed of terminal cancer and then I have prayed for people with a headache which were not healed. Some people are easily motivated to trust God for a small amount of money; however, the moment the numbers is raised and some zeros are added, doubt and unbelief enters. Why is this? People evaluate the possible avenues in which certain things can manifest, and as soon as they run out of ideas, then practicing their faith becomes practically difficult or impossible. What are we saying then? Mostly, people 'practice faith' with the possible avenues in mind; in other words, that

Dr. Adolf Jonker Ph.D

which can be seen. This is called pragmatic faith. This may very well even be happening subconsciously, whilst having a true heart and desire to trust God, irrespective. Another truth; remember that we said the purpose of this book is to discover true faith. Faith is the focus, and it is NEVER evaluating or meditating on the possibilities of the things hoped for. The focus is on faith. We established, thus far, that faith comes from God to man, and is then redirected from man to God (The reciprocal transmittal concept).

Directing your faith to God is pivotal, and the secret lies in focusing on the faith and not the things hoped for. We'll discuss the things hoped for later. Concluding, we say that by putting your faith in God, the focus shifts to God's 'dunamis' power, (HEBREWS 1:3 KJV) to accomplish the manifestation of what you believe God for. Again, your request, your visualization is not the dominant factor of the equation. Your focus is faith as substance in believing God.

I have observed that many folks, in the execution of their faith, look at their lives in regard to past sin, or evil, wrongs, mistakes and failures. They allow this to then influence and also determine their expression of faith. In most cases people refrain from a 'faith walk' simply as a result of the above, and disqualifying themselves because of it. Some will even consider their social status, education, socio-economic situation when considering walking by faith or not. Let's discover another true faith factor. God makes it crystal clear; He is no respecter of persons. (ACTS 10:34 KJV) It continues in James 5:17, that Elijah, the super spiritual biblical hero, was a normal human being like everybody else. He had his ups and downs, his wrongs, his failures etc etc. However, he walked in sublime faith, simply because his focus was God, and not the situation or things hoped for. The request takes a secondary role in the participation. Man's focus shifts to 'faith in God', and God's role is the 'actualization of the request'. If man focuses on the request we reverse the biblical will, ways and patterns of God, and can kiss our request goodbye. God honours His Word.

The Bible defines faith as something that doesn't release a conditional list of prerequisites. On the contrary, it is very basic: the focus is God, the currency is faith (more in the next chapter). I encourage every reader, whatever assumption you previously had. STOP. Don't allow assumptions as results of education, culture or tradition to keep you from glory.

**Matthew 15:6 NIV** says *"Thus you nullify the word of God for the sake of your tradition".*

Don't follow my example, as explained in chapter one, of the pork bone marrow illustration. Lay down your perspectives, the church traditions, if contrary to the above explanation. Take up your shield of faith, shift your focus from what needs be accomplished, and direct it to God. Come on, go for it. You will certainly reap the harvest.

## WHAT IS FAITH

Let me take you to other illustrations. In the US people are building their houses mostly with wood. Looking at the houses, and their architectural style, the substance is primarily wood. In South Africa the substance differs and is primarily bricks and cement. Elsewhere in Africa they build what is called mud houses, and the substance is soil. We can go on and on. The Bible says "Faith is the substance" (HEB.11:1 KJV) and this substance (faith) is the evidence.

Go to the above illustration. The houses in SA, the substance are bricks and cement and the brick's and cement are the evidence. Thus an architectural drawing of a particular house is not the substance and has no evidence. Therefore, we can conclude that faith, as substance, is not just a wild idea hanging in the air, or philosophy of some kind, or even just pious spirituality. Faith, like the bricks and cement to a house, has substance and is the evidence of our belief and walk with God.

Dr. Adolf Jonker Ph.D

# SPIRIT

God is spirit. We all know that. Has anybody seen Him? No. Touched Him? No. Smelled Him? So in the natural we cannot materially define or describe His substance. But His substance, according to the Bible, is SPIRIT. Faith comes from God, thus faith's substance is spirit. It is not a religious, abstract concept or church doctrine. It's not a mystical idea. The heavens are not going to fall on you and you wear a blue cap, or a wind blow over you and you receive angels' wings. It's real, it's concrete and it is spirit. The substance is spirit. Therefore we refer to the analogy of the house built with bricks and cement being the substance. The materialization of the things hoped for will correspond with the house; the substance is faith, in relation to the bricks and cement. Now we can move on with an understanding that the focus is God and faith and not the 'things hoped for'; and therefore faith is real.

# SUBSTANCE

The word substance is of major importance, and soon you will understand why we have spent so much time on semantics. The Greek word for substance is 'hypostasis'. (STRONGS, G5287) There are a variety of words available to compliment the translation. However, I want to settle on one word as the only interpretation. The rest are cluster words, their meanings all the same. The word to translate is 'confidence'. With this statement we now say that this substance (which is of a spiritual nature) is confidence. So faith is the confidence of things hoped for, or differently said, confidence is the characteristic of the divine spiritual substance that the bible refers to as faith. It necessitates a further investigation into confidence.

There are a group of words that relate to confidence, synonyms if you wish. These words are assurance, certainty, courage, determination, poise or reliance. These words are an intertwined network, interdependent, interactive and cooperative, regarding the concept confidence. Words are ideas, in order to give a better understanding, and, in this instance, of faith. Confidence is a foundational key truth in the equation of faith. Confidence is then a complete trust, fully reliant on somebody or something.

I want to highlight the word 'assurance' to help you with a better understanding. Confidence is the assurance, which applies more surety of self, something or someone. It is vitally important to note that nowhere do we talk about a feeling. It's not a feeling! Some folks have a good 'feel' toward their belief, others say: 'I don't feel it will work or come to pass'. Well people, to be blunt, both are wrong. Nowhere, in the equation of faith, does feeling play any role whatsoever! Not in God's mind. It is a human way of expression, but in reality it opposes the truth about faith. Wherever I came in contact with people, many will report concerning their feeling, with regard to what they are experiencing, and trusting God for, in faith. Feeling has nothing to do with faith. On the contrary, feeling is a deceptive detour turning us away from faith. These are mere compilations of good feelings or bad feelings, both defying faith. Whenever or wherever feeling becomes part of your trusting in God; your focus needs to be redirected, and you must pray and reconsider whether you are still on the right or on the wrong track. In the vocabulary sphere of faith 'feeling' does not exist.

## INNER KNOWLEDGE

My observation, then, is that confidence is an inner knowledge. Thus we have to firstly determine what 'inner' entails. Allow me to say that man is a triune being, with spirit, soul and body (more later). 'Inner' boils down to a combination of spirit and soul. This 'faith-confidence' is a gift of God, which we have already established as a fact. In context of the soulish realm, this gift is received and embraced. 'Inner' defines, then, the idea that the gift of God is embraced by man. Put differently, man made this gift his own.

Dr. Adolf Jonker Ph.D

As a result of the above, we say God is spirit, and gives us a spiritual gift (faith). Man receives it in his spirit; the brain registers its reception and man embraces it in his soulish realm (mind, will and emotions). Therefore a spiritual entity is released into the natural. When man releases this gift of faith, and directs it toward God, the reverse takes place. From the natural in man's soul, he decides to put this confidence in God, now man's soul intertwined with his brain formulates the concept, and through his spirit releases it back to God. Psalm 42:7 KJV refers to deep (spirit) calls unto deep (spirit). Remember that Jesus said that in the last days, true worshippers shall worship God in spirit and truth. This excites me enormously and I know it will do the same for you.

We now come to the second word, 'knowledge'. This inner knowledge is the spiritual substance received, and as a result makes this inner knowledge spiritual, understood within the parameters of the natural realm. Can you see that 'feelings' have no part? Can you also see that faith does not come from your mind by way of your IQ, intellectualism or acquired knowledge? Therefore it is not carnally minded but it is spiritual by nature. Your mind becomes acquainted as a result of perpetual practice.

We can describe it differently by saying that your soulish man [2 COR.10:4 KJV] bows to or submits to your spirit man. In any other way you bring in human factors, such as feeling, rationality or pragmatic faith (carnally minded). Romans 10:10 confirms this by saying that with your soul (heart) you believe (have confidence originating from your spirit) and with your soul (mouth) you speak. It's a working together, but in order of submission, when your mental capacity submits to your spiritual conviction. The confession says that man proclaims, declares or prophecies in the natural, of the working of the Invisible God in spirit.

The pestering concept 'doubt' enters when man allows mental attitudes to take control and argues against the spiritual truths of God. For argument's sake, let's say an unbeliever asks many questions and makes serious statements against the spiritual knowledge of God, then ends up not believing. In other words, there was no submission to spiritual truth, and heart and mouth couldn't unite together, therefore doubt entered and unbelief manifested. Differently said, God wants everybody to be saved <sup>(ISAIAH 45:22 KJV)</sup>, so the gift of faith is available to all. However, the unbeliever cannot embrace or make the gift their own. Same with you and I as believers. When we put our arguments, reasoning, assumptions or feelings above God's spiritual knowledge, we create the opportunity for doubt to sink our faith ship.

During 2005 God led me to sow my three vehicles into the lives of three other people. All of a sudden I had no means of transportation, and while extremely difficult, this lasted for 5 years. In May 2010 God spoke to me one Sunday morning and said, "Today will be different; you won't understand now, but go to church in faith. Before the service started, a gentleman approached me and handed me the key of a million rand BMW 745I. Can you even imagine or understand my shock and surprise? In the natural, nobody in their right mind would do that. In the natural, there was no way for me to buy that car. Simply said, every natural avenue was non-existent. I could never put my faith in the natural possibilities, because as far as those went there were none. They were non-existent, and my faith was only in God. I praise His name by His power that He accomplished the impossible for me.

## ASSENT

In order for believers and unbelievers, (in other words for all of humanity) to walk in faith, think faith, act faith, and live faith, our natural minds need to agree with the knowledge of God's existence. Our minds need to give in to God and His Word, to adhere to it, and as result, come into agreement with the spiritual knowledge. This assent draws a fine line. Let me then say that it spells out complete confidence in truth alone and absolutely not on assumptions which are based on a myriad of possible reasons. This confidence is not intuition, not a feeling, and definitely not divination. It is not presumptuous either. It's an inner knowledge.

Many people walk in presumptuous faith. They will normally argue that God knows their hearts, and will lay out what God will and won't do to and for them. Presumption will easily say: "God won't allow that to happen". Some might go as far as reasoning that because of how they perceive themselves and their righteous walk, that God will do it for them, because they are righteous people. "I am a good person", is another reason presented to suggest what God will do, but unfortunately all the above are untrue assumptions. Faith has nothing to do with your spiritual status or any other idea, nor is it bound to it. Many will tell that their supreme level of holiness will leave God no other option but to answer them. Sorry friend, it is religious baloney. Presumption is nothing more than people assuming, without any biblical ground, that God would act on their behalf because of unwarranted claims.

Let's say there are two sport teams and they are all Christians. They both ask God to let them win the world cup. It happens all the time! We all know there will only be one winner. Arguing that you are a Christian won't make God answer you. Arguing that God would allow a Christian politician to become the country's president because he favours his Christianity per se, warrants nothing but disappointment!

Some people mistakenly, and for various reasons, say: "But God said to me that it will happen". This behaviour can be described as mistakenly misusing and even abusing the authority of God in your statement, and doesn't verify anything, and you'll be disappointed. I think we have to come out publicly and confess that all Christians, at some or another time, claimed to have heard God but were mistaken, and at times even deceived. Nobody on earth, outside of Jesus, was, is, will ever be perfect in this dispensation. Its best we just acknowledge and move on with repentance. Well-known prophets from mega churches, good Christians, were proven wrong, and did some serious damage with wrong prophecies, but the worst are the unrepentant. Their falsity normally leads to corrupt doctrines and churches or movements. The Old Testament is deluged with false prophets, likewise the New Testament. Let's acknowledge our mistakes and move from presumption to truth. Some state they will believe when they see. That is not faith, but facts proven or something actualized. This so-called pragmatic faith is not faith at all.

Confidence in God is, then, the inner knowledge of God. But what about God? What is it to which we are referring?

## FOUNDATIONAL CONQUEST

We have established now that this substance is a confidence encompassing an inner knowledge. Hebrews 11:6 ISV makes three things clear:

I. Faith pleases God
II. Belief in His existence
III. He is a rewarder.

The backdrop or starting point of wherever and whenever faith is concerned, includes the three points in the above statement. I encourage you to make yourself little cards with these statements and put them at strategic places in your house. Whenever you see them, speak them out, proclaim them, embrace them and meditate on them! I guarantee that they will revolutionize your entire existence. Test this for yourself.

Firstly, the above three statements are the initiation markers to your faith statement. Understand that this pleases God! Its intricacies have been mentioned in great detail in Part 2.

The second statement is that you believe in His (God's) existence. Allow me then, to make a statement that your belief in His existence is paramount. You have to believe in

Dr. Adolf Jonker Ph.D

- ➤ His existence
- ➤ His presence

These concepts bring God into real life, making Him part of every second of every day. It makes God part of who you are and what you are doing. You believe in His being, 'I am who I am. I am sovereign, I am supreme, I am your source, I am your provider, I am eternal, I am the only God, I am creator and I am all you want Me to be'. This is so precious! You know He was and will be, but for Him the importance is 'NOW', Today! He is! Present tense! 'I am with you at this very specific moment!'

Thirdly, you believe He is the rewarder of those who diligently seek Him. Diligently implies continually. It saddens my heart to see how many Christians meet with God occasionally. He is only important when they want something from Him. I recently met with a lady who came for prayer. We hadn't seen her in church for about a month, and she said she had no apparent reason for not coming. However, that morning, she was in desperate need for finances and attended especially so that I could pray with her. I didn't! We cannot displace God out of our lives until we need Him. This is certainly not 'diligently', in fact it is far from it. Diligently seeking the face of God is the key.

Let me close with a thought on pleasing God with your faith. I'll give you two ideas on which to ponder. One of our church members passed away after being confined to a sickbed for a long time. Every single day, even up to her very last day on earth, she uttered words of faith, and whoever went to see her was confronted with her expression of faith in God, proclaiming that He is faithful and would healing her. The result? She died, and God did not heal her in the natural realm. Was her faith in vain? A million if not trillion times No! No! No! The focus of faith is primarily to please God, irrespective of the outcome of what we perceive or trust Him for. She pleased God with her faith every single day that she was alive, and the day she met with Him He was her rewarder. Allow me to say this: I have not seen so many people attending a burial service as on the day with this specific lady. You only get to see it when famous people die. However, even though on a sickbed, (and also before that), she impacted the lives of many, many people in the community, leading them to Jesus Anointed Son of God. It was evident that the honour and glory was towards God—and to God only.

What are the ideas I want you to ponder over?

We should remember that God is Sovereign. This has been a hurdle that many people tend to find difficult to clear. He is God, YHWH, He is I AM and does what He wills. 'He is' has a unique plan for each and every individual. Fact! He is omniscient. He knows best. The lady I spoke about submitted to God, and regarded Him as sovereign and omniscient. Her heart's desire was to always and only please Him. She pleased God, and the reward is in His hand.

My last thought: we believe God for salvation, for deliverance, for protection, for providence, and the list continues on and on. Allow me to encourage you to release your faith in God, and not per se trust Him for anything specific. Just open yourself to Holy Spirit and say; "God, I believe in You, I know You are, You are the beginning and the end. Enable me to walk a simple day to day, 'faith walk', Lord, where there is nothing in it for me, and the primary focus is: TO PLEASE GOD." In complete surrender and honour of God's Name, in faith, you will surely sow seed in receiving a harvest of being pleasing unto God. However, that is not the focus, yet God is such a gracious Rewarder that even before we ever thought to do something good He already gave us all we will ever need.

Dr. Adolf Jonker Ph.D

## CURRENCY

**KEY SCRIPTURE:** Revelations 3:18 KJV "I counsel thee to buy of me gold tried in the fire, that thou mayest be rich; and white raiment, that thou mayest be clothed, and that the shame of thy nakedness do not appear; and anoint thine eyes with eyesalve, that thou mayest see."

**KEYWORDS:** Trading

Exchange

**KEY CONCEPT:** Faith is the only currency between God and man; heaven and earth.

# CURRENCY

Since the creation mankind has been busy with some sort of business deal. All transactions in the trade-off, they made use of a specific 'currency'. The currencies applicable were decided upon during the different ages and time zones. Today it is still the same. In previous ages they made use of goods in their interchange as a form of payment. A Christian artist was eating at a specific restaurant, and when he had to pay he offered the owner one of his CD's to settle the account. The owner accepted, but I think it was more an act of decency then conviction. Today it's inappropriate. We deal in paper or metal.

Let me elaborate a bit for greater clarity. Let's argue that you live in the USA where the currency is the dollar. If any person from Japan comes to the USA and wants to buy something, and offers the seller Japanese yen, even the exact equivalent of what it is in dollar, the seller will blatantly refuse. The reason is the currency. If it was dollars, fine, anything else in the US won't do.

Sometimes we, as Christians, take life for granted and have our own misconceptions. Imagine going to the grocery store and telling the owner you are a Christian, you live a good life, you do good to others and you are in a smart mega church, where God is doing signs, wonders and miracles. Then, as result of the above, you ask if he would give you the groceries for nothing. He'll refuse, and thank you for your great testimony, but will tell you: "I need to see dollars before I give you the groceries"—the trading currency being dollars. Again, you go to the shop to get goods and you tell the owner that God spoke with you, you fasted for five days, and that the owner should give the goods free of charge. He will refuse, bless you with your walk with the Lord, and yet still insist that you first need to render dollars. It's the set norm instituted by the US government, dollars are the only legal currency. In every trade-off there is currency involved, no matter where you are in the world. The above scenarios are a little outrageous but in the Christian world, in general, at times

Dr. Adolf Jonker Ph.D

a norm. However, in the Kingdom of God, in trading with God the currency is determined by divine rule, as faith and faith only!

## FAITH THE SPIRITUAL MEDIUM OF EXCHANGE

Matthew 9:29 describes the story of two blind men visiting Jesus. He touched their eyes and made a significant statement: *"According to your faith, be it unto you."* Let's talk about it. First, let me say that this is clear evidence that the exchange medium between Jesus and these two blind men was faith. Jesus had the power to heal and restore and said to them: "All I ask is; do you believe?" In exchange, they boldly pronounced 'yes' and released their faith in the one with the power. He didn't ask them about their eyes and their experience, how long they had been blind or whether they had any medical report. Did the medical report state it was a cataract or some form of macular degeneration or something wrong with the ganglion cells? Neither did He want microscopic information on the cone cell's status. He didn't sympathize and counsel them on their terrible experience. He did not tell them about the multitude of sins committed. He didn't even ask if He could pray for them, what church they belonged to, the name of their Pastor and, and, and. He directed their focus towards Him and His POWER, away from themselves. Then when they responded He said 'your' faith—nothing else—'your faith'. Folks, let me address your hearts: **Your** faith is vital. This is when it doesn't matter who your neighbour is, what your nationality or ethnicity entails, what church you go to, and, and, and. This is where neither your parents, nor your pastor can help, and you don't even phone the counsellor or resort to Christian television. This is where only you can help yourself. You need to execute your faith, focused on God, who will exalt His power, and you have a done deal.

Wherever Jesus was involved, scripture is deluged with evidence of the above. Jesus said to the centurion, 'It will be done as you believed'.(MATT.8:13 KJV) Do you see the reference to the individual?

The responsibility is yours. Too many Christians rely on somebody else's faith to accomplish something. That's why we put 'certain faith people' on ungodly pedestals. It's wrong. You and I need to make a mindset alteration, take responsibility and discover the truth of faith. In Acts 27:25 KJV Paul urges the people saying, "Keep up your courage men, for I have faith in God that it will happen just as He told me."

Do you see that the focus is on God and not the situation? I encourage you to take responsibility of your own life; you owe it to God and yourself. Walk, live, act and think faith. Once you have taken responsibility and start acting on your own, then the support, (faith support), of others will be of great benefit to you. Then only will you enjoy those around you with their upliftment.

## WHAT ARE ALLOWED TO BE ASKED

Many times Christians are in the dark as to what they may or may not ask the Lord! This is as mainly a result of two things:

- Religious assumption and
- Lack of knowledge.

It is unfortunate, but many people in some way or another, grow up with a complete misunderstanding of God, His will and ways. In growing up, my understanding of God was that He is this unmerciful judge who sits on His throne like a school principal, and that He was just waiting for me to make a mistake so that He could enforce punishment on me. Was or is this your opinion of God? You may deny it but I do want to make this statement. If we only see Him as a loving, giving, forgiving, protecting and merciful Father, why would we, from time to time, or in certain situations, walk with shame or in condemnation? That God is a critical, judgmental judge on a throne is the most perverse assumption ever, and indeed so incorrect. On the contrary, He wants to bless you more than anything else.

The Greek woman, Syrophoenician by nation, in Mark 7:27-30 KJV is a great example. She came to ask Jesus to heal her daughter, who was tormented by a demon. She communicated with Him, expecting a response to her faith request. In Jesus' answer to her we can infer a slight unhappiness with this woman. However, she was adamant, as she reasoned with the Son of God, with great respect. The reason for this was that she was completely convicted that Jesus was and had the solution to her problem. Jesus saw her persistent faith demanding a positive response, and He acted accordingly.

My point, friend, is that we shouldn't allow any form of resistance from people, institutions, society, our family, close or extended, and even, with great respect I say this, from the church world, to influence us in our walk of faith—thinking, acting and living faith. Faith has no limitations, because God has no limitations. Years before I became a Christian (born-again), I went to the bank to apply for a loan. They declined my application. I went home and started praying. I was a horrible sinner, didn't know God, nor had anything to do with God, except warming the pews every Sunday. I surely didn't know how to pray. But, in my distress, I went on my knees and said: "God, whoever You are, I believe you can help me; please do. I will go back to the bank and apply again." The same day I went back and saw the manager. He looked at me and said: "I shouldn't do this, but I will grant your request." This was purely the intervention of God, but why? He is faithful to His Word, irrespective of my horrible status. I wasn't planning to serve God; I only wanted Him to help me!

What are we allowed to ask? Mark 9:23 will give you a clear picture. May Holy Spirit flood your whole being as we discuss this. The scripture states that "everything is possible." (MARK 9:23 ISV) The Greek word 'pas' (STRONGS, G3956) in this scripture translates as 'all, every, any or whole'. This is an all-inclusive concept. What can I add to the above? Let's reverse our interpretation and say, the scripture removes any idea, any hint of any restriction as to what you are allowed. There is no limitation. In other words what is on your heart God will grant, (PSALM 21:2 / MARK 11:24 KJV) providing you do it by faith. The possibility for Jesus, in God's Word, lies in **'all things'**. This is not rocket science, but plain and easily understandable. We exuberantly conclude that there are no restrictions!

**Matthew 19:26 KJV** states *"All things are possible."*

the prerequisite to the limitless possibilities in God is faith.

**Mark 11:22 ISV** *"Have faith in God!"*

It's in your face and crystal clear. In Matthew 21:21 Jesus speaks about what is allowed, and confirms 'all is allowed'. He said that anything, even analogously with difficult levels as high as mountains, is no problem with God but only faith makes it surmountable.

As result of the above, we can conclude that Jesus says, 'there is nothing too big or too small for you to ask God'. Nothing at all!

**Matthew 18:19 KJV** *". . . That if two of you shall agree on earth as touching any thing that they shall ask, it shall be done for them of my Father which is in heaven."*

There you have it folks! If you replace 'any' or 'every' in God's Word, with any restriction, you are adding untrue assumptions.

## SIZE OF FAITH

This is another huge stumbling block for people, and one clearly misunderstood! Most people have the incorrect idea that before God answers your request you need to become a superhero in faith. They think you need to have grown to thumping faith, before God even considers listening to you. Some think they need to qualify with a doctorate degree in faith before God will respond. All of these ideas

Dr. Adolf Jonker Ph.D

and reasoning are untrue and ultimately false. Some think the greater the level of difficulty, the greater the demand on producing more superior faith.

The Bible differs from the above. Jesus makes it clear that whatever the level of difficulty you are experiencing, or those that prevail, you can overcome it by faith. Then He compares the level of faith with a mustard seed. Friends, a mustard seed is more or less 1,5mm in diameter, if not less. What Jesus is saying, in actual fact, is that we are not talking levels of faith, or specific measures or whopping gigantic degrees. No, He clarifies the size: 'mustard seed'.

The mustard seed's size is almost insignificant. Jesus tries to tell us to get away from a worldly concept or religious idea. Just release your faith. He says the smallest amount or degree will work. But how come does He say this? You see, friend, the accomplishment is done by God. Your faith is the currency. Using my own illustration, it is as if God says to us, one cent of faith will 'pay' for the job. Your faith is the currency; the level and the amount of faith are not the determining factors as to what God can do!

Faith then is like a business deal, spiritual by nature. God is the supplier, the source, the provider. Faith relates to the currency, and the goods in demand represent your request. There is no limit to what you can ask of God; all He needs is faith.

Every morning when I wake up I greet Father, Son and Holy Spirit, thanking God for His kindness towards me. Then I express my belief in Him as the only true God and Creator. I release my faith daily. Will you allow me, on this note, to ask you to consider doing something similar? You can spice it up with your own workings. But in doing so you start living, acting, thinking and walking by faith on a daily basis. Remember, the just shall live by faith.

**Oncept 8** | JURIDICAL

**KEY SCRIPTURE:** JUDE 1:6 ISV

"He has also held in eternal chains those angels who did not keep their own position but abandoned their assigned place. They are held in deepest darkness for judgment on the great day."

**KEYWORDS:** **Constitutional**

**Enforceable**

**Statutory**

**Proof**

**Conviction**

**KEY CONCEPT:** Relating to the law (principles/patterns/ways of God) to the administration of justice execution

# CONSTITUTIONAL

It is my strongest conviction that faith, as divine interactive currency between natural and spiritual realms, puts us in a right setting before God. Differently said, faith gives us justice before God. It's a lifestyle and not an episodic occurrence. It's God's heart that we should live by faith, therefore binding to us in the natural, thus making faith a judicial concept. We are co-heirs with Jesus the Anointed One.(ROMANS 8:17 KJV) Being heirs postulates a covenantal testament.(HEBREWS 8:8 KJV) A testament is a legal document forcible by nature. What's stated in the document binds the parties in agreement. We have God, who writes the constitution for our lives, in His testament. What He says will be. He's not a man that He can lie. (NUMBERS 23:19 KJV) He continues to proclaim, with divine authority, that heaven and earth will pass away but none of His Words will. (MATT. 24:35 KJV) Furthermore, there will one day be a judgment seat for all of mankind to face. (REV. 20:11-12; 2 COR. 5:10 KJV) This proves my point, that faith is also juridical and not a Sunday morning philosophy or midweek discussion of the hopefuls.

If you were to be judged, you'd need to be judged according to something that holds you accountable. Thus God gives us His Word to 'image' after it. In other words, the Bible is our constitution for life. During the judgment our lives will be judged in how they correspond with our constitution. Therefore what God provides as lifestyle has statutory consequences. Said differently, it is enforceable and true, and thus judgment is God's.

> **2 Chronicles 19:6 KJV** *"And said to the judges, Take heed what ye do: for ye judge not for man, but for the LORD, who is with you in the judgment."*

Judgment is God's. In our analogy we'll refer to the perfect Judge. On what does He base His judgment? The constitution has divine statutory principles. Wherever you move on earth, the omniscient, perfect judge will always be around to address your case. Jesus being your advocate, expert in law as He is 'The Word' <sup>(JOHN 1:1 KJV)</sup> and Holy Spirit yet again another expert to assist you in whatever degree of difficulty or situation in life. He is your helper and the good thing is that He leads you in all truth. <sup>(JOHN 16:13KJV)</sup> Life, circumstances, situations, diverse issues and the demonical realm will always be there to accuse you with a guilty conviction. They will throw any and everything into the intermixture to destroy, kill and steal from you.<sup>(JOHN 10:10 KJV)</sup> The battlefield or the courtroom is your mind, the impartial jury, the Word of God.

The spirit of this world (lust of eye/ flesh, pride of life) <sup>(1 JOHN 2:16 KJV)</sup> goes out of its way to influence you and accuse you of wrongdoing. But we have an impartial jury, a great helper who knows truth by divine measures, and an advocate in great standing with the eternal perfect judge. Only the Word of God has the power to convict us.

I will show you that the very first thing on which you are judged by God is NOT your multitudes of wrongs, your sins, your inadequacies, or even your good deeds, your achievements plus, plus, plus. I guess John 3:16 is the scripture that all of humanity knows: God sends His own Son. Those that believe are judged and the judgment is eternal salvation. God's salvation plan acquits man of a guilty conviction, due to a release of faith. Those who don't believe are also judged with eternal condemnation. The judgment for such has already been passed in the constitution of God, His Word. Thus the primary principal entity that draws judgment is faith (pleasing God or eternal condemnation). John 3:36 ISV "The one who believes in the Son has eternal life, but the one who disobeys the Son will not see life. Instead, the wrath of God remains in him."

## JURIDICAL CONCEPTS

Why don't we look quickly into a courtroom scenario? Most prominent of all is, that you have your sitting judge, court clerks and

Dr. Adolf Jonker Ph.D

police officials to oversee and force down the following of correct court procedures. You have the accused represented by a lawyer. This lawyer is an expert on law who assists the accused to have a fair trial, to receive an appropriate verdict. You have the state prosecutor to represent the state in order to get a guilty conviction. Then lastly, the jury, they are impartial, and will make the final decision; convicted of the crime or not. I realise that you know these things. However, I want to use the above analogously to draw the parameter of the court further than brick walls, to the sphere where you live, the circles of society where you are involved, the market place, your family life, your personal space, your entire existence on a daily basis, delineated in the framework of your life from beginning to end.

Friends, the Bible is explicit, vivid to the bone in divine matters. "The judgment is God's" (DEUT 1:17 KJV), even where man is concerned in judgment. This conviction is legally binding, fair and enforceable.

Allow me a few minutes to take you through the judicial aisles from a different angle; a new perspective. You and I have certain things we hope for, things of necessity or desires, whatever they may be. Let's walk into the courtroom, advocate and helper; an impartial jury already there, available at all times, by God's design. Imagine we approach the bench. The question asked: what is your request? Together we address our request to the ONLY judge, God Almighty. He will firstly evaluate it on the evidence that you produce, if it's statutory. What do I mean? 1 John 5:15 says that should we ask anything corresponding to His will—His Word, our constitution for life, He will answer us favourably. However, friend, the judgment is not passed. There is no conviction yet. Allow me for now to go ahead of myself. Conviction in God's ability always precedes and also accompanies faith. God is clear in His Word; if you petition God, He will ask you: "Where is your faith?" (LUKE 8:25 KJV) He is clear that those that approach Him, with whatever request, must know that faith is the prerequisite. He will not answer unless we fulfil His divine standard. Jesus knew it and therefore when He saw the absence of faith in Nazareth, He did only a few miracles and walked away as a result of their unbelief. <sup>(MARK 6:5-6 KJV)</sup>

Jesus' power and ability wasn't the problem but the unbelief, showing in God's courtroom, when the evidence of God's will is proven when faith is on the table the deal is sealed with divine authority. Functioning outside of the above equation and the verdict for you and I will be the same. The currency unlocking God's working and miracle power is faith! Mark 2:5 *says "When Jesus saw their faith"* He responded. When does Jesus respond? He responds the very moment when faith, which is the key to unlocking the power of God, is released.

**Mark 5:34 NIV**    "Daughter your faith has healed you."

**Mark 10:52 NIV**    "Your faith has healed you."

**Luke 7:50 NIV**    "Your faith has saved you."

**Luke 17:19 NIV**    "Your faith has made you well."

**Luke 18:42 NIV**    "Receive your sight; your faith has healed you."

## DIVINE LAW

There isn't an end to the list that faith is the legal entity which God established in the interaction with His children. Even God Himself maintains this earth by a word of faith. <sup>(HEB 1:13 KJV)</sup> The word used in this scripture can be translated 'Rhema', meaning a revelation of utterance.

There is, however, one thing you and I need to address in this judicial process, and that is conviction. Conviction, very simply described, is the state of being convicted, but it can also be addressed as an act of confidence. This word carries authority and finality with it. You have to grasp in your mind and spirit the concept 'finality and authority'! It is vital in your faith walk. Therefore, I believe conviction is an act that places someone in a specific state of being confident in God. The state is the result of an act. The act is you finalizing in your being "God shall!" It's the judge's gavel (hammer) that he hits on the bench, announcing that the case is closed.

For you and I to function in faith, we need our minds to be firmly fixed on who God is, and His Word as being the ultimate truth. If He said the whale swallowed Jonah, then we believe it. Faith is something that happens outside of natural rationality, because it is produced with super-natural-wisdom. It is an entity beyond the parameters of human intellect and scientific arrogance and even religious stupidity. I'm talking about definiteness in your persuasion; a fixation in yourself of the knowledge you have of God and His Word. When you step out in faith, you have concluded, 'this is what I believe God for', and in boldness you assertively step out and believe God. You 'hit the gavel on the bench' saying 'it is final.' The Book of Matthew says my 'yes will be yes'.(MATTHEW 5:37 KJV) God created in Genesis 1 and every time He created something He boldly and assertively said, "and so shall it be." The conviction in His being was that nothing would stop Him; it would happen as He believed it would.

In barratry (common law) during cross examination lawyers make use of some characteristics relating to barratry. No other system's characteristics will do only that which apply to barratry. Diverse types of evidence should be produced and in modern history we see the critical role that genetic evidence (DNA) plays; its relevance, authentication all plays a role in the final judgment. Witnesses testifying will be classified as bona fide (good faith) or mala fide (bad faith). In Christianity I would refer to the above as believers and non-believers. In dealing with God, we have divine law and the characteristics evident as producing evidence of faith, proclamation of God's Word (irreversibly always perfect truth), authentication, personal prayer request, and prophetic utterances.

In the game of cricket, each team receives two opportunities to appeal against the decision of the umpire on the field. So you need to make sure of your reasons for appeal. The television umpire will make a decision based on the replays of the incident in question. I saw a game where the captain of the team went to the rest of the team to decide for or against a referral. Clearly, the rest of the team, with facial expressions and hand signals, verbally told him not to refer and thereby jeopardise the next opportunity. The next moment, against all odds, all advice opposing it; he turned around and with outstanding boldness referred the matter. To my surprise, the television umpire decided in favour of his appeal. I realized that day that no matter what happens around you, be convicted by your faith of God, His mercy, grace, goodness, kindness and a list of attributes with no end. Do not be passive but step out and release your faith. No circumstances in this world, whatsoever they may be, are too hard for God and cannot be 'believed possible to change'. Even if all the doctors' medical prognoses say that you are terminally ill, but you stand and believe; God can heal you. Do not hesitate to step out in faith. In stepping out, and releasing your faith for God's healing, you surrender and give God the right to heal you in whichever way He sees fit. You refrain from 'boxing' God into a specific methodology. Whether He leads you to drink medicine, or take herbs, or preventative natural products, or whatever medical or surgical procedures, just wait on Him to supernaturally touch you, it is all God's healing! Thus none can be attributed to superior faith on its own. God will heal you because you follow His direction in faith. Just step out and be amazed at the wondrous ways He can work in your life.

If you are declared insolvent, step out in faith, start over again. Slam the door on yesterday's failure. It doesn't define you. You will make it in God. Don't doubt God's ability to give you a new start. If you have believed God a million times for something and you have not yet seen Him answer you, boldly step out in faith and be ready to trust Him ten million times more. If you have failed in all you have done in your life, as far back as you can remember up to now, step out and know the day is coming; it certainly is coming for you! It is the day when God will reverse things for you. Never ever give up. Shout it out, trumpet it into the air, and write it on your wall, print cards and put it everywhere—"I will never ever give up."

Never turn to negativity and moan and groan about your marriage, family, friends, your job, your personal being, your hometown, your country etc. Never! A negative mind cannot function in faith. Negativity will only serve as a disqualifier to walk by faith. Make sure that you understand this. Do not succumb to it. Never ever! Negativity only produces misery. Negativity is an evil diabolic functioning. It has no power to alter your situation. You can be negative your whole life and I guarantee you that none of your circumstances will change for the better. Do you want to take that chance?

## OPPOSING FACTORS AGAINST FAITH

The opposing factors to conviction are all negative concepts and take the form of words like 'uncertainty'. It's a killer; a mighty destroyer of faith. Why do you want to be uncertain, if God can split the sea, if God can stop a river in flood to make way for His children, if an axe head can float on the water, if a whale can swallow a man and spit him out after three days, if God can heal the sick, if the lame can walk, if the blind can see, if the deaf can hear, if the dead can be resurrected from the death to life? Is there even a remote indication of a part of life that God has not proven Himself as Almighty? Can you think of any? One? There is not one. Whatever is believed indifferent to the Word is because our understanding is covered with deception. Uncertainty, hesitation and negativity have no place whatsoever in the vocabulary of a Christian. Why? They are not Christian words! They oppose faith. These are deceptive concepts darkening our faith perception.

On the contrary, a positive attitude can turn the world over. It levels the playing field. It puts you on a platform of belief. It creates hope, stirs your inner being and motivates you. It is a godly force of unimaginable proportions. There is no limit to any accomplishment or resource or miracle to those who are positive in what they say, do and live. Positive people will see negative things, but they have the ability in God to process them and allow Holy Spirit to support them to overlook negativity with a different perspective and then continue with a positive approach. Negative minds give in to the manipulation, dictation and intimidation of a negative approach. Positive people have only one approach and that is to rule over any negativity. They are never intimidated by negativity. Positivity is a runway for faith; it launches you into achieving the impossible.

While in the process, let's also kill Goliath, cut off his head: Goliath represented by the word "questionableness". There are people who question everything. It is part of their mindsets and lifestyle. I had people argue with me one day about the splitting of the Red Sea. Their argument was that the wind blew the water apart at a very shallow place. Wow! What an argument. However far-fetched it seemed that it was a possible reason for the Red Sea to split apart, I don't care. What is more far-fetched and complete ignorance, is arguing and watering down a true miracle to a humanly explicable situation. God is entitled to do whatever He wants and however He wants to do it. All I know is that the sea split apart because of the supernatural intervention of God. Some people want to argue past their unbelief. Faith is a conviction in God's ability; it is an act. The miracle or God's response to my faith request is answer enough. If the Bible says the dead were resurrected, then that is what happened.

Let me assure you then that this awesome God can do for you what He has done throughout history, beyond the borders of the Bible, to millions of people. He is the same yesterday, today, and forever (HEB 13:8 KJV) for you, me and any other person. I once fell and split the patella in my knee. The pain was excruciating. All the people around me, my wife and my family told me to go for medical help. On the contrary,

God gave me a clear word not to go, He would heal me. I walked for three months without being able to bend my knee at all. People spoke to medical acquaintances who said to me, "You have damaged your knee forever." After about 6 months I could hardly bend it, and one morning I prayed and said to God: "You said You would heal me and I believe you." I couldn't bend my knee in the natural as it had been said that the damage was irreversible. I had the impression from God, at that moment, to take a rope, tie it around my ankle and jack it up towards my buttock. It was seriously painful. Nothing happened. The next morning I tried to lift my heel towards my buttock by itself. I could have jumped through the ceiling when my heel touched my behind with no trace of any pain! Years later I ran a 200m sprint in the South African championships, won and broke a provincial record. Truly, nothing is impossible for God, not in the least!!! Where were the doom prophets that prophesied destruction to my patella (knee)? Nowhere! Where were science, and its scientific proof? My winning was a testimony of God not because I could run fast, but that He healed me completely, and enabled me to run. Do yourself a favour, cast off all doom prophecies from you.

Conviction is the act of confidence; in other words you make a decision, "I believe God." That places you in a state of conviction. Stay there by understanding this juridical concept; God's Word is His divine covenant with us. He is not like man who can lie. Hence, His Word is the ultimate and only truth. It is God's heavenly statutory law binding God to it and thus become a point of conviction for man releasing his faith in God and His Word.

# PART 2

**KEY SCRIPTURE:** JOHN 14:15 ISV

"If you love me, keep my commands."

**KEYWORDS:**

Dead works

Faith

Baptism

Transference / Ministry

Resurrection

Judgment

**KEY CONCEPT:** First principles are the basic fundamental entry level essentials into living true Christianity as ordained by

# FIRST SIX PRINCIPLES
## Introduction to the foundational Principles of a Christian walk

No person on the face of the earth can change God's order. To ensure God's protection and blessing over our lives, we have to follow His ways. The very first thing we need is to be fed with God's milk. Without it you will not be able to mature in God. Any born again child of God, who promptly follows the principles of God, will surely experience great spiritual growth, and will with ease be able to exhort and edify people, encouraging them to follow God's Word, His order and His ways. The significance of the first principles is found in God's Word. God's Word, and no other, is the premise for the study of the doctrine of First Principles. I encourage you to read and study what is being shared about the First Principles prayerfully, under guidance of Holy Spirit.

Let us first examine why it is so important to follow God's ways as prescribed by Him. Many folk will explain that the way they do it is not exactly the way the Bible says, but reason that God will not be offended by this, as it diverts only a minute part and after all, most Christians are doing it as well. Well, friend, most of Israel, apart from two, believed the ten unbelieving spies and the report they sketched about Canaan and the possibility of possessing it. If you have not heard of this before, go and read it. All who believed the unbelieving spies died in the desert, and God did not allow them the opportunity to enter with those who believed the report of Joshua and Caleb. Not the majority vote, celebrity pastors' approval, nor people we love and trust will ever have higher authority than God's Word. None of these will ever justify anybody from believing, doing and acting contrary to God's will. God gave Moses instructions in how to build the Tabernacle:

> **Hebrews 8:5 ISV** *"They serve in a sanctuary that is a copy, a shadow of the heavenly one. This is why Moses was warned when*

Dr. Adolf Jonker Ph.D

*he was about to build the tent: (See to it that you make everything according to the pattern that was shown you on the mountain)."*

Friends, God said to Moses, I am the Great I am, the only I am, YHWH, do whatever you do exactly the way, I, God, want it to be done. The Word of God has been ordained by God and not by the interpretations of theologians, pastors or churches. We are here to please the Master, because certainly the student is not greater than the master. (MATTHEW 10:24 KJV)

The writer speaks of First Principles in Hebrews 5:12-14, and it is obvious that he is indicating this to be the starting point which refers to a specific order. After the first principle comes the second, then the third. No person can enter a building of many levels and go to floor 12, if they have not started at ground level. This is also very true of our spiritual life in God. We cannot skip the first biblical principles, ignoring their value, and move on to the second or third. It will not only delay our spiritual growth but will ultimately compromise the quality of our relationship with God. What is very important here is to understand that one needs to follow God's order according to His Word. Without a strong and proper foundation, no building will be able to stand or exist for a long time. Isn't it sad that so many Christians want to live for God yet have not laid a proper foundation in God and His Word and its purpose for their lives? You lay this foundation firmly in your life, and only then can you start building. Building without a foundation is only building to see a collapse sometime soon. Ever wondered why so many Christians, with a true desire to walk with God, will seemingly so easily fall along the wayside?

Just like any building in the natural, our spiritual buildings (bodies referred to as temples of Holy Spirit) need a proper foundation, a plan, strategy and goals. In order for us to grasp First Principles we need to discuss them step by step. However, the goal is only to familiarise you with the concept, and we cannot elaborate in depth in this book.

Once again we see how we are urged to grow towards maturity in God, and it is evident that the Doctrine of the First Principles is foundational and not optional. "For indeed because of the time you are due to be teachers, yet you need to have someone to teach you again the rudiments of the beginning of the Words of God, and you came to be having need of milk, and not of solid food; for everyone partaking of milk is without experience in the Word of Righteousness, for he is an infant. But solid food is for those full grown, having exercised the faculties through habit, for distinction of both good and bad." (Heb 5:12-14 LITV)

Hebrews 6 refers to the different doctrines:

> **Hebrews 6:1+2 ISV** *"Therefore, leaving behind the elementary teachings about the Messiah, let us continue to be carried along to maturity, not laying again a foundation of repentance from dead actions, faith toward God, instruction about baptisms, the laying on of hands, the resurrection of the dead, and eternal judgment."*

# DOCTRINE 1: REPENTANCE OF DEAD WORKS
## This doctrine covers repentance from dead works

Repentance from dead works is mentioned first. Ephesians 2:10 makes it clear that God has called His children for good works. However, no person can do good works without understanding the meaning, and having repented of dead works. We are saved only by grace, and God's heart is that we understand that this is a free gift He has given us. Holy Spirit draws us near, executing all that Jesus the Anointed One with His anointing has done for us on the cross. (JOHN 19:30 KJV) Jesus did it for us. No matter who we are, Jesus the Anointed Son of God took our sins upon himself and paid the full price for all our sins. He died on the cross for everyone, once and for all. The Word of God says that nothing besides faith can be done in order to be saved; we are only saved by grace.

Nothing that we ever do will add to us being saved: not our background, our religious diligence, bible reading, church attendance or whatever we do that is important to us. Why are we saved? Why do we need to be saved? We have been created by God, in Jesus the Anointed One, for good works and we are His workmanship. We can say that through the crucifixion of Jesus He justified us. (ROMANS 3:10-22 KJV)

People may argue about the necessity of being saved. Why do we need to be saved? Is the purpose of being saved to avoid going to hell, or to ensure going to heaven? Our salvation is primarily so that God can reconcile us with Himself and restore the mandate He had originally given to Adam and Eve. His order was: be fruitful, multiply, subdue, rule the earth and have dominion, yet Adam and Eve, because of their sin, handed God's mandate for mankind on a tray to satan. God's love for us is so enduring and completely unconditional, that He sent His Son, the Lord Jesus, to die on the cross for us, symbolically the second Adam reclaiming the mandate of God.

Every action has a reaction. Every choice we make in life will have a result. Therefore, should human beings decide to not accept Jesus the Anointed Son of God as Lord and Saviour, it will lead to harsh consequences, leaving them under the power of satan, never reconciled to God but with the Lake of fire as their eternal destiny.

We have to make an important distinction between good works and dead works. What is the difference? Good works are done in Jesus the Anointed One, and dead works are always outside of Jesus the Anointed One. Good works, such as giving to the poor, serving God by teaching, preaching and many other things can easily be labelled as dead works because anything 'outside' of Jesus the Anointed One and His will is dead works. Outside of Jesus can refer to not being born again, but also living outside of His will, according to the flesh and religion, and not completely relying on Holy Spirit. Let me explain this: God's will for your life may be to become a medical doctor, farmer, teacher (to mention a few) but you decide that it is not the career you anticipate, then whatever you do will be dead works. If God's will for you is to be a teacher and you study to become a medical doctor, you are in dead works. It is of paramount importance to seek God's will for your life, and also the lives of your children, so that their lives can be built on the right foundation. Doing your own thing $^{(JUDGES\ 17:6\ KJV)}$, and following 'your heart' and not God's plan for you, is direct disobedience towards Him. The above serves for every sphere of your life.

We find a perfect example of this in 1 Chronicles 13 &15, where King David went to reclaim the Ark of God which the Philistines had captured. God's will was for the Ark to be returned. It symbolised His presence with them. Because of lack of knowledge, David brought the Ark of God back according to his own way and not God's way, resulting in the death of many people. This was dead works. In 1 Chronicles 15 David first inquired from the Lord how to go about bringing back the Ark. He followed God's way and returned the Ark safely and with no casualties. This was good works. If a person is continually living outside of good works (the will of God), then it is evident that the first foundational block, repentance from dead works, has not been laid properly, if at all. Without this foundational block you will not be able to grow to maturity in God and will be stuck in the 'milk phase' of being a child of God. A key reminder is to always seek counsel from God first. God has given us leaders and counsellors to go to for advice; however, the prerequisite is that we always go to Him first. Dead works are then anything you do, will do, or have done without inquiring from the Lord first.

What if we have walked in dead works? The Bible says clearly that all of us have sinned . . . . repentance is God's key for us to turn around and walk the opposite way. His grace paves the way for us to confess and repent and then He will, by Holy Spirit, enable us to walk in His ways, doing good works. Repentance (metanoia) is to change your mind and direction and to think and do differently. $^{(HEBREWS\ 9:14\ KJV)}$ The Blood of Jesus, the Anointed Son of God, cleanses us from all dead works and gives us a new start and opportunity, in God, to do good works. My dear friend, God only blesses that which is His will for your life. Do His will and it will carry His blessing!

Dr. Adolf Jonker Ph.D

# DOCTRINE 2: FAITH IN GOD
*This doctrine deals with a steadfast faith and complete trust in the existence of God*

This doctrine deals with steadfast faith and complete trust in the existence, sovereignty, nature and Trinity of God. God is from eternity to eternity. Eternity can be likened to a ring. It does not have a beginning or an end.

Having faith in God's nature is knowing that He protects, cares, leads, looks after and cares for you and gives life. Simply said: He is a good God. Our belief in the fact that God has existed from all eternity past, and that He existed before anything else's existence, means that God is sovereign. Sovereign means He is governor, above all, the highest; all powerful and supreme authority. This means that if God is sovereign He demands our submission. Hebrews 13:8 says that God never changes, but His sovereignty in our lives causes change in us. The Trinity means that we have faith in God the Father, God the Son and God the Holy Spirit. To explain Trinity we use the example of an egg. Even though we have one egg, it has three different parts: the outer, the yolk and the egg white. God lives, as Trinity, in perfect harmony, perfect unity, perfect togetherness and perfect love. It is most important to understand that God is ONE, but three different persons. (JOHN 1:1-5 + 2 COR. 13:13 KJV)

Faith is essential in our walk with God, and enables us to turn to Him. We need to grasp that we cannot please God without faith. (HEBREWS 11:6 KJV) Pleasing God with faith follows simply by making a decision to trust God and believe in Him and His sovereign will, ways and workings. Walking with true faith in God, your perception and attitude will change and He will become your source, life and security. True faith will see people, schemes, institutions, medical science only as the means through which God can work if He so chooses, and in no way the source. (JEREMIAH 17:5 KJV) We do not trust in things or people but in God! When God becomes your source, He becomes your focus. Focusing on the means, rather than on the source, will only divert focus from God as the only source and will easily cause stress, tension, misunderstanding and confusion. God as your source, becomes your life. Your life is then Jesus. (COL 3:1-3; MARK 12:30, JOHN 14:6) It is no longer primarily about yourself but all about Him. Whatever you attempt in life will be for Him, whether you excel in sport or in the business world, or whatever; you will turn all glory back to Him and not be concerned about making a name for yourself. You wake up with a zeal for life because you are living in Him. Your life is not about family, friends, sport, work or even making money, but it is about Jesus the Anointed One with His anointing, through Holy Spirit; to follow Him, to know Him and to become like Him, bringing all the glory to God. Your family and any other thing you are involved in comes second to the above.

God, as our security, guarantees safety and assurance and we need not seek it elsewhere. Anything outside of God means that we are building on a false foundation. God is our only God.

We say God has become:

~ our source
~ our life
~ our security

and when God is our source; we do not trust in:

People
Schemes
Institutions
Insurance
Medical Science (JEREMIAH 17:5 KJV)

All these things then become the means through which God can work if he chooses to do so! He never changes and specialized in doing the impossible!

Dr. Adolf Jonker Ph.D

It is we who have to change. We have come to the place of acknowledging and embracing God as our source and must allow Him to be our constant focus.

It is guaranteed that our lives will not be the same any longer. God will decorate them with the manifestation of seemingly impossible promises and miracles, whatever and whenever we need it.

## DOCTRINE 3: THE DOCTRINE OF BAPTISMS
*This doctrine deals with facts concerning baptism.*

This doctrine has caused many disputes throughout the centuries; between the Catholic, Reformed, Pentecostals and Charismatic people of God causing serious divides. Despite all the disputes, I am convinced that the answer lies in Matthew 28:19-20. This scripture has been used by most as evidence of what they believe, yet it has been misunderstood and practiced in diverse erroneous manners.

In the doctrine of baptism, we will not focus on its methods and ways, especially not those presented outside the truth of the Word of God. It is of paramount importance to remember that the emphasis is on the concept 'baptism', its true meaning and power, and not on the many religious forms.

In Matthew 28:19-20 KJV it says: "Go ye therefore, and teach all nations, baptizing them in the name of the Father, and of the Son and of the Holy Ghost . . ." I would like to draw the following analogy. Think of an egg. You will have one egg but it will have three different parts: the shell, the egg white and the egg yolk. The baptism is similar. It is one idea, with more than one facet. The facets of baptism can be defined as:

✓ Baptism in the Father
✓ Baptism in the Son
✓ Baptism in Holy Spirit.

The above is the core of the principle of Baptism. Does this not ring a bell? Baptise them in the Name of the Father, in the Name of the Son and in the Name of Holy Spirit. Divides in baptism have come because of the focus on different forms instead of the purity of the doctrine.

The Greek word for the baptism is 'baptizo', and it comes from the root 'bapto' (STRONGS; G907) which means to be completely covered. However, let us dissect the scripture of this foundational teaching, the doctrine of baptisms in Hebrews 6:1-2. Note the word 'baptisms' which everybody will agree with me is plural. Said differently: there is a doctrine of more than one baptism; thus diverse forms, (purposes and elements), but one concept: immersion. Remember the Greek word for baptism; 'baptizo'. Jesus said to His disciples in Matthew 20:22 and in Luke 12:50 KJV "But I have a baptism to be baptized with; and how am I straitened till it be accomplished!" The CEV translation says: "And I will have to suffer a lot of pain until it is over."

The baptism in Jesus name speaks of:

> The exact same word used for water baptism and baptism in Holy Spirit: 'baptizo', however, the baptism Jesus speaks of, is in reference to a baptism of fire; an immersion in fire.
>
> **Matthew 3:11 KJV** *"I indeed baptize you with water unto repentance: but he that cometh after me is mightier than I, whose shoes I am not worthy to bear: he shall baptize you with the Holy Ghost, and with fire."*

I am trying to show you that it is because of the preference of interpretation that we refer to Matthew 28:19-20 as water baptism only. However acquaint yourself. There is no context or indication referring to water but to the Triune God as fundamental principle. The disciples (the New Testament Church) understood and therefore they baptised only in the Name of Jesus and through immersion in water, throughout the whole book of Acts. Nobody will find any other reference in Acts that are different. However, we make use

Dr. Adolf Jonker Ph.D

of only one verse in Matthew 28:19-20 as evidence, which is more speculative, against 5 specific references in Acts that water baptism is in the Name of Jesus only. (ACTS 2:38, 8:12, 8:16, 10:48, 19:5 KJV) There is not one hint indicating of one incident where the combined names of the Father, Son and Holy Spirit are used in water baptism! This initial method of water baptism in Acts stretches over a time span of approximately 32 years. It makes one think, doesn't it? Some `theologians will argue forever about the baptism of John. Friends, John was already dead a long time and part of the old covenant. Hence, why would the disciples hear and learn from Jesus and then ignore what He taught and follow John? Rubbish! John's work was done and we clearly see it in Acts 13:25 NIV ". . . John was completing his work . . ." And if the disciples were wrong about the way they baptised, why did God not correct and punish them in the same way He did with Ananias and Sapphira, when they only lied once concerning offering and fell down dead?

Baptism in Greek 'baptizo' speaks with clarity of immersion. The root word 'bapto' means 'dip'—or 'cover'. The word by itself is not indicative or specifically referring to water, fire, blood or Holy Spirit. John says, I 'baptizo' with water (element) but Jesus will 'baptizo' with Holy Spirit and fire (different elements). Thus, seeing the word 'baptizo' or baptism does not by itself speak of the element of water only. I believe you are intelligent enough to discern the facts. First of all, by this time Jesus was already 'baptizo' (immersed) in the element water. You certainly do not suffer great pain when you are baptised in the above manner. The baptism of Luke 12:50 refers to a second 'baptism' (baptisms—plural according to Hebrews 6:2). The pain, then, in reference to suffering, relates to Jesus going to the cross; a baptism of fire. One verse by itself is not evidence. In concluding, I do not care whatever celebrity theologians said! Their traditional status, cultural persuasion or religious assumptions never supersede the authority and truth of God's Word. Let us then look at the doctrine of baptisms (immersion) by nature into an element, stated or referred from a specific context. Baptisms point to the different elements and purposes.

# BAPTISM IN THE NAME OF GOD THE FATHER

We lost our position in God in the Garden of Eden because of sin. In order to be reconciled to God we have to be washed by the Blood of our Lord Jesus signifying our spirits being born-again. Being born again means we have been saved from our fallen position; our spirit is alive yet again, our position with God is restored, and we are reconciled to God. We are washed in His blood and baptised into the Body of Jesus the Anointed One. The baptism in the name of the Father simply means 'rebirth'.

Through this baptism everyone who accepts Jesus the Anointed One is then taken into the Body of the Anointed One. (ROMANS 12:5 KJV) John 3:5 confirms that rebirth is the baptism in the name of the Father.

# BAPTISM IN THE NAME OF JESUS

Our sole source of information is the Word of God, when looking at the doctrine of baptism, and it is not based on controversial arguments. We trust that Holy Spirit will give revelation of the Word of God through His Word. Acts 8:16 KJV clearly indicates that they were only baptised in the name of Jesus, and not the name of the Father, or in the name of Holy Spirit. It only speaks of baptism in the name of Jesus. Read and conclude if you also see what I do.

We see in

> **1 John 5:7-8 ISV** *"For there are three witnesses—the Spirit, the water, and the blood—and these three are one."*

Do you agree with me that the above speaks of three witnesses, individually different, yet one by nature? In other words it is clear, there are three different elements; first element is spirit (Holy Spirit);

Dr. Adolf Jonker Ph.D

second element is water (Jesus); third element is blood (Father). Be reminded that the blood was the Father's idea.

We see in Acts 8:14 that the Word of God is accepted, and this indicates the baptism of the Father in blood, ultimately, salvation. In verse 16 they were baptised in Jesus' name and in water. In what were they baptised? Water. Water is the object of cleansing used. What object is used in salvation? Blood—The Father sent His Son to die on the Cross and shed His blood for our salvation: rebirth. In verse 17 we read about the laying on of hands and it speaks of the baptism of Holy Spirit. We are baptised in spirit. In looking at these scriptures we see that they all speak about the doctrine of baptism. The order of baptisms may vary. However, the baptism in the name of the Father is and will always occur first, as it is rebirth.

A short summation of the different baptisms:

- ✓ Repentance speaks of rebirth and the baptism in the Father and we are cleansed with blood.
- ✓ Forgiveness of sins occurs when we confess and repent and are symbolized when we are baptised in water in the name of Jesus.
- ✓ The element of the baptism of Holy Spirit is Holy Spirit Himself and it opens the door for the gifts of Holy Spirit and His manifestation of power in our lives.

The baptisms are an entryway for the gifts of God to manifest in our lives, therefore it is important to look at the gifts of God:

**Romans 12:6-8**              *Gifts of God the Father*

**Ephesians 4:11**             *Gifts of God the Son*

**1 Corinthians 12:7-11**      *Gifts of God the Holy Spirit*

These are diverse forms of gifts yet, by nature, they are the same. There is one Lord, one faith and one baptism. (EPHESIANS 4:5 KJV) Acts

10:43 clearly indicates the different baptisms. Firstly, they repented and accepted Jesus. This indicates rebirth, thus baptism in the name of the Father; (44) and Holy Spirit came upon them, which is the baptism of Holy Spirit; (47-48) and the command was to baptise in water in the name of Jesus. Here we see again that although the order differs, the doctrine is the same. Thus, we cannot deny that there is more than one baptism and Matthew 28:19-20 is not whatsoever an all-inclusive scripture validating baptism in water in the name of the Father, Son and Spirit. Matthew 28:19-20 does not exclusively deal with a baptism in water! It never has and it never will!

Matthew 28 is a clear call to go and make disciples. Acts 8:36-37 indicates who is allowed to be baptised in water and it says: "whoever believes with their whole hearts." The only pre-requisite for being baptised in the name of Jesus is to be re-born, which is the baptism in the name of the Father. Nowhere in the Bible have we found a direct command as to a specific form or method.

Baptism in water, according to the Bible, speaks of submersion into water. Disputes and differences about Mark 16 left many questioning its truth. However, it is part of the Bible and therefore we believe it is as truth. Baptism in water, in the name of Jesus, does not bring eternal life. Romans 6:1 speak of us being dead to sin. Baptism in the water is symbolic of dying to self and sin and it follows in the example Jesus set. He died and rose from the dead. So we identify with Him through baptism in water, in the name of Jesus. As Jesus the Anointed One physically died and rose again, so we die symbolically, in the physical and lay our sins and very soul dimension in the water. Then we will rise up in the name of Jesus the Anointed One and sin will no longer rule in our souls.

Dr. Adolf Jonker Ph.D

# BAPTISM IN HOLY SPIRIT

We have settled the baptism in Blood and water. The remaining one left is the baptism in the name of Holy Spirit. The Bible uses quite a couple of terms referring to Holy Spirit. Some are: 'the spirit of God'; 'the spirit of the Lord'; the 'spirit of Jesus' and the spirit of Christ (Anointed One with His anointing). Paul uses various ways to describe Holy Spirit, but is never consistent in using only one specific term. The Hebrew word for Holy Spirit is 'ruach', and the Greek term 'pneuma', both meaning breath. Where the Greek speaks of 'Pneuma Hagion', it is a direct reference to Holy Spirit. It is important for us to understand that whichever way Paul and the Bible describe Holy Spirit, they are simply making use of diverse manners of vocabulary preferences, but still speak of one and the same person: Holy Spirit. The Bible, even at times, refers grammatically to Holy Spirit as 'the Holy Spirit'. Similar to when we refer to God as 'the Father', it is simply in grammatical context, and has no reference to denying the person. When we are in conversation with God the Father, we address Him as Father, and it would be ridiculous to address Him 'the' Father and this is also true of Holy Spirit. We should not in prayer and personal conversation with Him, address Him as 'the' Holy Spirit. It is of paramount importance to understand that Holy Spirit is equally part of God as Trinity, and not as a spiritual power or force of the Father or Jesus. He is a personality and He is God in His own right.

In the current economy, God the Father sits on His throne in heaven and the second person, Jesus His son sits at His right hand. The third person Holy Spirit has been sent by God the Father to earth, thus pointing to three distinct personalities and functionalities of each. More intimately, we can say Father sent Holy Spirit.

We see clearly in John 20:22 KJV that Jesus breathed over His disciples and said: "Receive ye the Holy Ghost!" The journey unfolds itself, and not a theologian, but the Lord Jesus Himself makes a profound statement in Acts 1:8 KJV "But ye shall receive power, after that the Holy Ghost is come upon you." The disciples gathered and there were 120 in the upper room waiting for this outpour. Acts 2 explains that the outpour of Holy Spirit, referred to as the promise; and as prophesied in Joel 2:28, has transpired.

> **Acts 2:4 KJV** *"And they were all filled with the Holy Ghost, and began to speak with other tongues, as the Spirit gave them utterance."*

What an interesting scenario. Let's investigate with John 3:3 "Except a man be born again, he cannot see the kingdom of God." Whatever happens; rebirth has to first take place in every person's life. Rebirth is the gateway or initiation into the Kingdom of God, and relates to the baptism of blood done in the name of the Father. The blood of Jesus is an element, which is primarily for cleansing. Faith in His name as Son of God opens the way to rebirth. Holy Spirit baptizes us immediately into His church.(EPHESIANS 4:5 KJV) The blood cleanses us and we become children of God the Father. (JOHN 1:12 KJV)

In John 20:22 Jesus breathed over His disciples? Why? He was going away and said that another Helper, Holy Spirit, would come. This breathing represented the rebirth (becoming born-again). They now had the Holy Spirit residing within them from that moment onwards, and their bodies became temples of Holy Spirit (1 CORINTHIANS 6:19 KJV), but their bodies were also members of Christ.(1 CORINTHIANS 6:15 KJV) Holy Spirit dwells within us representing the Son of God.

In Acts 1 Jesus made a seemingly strange statement. They had just received the indwelling Holy Spirit, and now He ordered them to wait for the outpour of Holy Spirit. This refers to a second experience, distinct from the first one. Friend, it is not so strange! In fact, for ages the devil wanted us to debate this statement to come to the conclusion: 'Did God (Jesus) really say go and wait? Is this for me?' Well, let's read the scripture, which is the only truth; they waited, and Holy Spirit came on **ALL** of those who waited. You release your faith, and He is no respecter of persons. After His crucifixion, Jesus met 500 on the road to Emmaus. However, in the upper room there were only a 120, including the disciples. Where were the other 392? He did not tell them what rituals and rites to follow to be liturgically correct. His strategy was very simple: wait on Me. I think those 392 gathered in the town hall, democratically discussing the 'wait on Me' with the debate: did Jesus really say it was for all his children. Their focus was there theological reasoning. The others (those in the upper room), a theocratic approach and acted on faith waiting in the upper room.

If you as reader argue, that for some strange reason, you might not fit into the 'ALL' category; then I want to ask you a question: "Where did you get the audacity from to declare God a liar?" If your pastor, church, family or friends (society knows in any case nothing about God) see it differently, please tell me, where did God give them biblical authority to alter His Word to suit their deception, lies, assumptions and denomination traditional, cultural effrontery. We need to grow up and mature as God's children and admit our wrongs and let God be God, and expel any other god, dethroning them as idolatrous demons.

The baptism in the name of Holy Spirit is to receive power. The Bible is so clear on it, power as Holy Spirit came upon them. We can all read. First He came 'in' when rebirth takes place; the next time 'on' but this time not to represent Jesus but to be part of the believer's life in his very own capacity as Holy Spirit.

Let's deal with the concept 'tongues' "glossa." (STRONGS G1100) Strong's translate the word as a language, specifically one not acquired, of uncertain affinity. Friends, it is clear that it is not an earthly human language you receive—please! You're not english speaking and now all of a sudden you speak eloquent French and silver-tongued German. Let's all wake up. It is a heavenly spiritual language: spirit as coming from God and not naturally acquired. It is a gift. It is given to you and you receive it by faith, not reject it by theological uppityness. It is strange, it is different and it is tongues. Words uttered that humanity doesn't understand, and praise God neither the devil nor all other evil forces. It has no intellectual, academic or grammatical structure. It is tongues. It is a language to primarily praise God. The question might arise but why the necessity? I think it will be good if we ask God, because it was His plan and the purpose is evident. He wants to aid the believer. The help is summed up as follow:

- ✓ Power
- ✓ Witness
- ✓ World

It is evident that it is not to show forth our spirituality but to empower us to be His witnesses throughout the earth.

How does the baptism take place? The truth is that there is no fixed way. At times it can happen spontaneously, at times with pastors and leaders laying on of hands, prayer or somebody who just pray with you. The prerequisite to the above is rebirth. Sometime it takes place before baptism in water and sometimes afterwards. The book of Acts shows no specific order. The important part is to understand that human involvement is just instrumental. The true baptiser in Holy Spirit is the Lord Jesus.

> **Acts 1:5 KJV** *". . . for John truly baptised with water, but ye shall be baptized with the Holy Ghost not many days hence."*

My prayer for you, if you are already baptised by Jesus, in the Name of Holy Spirit, that you will receive a fresh awakening. If you, as reader are not, I pray that He will enlighten your heart and you pray that Jesus will baptise you with Holy Spirit. You are part of the ALL group, bless His holy Name.

We end with a diagram to summarise what we have shared.

| Witness of Salvation | Recipient Man | Baptism in the Name of . . . | Working | Function | Who baptizes? |
|---|---|---|---|---|---|
| Blood | Spirit | Father | Rebirth | Righteous | Holy Spirit |
| Water | Soul | Son | Laying down of sin | Cleansing | Minister (man /woman) |
| Spirit | Body | Holy | Empower | Godly | Jesus |

## DOCTRINE 4 (Hebrews 6:1-2)
### Laying on of hands

This doctrine is all about the laying on of hands and it is visible right through the Old and New Testament. In order to have a complete understanding we should understand how God created us. A very powerful scripture is found in 1 Thessalonians 5:23:

We are Spirit,

Have a soul (will, emotions, and thoughts)

And live in a physical body.

Your body (temple of Holy Spirit), is the carrier of your spirit man, and has a soulish dimension, which consists of your personality and character. Think about this: you are a spirit being . . .

**Spirit**     –     *cannot be seen*

**Soul**     –     *can be experienced*

**Body**     –     *the carrier of both and is tangible*

In understanding that we are spirit, soul and body the next appropriate question would be: "What is laying on of hands?" It simply speaks about:

- Transference of spirit.

Spirit is being transferred. In other words: What can transfer? Spirit. It can transfer from a person or an object. Let us look at an example. Person A has severe depression (spirit) and person B does not have depression, but has a lot of contact with person A, e.g. working together, visiting or even praying together. B will start experiencing depression because of contact with A, and will receive what A has, unless B prays against transference.

In short—The laying on of hands is transference. Now there are a few very important points to look at. Which spirit is being transferred? Remember that the laying on of hands means that transference of spirit takes place. Why is it so important? We are dealing with the lives of people and eternity. 1 Timothy 5:22 warns that we have to be cautious and know that we are dealing with people's lives.

## Important!!!

1. Who is laying hands on you?
2. How are you laying on hands?

How should our hands be? We should ensure that our hands are cleansed by the blood of Jesus and that they are pure. (PSALM 24:4 KJV) How do we get our hands clean?

> **Psalm 26:6 ISV** *"I wash my hands innocently. I go around your altar, LORD."*

> **Psalm 73:13 ISV** *"I kept my heart pure for nothing and kept my hands clean from guilt."*

Dr. Adolf Jonker Ph.D

Before you lay hands on anyone, wash them in the spirit, in the blood of Jesus through Holy Spirit. Before anyone lays hands on you:

a.   Cleanse that person's hands through prayer.
b.   Wash them in the spirit with the blood of Jesus.
c.   If led by the Holy Spirit, refuse kindly and in love.

Must we ignore what we transfer via our hands? No!!! Are 'holy hands' (clean hands) important? <sup>(1 Timothy 2:8 KJV)</sup> Definitely!

## TYPES OF LAYING ON OF HANDS:

1.   Blessings from people (Genesis 48:14-15)
2.   When bringing offerings (Numbers 8:10-11)
3.   Inauguration (Numbers 27:18, 23)
4.   Transference of spirit (Deuteronomy 34:9)
5.   Blessing families / children (Matthew 19:14-15)
6.   Healing of sick (Mark 16:18)
7.   Signs and wonders (Acts 19:11-12)
8.   Transference of gifts (1Timothy 4:14)
9.   Baptism in Holy Spirit (Acts 8: 17-24)

Laying on of hands will and should always be done under the guidance of Holy Spirit and the presence of God. Even although this was also implemented all over the Old Testament, it was never a dead ritual. Hands speak of contact and contact speaks of activity. Thus, I refer to the 'laying on of hands' as a ministry of the life of Jesus; in spirit and truth.

## DOCTRINE 5: RESURRECTION FROM THE DEAD
### This doctrine is all about resurrection from the dead

In Ephesians 1:13-14 we read that God comes to redeem his property—you and I! Did you know that you are his property—God's treasured belonging? Thank Father God that you are His! God teaches us His redemptive plan, which includes our whole being, and it is so important not to forget that we are spirit, soul and body. Death has separated us from God.

God's redemptive plan is a 'holistic' approach to save us:

Spirit = Re-birth

Soul = Sanctification

Body = Resurrection in an incorruptible body

## <u>DEFINITION OF DEATH</u>

The inevitable question is to define death. We were created to be one with God. However after the tragedy in the Garden of Eden, an unknown concept to Adam and Eve occurred: death entered their lives. Accordingly, we can define death as separation. The diversity is clear, (a) Separation from God and thus the purpose you have been created for. This is spiritual death. (b) Death occurs as your physical body dies and returns to dust.(GENESIS 3:19 KJV) Your spirit and soul remain immortal, ending either in: (1) heaven or (2) hell, depending on your spiritual status. Those believers, who died since Adam, went to a resting place, paradise, also called Abraham's bosom. They stayed there till the resurrection of Jesus, and went to be with God in heaven. The unbelieving went to hell and will stay there till after the millennium of peace. Thereafter, they will be cast into the Lake of fire.

Let's clarify and define hell first and unequivocal. English translators were inconsistent for unknown reasons, in their translation of many Hebrew Greek words which are different in meaning and purpose. However, they made use of the same word choice but the meaning refers to different concepts. Hell and Paradise are two completely uniquely different words, but at times, both were referred to as Hades, yet only translated as hell. In the same way translators called the 'abyss' and other places also hell, but it is certainly different in location and purpose. Paradise is in close proximity with hell, and a chasm in between separates one from the other. The one contains the unbelievers even up to today; and the other the believers until Jesus' resurrection, where they are now with God in heaven.

Separation between believer and unbeliever also play a specific role in as far as destiny is concerned. Believers have eternal life, whereas unbelievers are eternally dead, and thus separated from God. Physical death is the deadline inaugurating every person's end destiny. (HEBREWS 9:27 KJV) Before physical death you have all the opportunity in the world to make right with God. Afterwards only the reward of the choices you make while still alive, remains.

At death, with the exception of unnatural occurrences, for example drowning in the sea, explosions, fires, etc; we are all buried in a grave. The Hebrew calls it 'gerber' and the Greek 'mnayion'. These are physical graves in the visible physical realm. (MATTHEW 27:60, GENESIS 35:20; JOHN 11:17; NAHUM 1:14; REVELATION 11:9 KJV) John writes in Revelation, that at the end of time, the sea will give up the dead.

## LOCATIONS OF THE DEAD

**HELL** is a place of punishment for evil spirits and unbelievers. Sheol and Hades are found in the following scriptures:

a. Sheol (Hebrew) (Deuteronomy 32:22, Job 11:8 KJV)
b. Hades (Greek) (Matthew 11:23, Acts 2:27&31, Revelation 1:18 KJV)

**PARADEISOS** (Greek): Paradise is also referred to as Abraham's bosom. I want to point out that paradise and hell are both, at times, translated as 'Hades / Sheol', and although it is not the same place, it is in the same vicinity. (LUKE 16:19-31 / 23: 43 KJV)

**TARTARUS** (Greek) is the place where fallen angels, who sinned before the flood of Noah, are kept. No human or demonic spirit will go there. This is not hell. This is a different place lower than hell. (1 PETER 3:19, 2 PETER 2:4, JUDE 1:6-7 KJV)

**GEHENNA** (Greek): This is the Lake of fire where all the fallen angels, satan, demonic powers and the ungodly will be cast into after death; and after they are re-united with their bodies. This is their final destination. Take note that Gehenna is the Lake of fire. It is a different place from Hades/ Sheol / Hell, and it is the final location of eternal punishment. (MATTHEW 5:22, 29-30; JAMES 3:6; REVELATION 20:4,15 KJV)

**ABYSSOS** (Greek) is referred to as the abyss, or the bottomless pit. It is immeasurably deep and locked up. (REVELATION 9:1 KJV) It is the place of the beast (anti-Christ); dragon (satan); and the false prophetess (Jezebel) (REVELATION 20:10 CPDV)

**EUPHRATES:** It is the abode of the four end-time angels that are bound under the Euphrates river. (REVELATION 9:14 KJV)

# FIRST AND SECOND DEATH

Now that we have taken a look at all the possible hereafter dwellings, it is also important to know that there is a first and a second death, and to point to the distinction between them. The first death took place in the Garden of Eden, when Adam and Eve sinned. They listened to the snake and rejected the Word of God. This means that their spirits died, and because of their submission to satan, their souls were now under his control and they became part of the world system. (2 CORINTHIANS 4:4 KJV)

# THE SECOND DEATH

This is when 'death' and hell were cast into the Lake of fire. (REVELATION 20:14 KJV) This Second death is only for unbelievers, and takes place after the White Throne Judgment.

# THE FIRST AND SECOND RESURRECTION

The Book of Acts 24:15 brings clarity regarding death, stating that there will be a resurrection of both believer and unbeliever. The first resurrection takes place for the believer only, and this will be before the thousand year millennium. (REVELATION 20:5 KJV) These saved ones incorporate those since the resurrection of Jesus, until His Second coming. Some refer to this as the rapture. (1 THESS. 4:16-17 KJV) This is also the time when the born-again believers will receive their eternal resurrected and glorified bodies. (1 COR. 15:38+44 KJV)

The second resurrection is different from the above. John elucidates in John 5:28-29, declaring that believers will be resurrected to eternal life, whereas at the second resurrection unbelievers will face the White Throne of God, and receive eternal damnation.

# JUDGMENT

There will also be a first judgment (bema), and a second judgement (white throne). The believer will be judged before the millennium at the judgment seat (bema) of Jesus the Anointed One. (2 COR. 5:9-10 KJV) This judgment is not punishment (1 THESS. 5:9 KJV) but it speaks of recompense. The word 'bad', is a bad translation in the scripture, and should rather read as things that are done of no account, or being meaningless. I want to rephrase it stating that believers will be judged for good works done in Jesus the Anointed One by Holy Spirit and for dead works (bad).

The second judgment is not for believers, but the ungodly—the wicked and it will take place after the millennium of peace, and the judgment of this will result in them ending in the Lake of fire. (REVELATION 20:13-15 KJV) Let us have a final look at what happened with Jesus at his death. (LUKE 23:46; MATTHEW 27:50; JOHN 20:11-18 KJV)

**Look again at:**

Step 1: Spirit   —   Father   —   | **DEATH**

Step 2: Body   —   Grave   —   | **MEANS**

Step 3: Soul   —   Paradise   —   | **SEPARATION**

Death means separation, whereas resurrection means re-uniting.

## DOCTRINE 6 THE ETERNAL JUDGEMENT
### *This doctrine is about the eternal judgement of God!*

There are a couple of Greek terms related to time, that I want us to look at:

- Chronos Aionios (STRONGS, G166) = eternal (time period) (2 TIMOTHY 1:9; ROMANS 16:25 KJV) It means eternity (period of time before beginning of eternity). (MATTHEW 18:8, MARK 3:29, JUDE 1:7 KJV)
- Eternal—Kairos (STRONGS, G2450), Krima (STRONG'S, G2917) = A judgment order

This is a judgment that will take place and the consequences will last for all eternity. Let us explain judgment and what it entails:

i. Determines the destination of every soul / spirit when it leaves the body—physical death.
ii. Determines the destination of every spirit / soul and body in the last days.
iii. Determines the rewards and judgment (penalties / punishment) of every single person. (COLOSSIANS 3:24, EPHESIANS 6:8, 1 CORINTHIANS 9:25 KJV)

Where you are right now, you find yourself already in an eternal state. Therefore, you must know that the eternal judgment has different facets, but you are already living in certain parts of these facets. You are here and now involved in making choices that will influence eternity.

**Example 1:** Deuteronomy 30:19—*'Choose life or death'*

A child of God has to make a choice concerning the Word of God. Malachi 3:10 states "give tithes and offerings . . ." but you have to decide whether you will be obedient. The very moment that you choose to obey God's Word, you choose life, and the blessings of Deuteronomy 28:1-14 are immediately upon you. If you decide to be disobedient, that very moment you choose death, the curses of Deuteronomy 28:15 to the end come immediately upon you and your descendants. In other words: the Word of God will judge you 'now', according to the choices you make. Today! Daily! Now is also part of eternity!

**Example 2:** Romans 10:13; John 3:16-18; *Choose life or death*

We, you and I, have a choice to accept Jesus the Anointed One as your Lord! The moment you accept Jesus Anointed One into your life, eternal judgment comes over you, and you are immediately saved. This also determines your destiny in eternity. Are you going to spend eternity with the Anointed Son of God, in heaven, or in eternal hell (Lake of fire) because you had not accepted Jesus Anointed One into your life?

**Example 3:** Choose life or death!!!

Let us take a child of God and say that throughout his life he was obedient to God in giving his tithes and offerings. However, this person had bad attitudes towards his fellow man, and treated them badly. Eternal judgment says:

1. He will receive judgment now (talking about the eternity concept).
2. He will again be judged one day when he appears before God for:

a.  His good deeds—finances.

b.  His bad deeds—bad attitude.

He receives this judgment because of his deeds:

Good (1 CORINTHIANS 3:12-15; 2 CORINTHIANS 5:10 KJV) or bad choices influence eternal destiny and reward. For which deeds will you be judged? According to your good deeds, you gather or store up treasures in heaven.(MATTHEW 6:19-20 KJV) The ungodly are also judged according to their deeds (good and bad), which will determine their final chastisement in hell.

You are judged according to your:

a.  Advantages:    (MARK 6:11; JOHN 15:22; JOHN 9:41; LUKE 12:48 KJV)

b.  Works:    (MATTHEW 16:27; PSALM 26:1-2; JEREMIAH 17:10; REVELATION 22:12 KJV)

c.  Secrets:    (ROMANS 2:16; HEBREWS 4:12 KJV)

Your choices determine your eternal destiny and reward!

## WHO IS THE JUDGE?

1.  God—(HEBREWS 12:23; PSALM 75:7; ECCLESIASTES 3:17 KJV)

2.  Jesus The Anointed One. (JOHN 5:22; ACTS 10:42; ACTS 17:31 KJV)

3.  You—Our present deeds influence our eternal judgment. (ROMANS 2 KJV)

4.  Authorities—now, here on earth. (ROMANS 13:2 KJV)

5.  Word—(JOHN 3:18 KJV

## WHERE DOES GOD'S JUDGMENT BEGIN?

Firstly—With the children of God and the church of Jesus the Anointed One. (1 PETER 4:17 KJV)

Secondly—With the lost (JOHN 3:18 KJV)

Dr. Adolf Jonker Ph.D

There are then different facets of judgement which will one day end at the white throne judgment.

## QUESTIONS:

    i.   How do your choices look so far?

   ii.   Are you bringing damnation on yourself and your family?

  iii.   Are you bringing blessings / curses upon yourself?

  iv.   In terms of eternity, how do your choices appear to you? (Dare to look behind your masks!)

   v.   What do the secrets of your heart reveal? (It will be judged one day!)

  vi.   Do you know that whether you allow God to search your heart or not, He still does?

 vii.   According to your works—what do you think of your prospects in eternity? (Remember dead works count for nothing—they remain dead! Works must be done in Jesus the Anointed One).

viii.   That which you are now doing for God . . .
Are they "good Biblical / Christian works which are nothing but dead works? Or has God instructed you to do it and is it verified by His Word? (Good works)

According to the command in Matthew 28:20, how obedient are you? You are going to be judged according to this "Great Command"! How many people did you disciple in the Lord and will you take with you to heaven? Have you ever been involved in bringing about division within the body of Jesus the Anointed One? There is judgment for that! Have you ever hindered anyone from serving the Lord? Have you ever consciously or subconsciously accredited the work of Holy Spirit to satan? You will be judged for this! Do you know that you will stand alone before the judgment seat? Do you know that there will be no excuse? Even nature will bear witness against you! (ROMANS 1:19-20) How does your future and reward in eternity seem when looking at your good and bad works? Do you think you can take chances? (HEBREWS 12:29 KJV) Take a quick look at the following:

Our physical lives on earth are but a few years in comparison to eternity. Everything has to do with eternity. Now think . . . Visualize yourself at the judgement seat of God. What will it be like? What are you going to do to change the situation you're in?

## SYNOPTICALLY:

First Principles is a foundational concept, analogously referred to as milk. Six key concepts serve as an elementary framework for the born-again child of God to understand the walk with God, serving and worshipping Him (PHIL 3:3, 8-9 KJV) within the framework of these fundamental principles.

## Dead works:

Is making sure that the old has gone and now you live a new life in Jesus the Anointed One; doing God's will and being transformed into the image of the Lord Jesus.

## Faith in God:

This is an absolute necessity for every child of God. Live, act, think and walk by faith. It is the divine trading currency between heaven and earth.

## Baptisms:

These are the initiation rites into Kingdom living. It invokes God's orientation as Trinity: Father, Son and Holy Spirit; and the witness they bear in heaven and earth. They are representative of the salvation plan of God, and reconciliatory by nature.

## Laying on of hands:

This is an essential concept in disciple-making, ministry to others and being the hands of God for someone else. It has diverse facets.

Dr. Adolf Jonker Ph.D

## Resurrection of the dead:

The last two are eternal end-time concepts. The first four principles are 'now'. This is about the concepts of first and second death and first and second resurrection. The allotted venue will be according to your spiritual status.

## Judgment:

This is the finality of dispensation and judgment of good and bad; believer and unbeliever. The determining factor is personal, earthly choices.

1. Confession, repentance:     ⟶   Dead works
2. Live by faith         ⟶   Faith in God
                YHWH
3. Initiation of salvation plan of God   ⟶   Baptisms
4. Disciple-making       ⟶   Laying on of
                hands
5. Death separation       ⟶   Resurrection of
                the dead
6. Determining eternal destination   ⟶   Eternal judgment

# art 3

## SUBJECT RULE 1: LIFE OR DEATH

**KEY SCRIPTURE:** Deuteronomy 30:19

"I call heaven and earth to testify against you today! I've set life and death before you today: both blessings and curses. Choose life, that it may be well with you—you and your children.

**KEYWORDS:**

Life

Death

Imbalances

**KEY CONCEPT:** God sets before you life or death: you choose!

# GLOBAL HISTORICAL OBSERVATIONS

I have made some disturbing observations throughout my lifetime. I have taken note of a group of people who excel in everything they do, and then a vast majority who do not excel, no matter how hard they try. It always seems as though nothing works out for them, and it appears as though no matter what level of skill, energy or expertise they apply their end result is failure. It is though the end result of failure has been declared before their beginning. Whatever effort, the perturbing result is an encompassing failure. A grim picture, but it is the truth.

I furthermore noticed the similarities in specific habits between parents and children. I see that children and grownups do the exact same thing their parents did, almost as though their actions were prescribed and set in place beforehand. Divorce, alcoholism, child abuse, sexual abuse and many others will run in the same family for generations. The medical world, for scientific reasons, shies away from the biblical terms, generational inheritances or curses. They define it as genetically inherited. There are flood waves of evidence, for example, that if a family member is diagnosed with cancer (or any other illness or disease), their children and grandchildren will stand a chance of being confronted with the very same thing. It is barely impossible not to notice such occurrences. However, I do acknowledge that there are exceptions to the rule. After all has been said and done, Science has been aware of the inheritable facts. Irrespective of the word 'choice' difference, between Science and the Bible; whether genetically inherited or generational; when it is split down the middle, the concept is one and the same thing. Science leaves no stone unturned to prove the existence, function and validity of the above, whereas the larger church domain pulls out the boxing gloves and vehemently resists it. Some will agree to the generic inheritance, but will be on guard with the attitude of "please, in Jesus name, do not mention the words 'generational inheritance' (blessings or curses)!" It destroys our 'moonshine and roses' teachings for

Christianity, saying that a Christian will only experience the proverbial 'heaven on earth'.

I have also observed that this is true of physical locations. Certain geographical areas will be poverty stricken, and no matter what is done, poverty will not diminish one inch. The Democratic Republic of the Congo is factually the one country in Africa with the greatest and best mineral deposit especially in the context of diamonds. However, I travelled there years ago, and not even the greatest positive attitude and outlook could protect me from the harness of the impact of dire poverty. It is everywhere you turn your head, and one is astonished that people are able to continue living in such horrendous conditions. The same rings true of Nepal. I've always admired the beauty of the Himalayas, and was excited to experience them in person. Nothing could have prepared me for what I walked into. I was shocked to the core to see the extreme poverty. In fact, I thought that what I saw was a hundred times more than the original definition of poverty.

In continuation of the above, I have also seen that certain places are always vulnerable and prone to experience military warfare, especially in Africa, India and Palestine. Kashmir is an area of intense conflict and dispute between India and Pakistan. By nature, this situation is volatile and potentially a bomb waiting to explode! Why particularly this area and not another? Himachal Pradesh lies just South. Why not there? My theory is contrary to that of most people, who want to define what is happening in this area within the borders of politics. The truth about this situation is that what is happening in Kashmir is curse-related. Similar to that, we have a situation in the Middle East which can be at complete peace one day and the very next day they are actively involved in full-blown warfare, giving the news media yet another breaking news story about another attack and subsequent retaliation. Plans of yet another peace process will accompany the battle that is raging out there, killing and cause yet again more death to people.

In South Africa we have yet another phenomenon. I assume that it will be similar in other regions. There are geographical areas where one can beforehand predict rape cases. It is as if certain areas are allocated to the occurrences of predetermined happenings. Have you ever been on a road trip, and when you enter a town you have a specific impression of what is happening there, without having factual knowledge? I experienced this many times. One time, while leading a prayer tour, we travelled from town to town, praying. I remember one specific town where we had such a strong impression that there were a lot of immorality and rape cases. We felt this while still a distance away from entering the town. Do you want to know what the first thing was that caught our eye when entering on the main road? Every signpost had posters, shop windows were decorated with it: it was newspaper headlines of rape cases. Any police squad will be the first to tell you that they always identify designated places where specific crimes take place. They will also have a general idea of where to start a search for criminals, depending on the type of criminal and crime committed.

Let's take it to another level. The United States of America has a population of roughly 300 million people. China on the other end of the world has almost four times more, and it equates to more or less a total of 1.1 billion people. Quite a difference, isn't it? Yet, if anyone refers to the powerhouse of the world, it is common knowledge that it is the USA. Although having significantly fewer people, it is still the superpower. What is our conclusion? Isn't it evident that the blessing on the USA, as a nation, outweighs that of China? Numbers and size do not play a role, even though it might be the outlook of some. We have to be smart and look beyond facts, and then find reasons behind the logic elsewhere.

If we look at the scenarios sketched above, the conclusion is simple. There are certain people, objects, locations, territories and nations that are experiencing suffering in extreme measures, and in all facets of life. Pain, hurt, failure and devastation, are all part of their daily existence, and what they have to face and fight against. And then, contrary to the last mentioned, I have seen people, places, areas and nations that are extremely prosperous and excel in every facet of life, despite what they do. My final observation is that the above scenarios; extreme suffering versus extreme blessing, occurs in the lives of both Christians and non-Christians. Allow me to say that I have noticed in countries such as Africa and India, where many gods are worshipped, the poverty and subsequent suffering, are more severe than anywhere else. Is this coincidental? Yes, it coincides with all biblical warning against idolatry!

The lengthy discussion above clearly points to the Word of God that speaks of life and death, blessings and curses. Irrespective of our argumentations regarding ethnicity, politics, socio-economics, educational or religious persuasions; the finality indicates nothing outside of blessings and curses.

Let me illustrate and forgive the vividness of my example. I have counselled many, many women over the years. If you were to ask any woman, anywhere in the world, who has been raped what the experience was like, what would their response be? Would they describe being raped as a blessing? It is absurd to even ask such a question. If this same question is posed to both Christian and non-Christian women, will their answers differ? I think not. I have not come across any woman, whether born-again or not, who did not suffer because of rape. The detail to the crime, the intellectual defining and or the media interpretation, and the diversity in the content is irrelevant. Any woman, who is raped, suffers, period. The only difference at the end will be in how they handle the situation, and I have heard marvellous testimonies of how God worked miracles for born-again women. The born-again child of God can, in all circumstances, rely on the help of God. Therefore, the difference in experiencing suffering (and many other difficulties or curses) is God, and the individuals standing with Him. Opposing suffering and curses we have to look at blessings. I introduce another scenario: Two students finish their University degrees. One is an outspoken Christian and the other denounces

Christianity completely. What will happen at their Graduation? Will their experiences or rewards differ? No, both studied and completed their individual studies, and both will be overjoyed, satisfied and greatly blessed. Yet again, we have to ask ourselves the question of where the difference lies. The Christian will experience this joy and blessing and give all the glory to God, whereas the unbeliever will pride in himself. These examples are only to portray a picture, and help in our overall understanding that whether blessing or curse. God is the centre point, and it all revolves around His involvement or non-involvement.

## POLARITY

History and society is deluged with the polarity as the above examples explained the reality of blessings and curses. People and leaders may want to reason it away, but anyone can reason as much as they want to, it will not change anything, nor will it alter the evidence of the experiences of people everywhere in the world. For this reason, we need to further investigate these concepts so that we will ultimately be at a place of walking in God's truth and blessing, in all spheres of our lives.

I am sure if you are willing to openly and honestly look at your own life, you will be able to identify areas of similarities between yourself and your ancestors. You may also become aware of, and acknowledge certain areas in you, the reader's life, which proves problematic, or even in a worst case scenario which seems insurmountable. The above equation excludes but also recognises that not every negative thing proves to be curse related. Added to the above is the fact that Christians are not excluded nor warranted to have a problem-free life. However, the Christian has the advantage of relying wholeheartedly on God's love, presence and support during troubled times. It is in this specific area where the role of faith is one of paramount importance. Having said the above, it is evident that every positive outcome always proves to be blessing inclined or related.

## IMBALANCES

The polarity of everything I wrote about, in the above introduction, is evident and it proves the societal imbalances regardless of background, education, nationality, spiritual status and so forth. The intellectual argumentation of the Anthropologist; the detailed counselling outlay of the Psychologist; the extravagant analyses of the Sociologist and the doctrinal methodology of the Theologian (to mention a few), or whomever else finds more vantage and efficacy in the aisles of the university, or the shelves of the bookshops than wholly and vivaciously, alternating the lives of people. The way we paint the picture never deals with the Biblical evidence, or the root of the problem, which is plainly described as life or death, and blessings or curses.

The imbalances are also further enhanced by the conduct of humanity. Many times the blessed person will, as a result of the blessing experienced, incur envy and jealousy from those around them and beyond. Such behaviour comes from those who are envious of the prosperity, or then blessing in whichever area of the person's life. My personal opinion is that it is as a result of the blessing postulating life. I reiterate that it is not an absolute rule but a generalization pointing towards the polarity. Some non-Christians, especially in the entertaining industry, are extremely prosperous but publically deny the existence of Jesus the Anointed One, and the Son of God. What is perceived as their present blessing will end to be a curse, which is separation from God for eternity. Thus, blessings for Christians and non-Christians have different end results, and it should then also be defined within the borders of God's Word. The blessing of the one is to glorify God and the nature of the other is narcissistic, solely glorifying self. From here onwards my focus will be directed towards blessings and curses, relating to believers.

I define believers as born-again children of God, embracing Jesus the Anointed One as Lord and Saviour, and believing He is the Son of God following Him, and surrendering their lives completely unto Him. (JOHN 3:5; JOHN 1:12; JOHN 3:16; 1 JOHN 5:1+10 KJV) The silence of the general church world regarding this topic, the hostile resistance of many, and the extreme ignorance and refusal to understand attitude towards it, necessitates an in-depth study on what the Word of God says.

## ORIGINATE FROM GOD

**Deuteronomy 30:19** *"I call heaven and earth to testify against you today! I've set*

*life and death before you today:*

*both blessings and curses.*

*Choose life that it may be well with you—you and your children."*

The King James Version refers to 'seed' in place of 'children'. As soon as a debate develops around this topic, and you dare quote from the Old Testament, trumpet cries go up and adamantly shout "We are not Old Testament but New Testament people!" Amen to that! It surely is the truth. Praise God that we **DO** have a New Covenant! However, in no way is having such an attitude, of subtly and deceptively denying the existence and relevancy of the Old Testament justified. The Old Testament has its place and role to fulfil. (2 CORINTHIANS 3:11-14 KJV) It serves as examples for us, or acts as a shadow of the New Testament. The author, God, who instituted the Old Testament, was one and the same author of the New Testament. It is disturbing, and uncalled-for, that people such as those in the office of a shepherd or those seen as lay people, move away from selected Old Testament statements, to fit and strengthen their own argumentations, doctrines or beliefs. They avoid such statements because it frustrates them in their quest to support their belief, especially when the Old Testament scriptures clearly show evidence pointing to a different conclusion than what they embrace. Some will go as far as saying that the Old Testament was written for the Jews only. Well, this argument will not suffice, because many New Testament books were written to people in specific locations, and where most of these churches ceased existing ages ago. Does this mean the New Testament was not written for us? With the exception of the Book of Luke, all books were written by Jewish authors. The above is factual and true, however, is irrelevant in context of Christianity. The entire Bible is written by God, for all of God's people. Amen. If anyone oppose this with a better idea, though very harsh, we would then be able to get rid of the entire Bible and not believe it at all! It is either all of the Bible, Old and New Testament, or no Bible at all! There are those who ignorantly interpret many scriptures incorrectly. It is not within the scope of this book to explore the reasons thereof. The tragedy is that many folks are stuck in their status quo of misery, failures etc.

I will dissect unapologetically Old Testament scripture, Deuteronomy 30:19, to ensure clarity, and we will then incorporate the entire Bible in its proper context. We refuse to be influenced by humanistic dissertations, and their analytical thinking, causing a worst case scenario by avoiding and eliminating certain parts of the Word of God. The aim of our research will be to point out to the reader the reasons for our introductory remarks and the imbalances in life. This rings true even of Christians who are confronted with the borders of blessings and curses, life and death. This solidly refers to an either / or situation. It is either the one or the other, but not some of the one and some of the other, In order to be able to do the above, we can and should go nowhere else than to the Bible and look at the origin.

Deuteronomy 30:19 is explicit and crystal clear. You need not be a theologian or a Hebrew scholar to comprehend its meaning. God refers to Himself as the designer of blessings and curses. He says: "I, GOD set before you . . ." Can it be any clearer that both blessings and curses are God's design and are part of His plan? There are, conservatively speaking, many people who are as quick as lightning to refer to the devil when they talk about curses. The final authority is God and His Word, and the statement makes it final that both are from God and no one else. We cannot assign that to the devil because it is not his, nor did he invent or initiate it. You need to understand one thing indefinitely. The evil forces can only function within the borders of God's Word. They have no special power or authority superseding God's Word. None whatsoever! We will discuss more about this later on. A small reminder: God has given us power over all the power of the enemy. (LUKE 10:19 KJV)

## CHOICE & EFFECT

The plan develops further when God finishes His statement. He individualizes it by saying: "I set before **YOU** . . ." Thus, friend, you and I, and whoever else can take out the 'you' and replace it with our own names. The words are directed towards the Jews and all of humanity, and personalised with one simple word: 'you'. In God's divine wisdom, He leaves us with a choice. The whole of creation, and humanity in particular, Christian and non-Christian alike, became subject to God's blessings and curses. Instead of forcing His Word down our throats, He gives us the freedom and liberty to choose by saying: 'You choose'. Let me then make a very harsh statement and say that we, as humanity, are where we are as a result of our own choices. You, dear reader, will become what you choose; either / or! In continuance of the above scripture, God alone; not man, not a Theologian, preacher of a mega church, or one of a small church, or whoever else; claims authority. We have no right to claim any form of authority outside of God. God says that your choices will influence 'your seed'. Your choices have generational effects. What you do will influence your children. Or we can say that what your ancestors and parents have done have already affected you and are affecting you today! Hang in there; we will elaborate in detail as we continue the journey. May I ask that you do not allow your mind to run wild now and ask too many questions? The modus operandi is to first establish certain principles, and then we will give answers to all the questions.

We can conclude by saying that decision-making is part and parcel of our everyday lives. We are daily faced with making some form of decision. The subsequent choices will have future ramifications. Thus, the plan is God's and the choices are ours to make. He forewarns us, in detail, of the potential result and outcome of our choices.

## PROTECTION OF GOD'S NAME

Every so often we will hear the remark being made to the effect that if God is a God of love why does He allow all the heartache, pain and suffering to continue on earth? Why does He not step in and change the situation, bringing relief to those in utter despair? Questions like these are made in ignorance, and devoid of understanding Scriptural reference, camouflaged with secular humanism and based on a complete lack of knowledge. This indicates the absolute importance of journeying with Holy Spirit continuously, allowing Him to elucidate all biblical truths on the road to establish valid answers. The quest of finding valid and true answers to all the intricate, and most humanly unbearable, is to have an intimate relationship with Holy Spirit and a love for the Word of God. Then you will understand that every answer you need can be explained and understood.

First and foremost we have to establish certain fundamental concepts. The Bible introduces us to the undeniable fact that God is the Creator of heaven and earth. This is explicitly announced in Genesis 1:1 KJV *"In the beginning God created the heaven and the earth."* This is surely a profound introduction, because this makes God:

I.   Supreme over His creation
II.  Sovereign above all

III. Sole owner of the Universe <sup>(PSALM 24:1 KJV)</sup>
IV. Designer and therefore transcendent
(all-knowing, all-powerful and all-present)
V. Conclusively, His being can be described as the epitome of
perfection.

Hence, the difference between God and man is somewhat indescribable. The subsequent consequences of the above are that whatever He says proves to be a command.

God created man; placed him in the Garden of Eden and commanded him to look after God's property as a steward (manager). <sup>(GENESIS 1:29 KJV)</sup> He continued by giving further instructions and stating the following in

> **Psalm 115:16 KJV** *"The heaven, even the heavens, are the LORD'S: but the earth hath he given to the children of men."*

Here we have a clear instruction. God created heaven and earth, and put man in charge of it all, to look after it. Sadly, man had already mismanaged what was God-given in the Garden of Eden. You see, friend, what we need to understand is that God, in His sovereignty, hands out the directions, and as we have already said, they go along with a decision. God gives instructions and he allows man to have the liberty in choosing whether he wants to follow the godly direction given or not. God's instructions are not a humdrum to occupy our lives but rather specifics on which He will command His ultimate blessing when we follow the particular way He wants things done. Have you heard? God commands His blessing on all we do according to His instructions and ways. However, should we resist and go against what He says with self-justifying; the regrettable after-effects will be curses accompanying our actions. Looking then at the whole earth, we see a mixture of blessings and curses; life and death.

Follow me now: the condition of planet earth at present is a direct result of humanity going against God's command. It is evident that the wrong is to be found within the borders of humanity and

Dr. Adolf Jonker Ph.D

not looked at God as the guilty party. He honours His Word. He functions within the framework of His Word to honour and protect His name. You and I and whoever else do not have the ability to alter His Word without accusative, rebellious pointing of the finger, suggesting God as the guilty party. This is exactly why God insists on confession and repentance. That is how we can reverse the curse as individuals and society. "If My people will humble themselves and pray I, God, will heal their land," [2 CHRONICLES 7:14 KJV] is God's invitation, even for nations, to come to Him in confession and repentance, and He will reverse the curse. Ezekiel the prophet clarifies the matter even more clearly.

> **Ezekiel 20:9 NLT** ". . . I acted to protect the honour of My name. I would not allow shame to be brought on My name among the surrounding nations . . ."

Wherever and whenever we dishonour God's Name we are in trouble, God makes it clear; His preference is to be merciful and bless us. This would involve His honour. A sure and guaranteed route to tapping into God's blessings is by honouring His Name.

# art 3 BLESSINGS AND CURSES

## SUBJECT RULE 2: SUBMIT TO GOD—
## RESIST ALL EVIL

KEY SCRIPTURE:    James 4:7 KJV

"Submit yourselves therefore to God. Resist the devil, and he will flee from you.

KEYWORDS:

**Defy**

**Refuse**

**Fight back**

KEY CONCEPT:    Daily living in God's overcoming victorious power.

# INTRODUCTION

The demonic realm is one area that stirs great interest; to discover truth in the maze of opinions regarding it. You have the polarity of some who resist even mentioning the name, devil, and, contrary to scripture, they will argue that it's best to leave the devil alone and he will do the same with you. Is this what God says? Certainly not! He instructs us to resist the devil, not practice the 'leave-alone' method. Another common approach is to overemphasize and over-compensate, acting as if the devil is in control and dictating our lives and daily affairs. The 'middle of the road group' won't even bother to make a statement whatsoever; in fact, they will do whatever to avoid such pressure. The Bible says that we should not be unaware of the schemes of the enemy's plans. (2 CORINTHIANS 2:11 KJV)

Humanity plays Sherlock Holmes and wants to find the culprit of the many things that go wrong in life, through its secular and humanistic detective work. Sad, but true, is that we completely rely on natural focal points and look at Socio-economic answers, such as Philosophy, Science and Religious social acceptable forms that are conformed to those of society. Whereas the answer to the root of it all has a spiritual origin, although, it manifests in the natural. When we see the rotten fruit in the natural, we act promptly to remove it, basing it on some of the answers we have found to the 'why'. However, fruit is always seasonal, and what you remove this season will simply re-occur next season. Why is this? We have not yet dealt with the problem. The only way to stop fruit from being produced is to cut off the life source: the root.

The apostle Paul makes problematic comments in:

**Ephesians 6:12 KJV** *"For we wrestle not against flesh and blood, but against principalities, against powers, against the rulers of darkness of this world, against spiritual wickedness in high places."*

Paul addresses some vital points. He uses a very strong word, 'wrestle', to re-direct our fight away from humanity towards the demonic. 'Wrestle' is no complacent indicator whatsoever. It indicates face-to-face conflict involving skills, strength, strategy, endurance and so forth. It is a 'contact' sport, and I fail to see the reasoning behind the idea of 'if I leave the devil alone he will not hassle me.' The overwhelming majority of people spend their time, energy and money in wrestling against flesh and blood, ignoring the signpost of scripture not to do this. In essence, fighting against flesh and blood is no more than fighting the wrong opponent, with no backing from heaven, and who would want that? Regrettably so, we as God's children are guilty, irrespective of clear Scriptural guidelines.

Peter solidly nullifies the idea of leaving the devil alone by stating the following:

> **1 Peter 5:8 KJV** *"Be sober, be vigilant; because your adversary the devil, as a roaring lion, walketh about, seeking whom he may devour."*

In laymen's terms, we can explain what Paul and Peter says: "Don't be stupid, you have an enemy, fight him, stand against him, defy his plans, refuse any intrusion from him into your life, give him no place, and wrestle against him face to face. Paul does not incline to either of these extreme poles: ignore the devil or the other to be completely obsessed with him. There is a time and a place for everything. (ECCLESIASTES 3:1 KJV) He uses strong words to elucidate the evil one's plans and he re-emphasizes strengthening scripture that the devil wants to kill, steal and destroy your life. (JOHN 10:10 KJV)

## PERSPECTIVE

None of the introductory remarks are remotely close to being correct. We need perspective to see evil in the context of the Bible. The very day that Adam and Eve, opened the door in the Garden of Eden, they influenced the rest of all humanity, and the devil walked right into our lives with one of His purposes: to convolute and abuse the promises of God. His ultimate purpose is obviously to defraud us from the beauty, prosperous plans and hopeful future God has for us. By walking into the lives of humanity, the devil claimed humanitarian authority and he became the prince of this world. (JOHN 14:30 KJV) What comprise the system of this world? It constitutes the secular, humanistic, religious and demonic domains. This is a system opposing faith in God, because in every possible way it will encourage you to rely on and function in the natural. This is a system that daily opposes, as well as influences, all of us, specifically you as reader.

I want to be absolutely clear on one thing, and want you to make sure that you truly grasp the meaning and extent of this: although satan is prince of this world, he does not own the earth! Got that? The system encompasses a deceptive structure of various evil devices, globally deluding the minds of people. (REVELATION 12:9 KJV) This warning is even to the elect, God's children, that '. . . *some shall depart from the faith, giving heed to seducing spirits, and doctrines of devils . . .* '(1 TIMOTHY 4:1 KJV) How much clearer than this do we want it to be? The plan of the enemy is to deceive the minds of the people, thereby getting them to believe false doctrines, which are then solely inspired and proclaimed by demons, and even subtly propagated through human beings, recruited as instruments, making use of earthly structures.(2 TIMOTHY 3:13 KJV)

I want to elaborate on the above, illustrating it by giving biblical examples to clarify the proper place and role of the one third of fallen angels and their diabolic nature. Let us have a look at the ten plagues. How did they happen? Were they just some random, out of the blue, happenings? Did the people know they would come? Yes, they had to, because God proclaimed His plan through Moses and predicted the ten plagues. He said to Moses that He would harden Pharaoh's heart and that would be the onset of God's signs and wonders in their midst. God promised to multiply His signs and wonders through what was about to occur. (EXODUS 7:3 KJV) The suspense unfolds as we reach the 10th plague, ". . . for I will pass through the land of Egypt this night and will smite all the firstborn." (EXODUS 12:12 KJV) Make sure you follow me in what I am trying to convey: "For the Lord will pass through to smite the Egyptians . . ." (EXODUS 12:23 KJV) The scripture continues with: "The Lord will pass over the door, and will not suffer the destroyer to come unto your houses to smite you." Hebrews 11:28 expounds on this: "Through faith he kept the passover, and the sprinkling of the blood, lest he that destroyed the firstborn should touch them." According to the above evidence, we unambiguously see that the plan was God's. Period. Who executed the judgement? Not God, but he summoned the destroyer. But who is the destroyer? We find the answer in Hebrews 2:14. It states: "that through death we might destroy him that had the power of death", that is, the devil. The destroyer, plain and simple, is the devil.

Let us move on to Job 1:8 where we come across a very interesting discussion, quite peculiar at first glance. God points out to satan the perfect life of his servant Job. The discussion evolves and it boils down to the point where God set specific parameters and allowed satan to have the liberty to harass specific areas in Job's life. God drew a line and said: "you can steal and destroy as much you want, but you cannot kill him." (JOHN 10:10 KJV) Without going into the detail, let's add the above to my previous elaboration and draw a conclusion. God is in complete control of His plan in the same manner it is constitutionally grafted and given as directional in the Bible. In view of this statement, it is evident that the demonic realm can only function within the realm that God specifies and allows. It has no secretive agenda, warranted of execution, outside of God's knowledge and authority.

Where does satan get his authority—the authority to kill, steal and destroy, as history so pertinently portrays? Paul says in Ephesians 4:27 *"Neither give place to the devil."* Analogously, I want to rephrase the above saying: "Do not open any door in your life to the devil." This door is seen as the battle of the mind. Ephesians 4:17-18 *". . . as other Gentiles walk, in the vanity of their mind, Having the understanding darkened, being alienated from the life of God through the ignorance that is in them, because*

Dr. Adolf Jonker Ph.D

*of the blindness of their heart . . ."* Paul further elucidates, now addressing the Christian, by saying in

> **2 Corinthians 10:5 KJV** "Casting down imaginations, and every high thing that exalteth itself against the knowledge of God, and bringing into captivity every thought to the obedience of Christ . . ."

We, as the 21st century modern day Christians, find ourselves in the exact place Adam and Even did when they were in the Garden of Eden. The structures of this world system raise a query as to the exactness of the Fall in the Garden. The similitude in then and now is that both questions God's Word. The popular phrase: "But . . . did God say?" It plays mind games and seduces our faith to disobey, thus rejecting God's Word. Being enticed, and part of such games, will cause us to ultimately walk and live contrary to God's Word. This is the only way you can give a place to the enemy. The more you question God's Word the bigger opportunity you give the enemy to find the opening and enter. He will surely not cease to abnegate himself of such an opportunity to claim a place of operation in your life!

## GOD'S PERSPECTIVE

To have a clear understanding of God's perspective, we need to analyze satan's working agenda. His demonic perspective is to effectively 'wrestle' with our minds. How does he do it? He tries his best to deceive us with his opposing biblical questions, in the attempt to cause us to doubt and ultimately reject God's Word.

Notwithstanding the above, we now have to look at things with a divine godly perspective. Society is bombarded on a daily basis with subtle, ignorant and or even blatant rejection of God and His Word. The media in all its multitudes of avenues plays a vital part in what is published. Many unbelieving scientists will boldly proclaim scientific discoveries questioning biblical truth or proof. They produce television programmes where they can preach and sow doubt as their global strategy. The rhetoric is aimed at discrediting God and His Word and to get as many as they can to willingly play a scientific 'follow-the-leader'. How is it that such a vast majority will succumb to this? We fall prey to the 'least-resistance-movement' because the lack and zeal for the knowledge of God is outweighed by what society presents on a tray.

Allow me to make a very clear statement: GOD IS!!! He is I AM, and was and will always be, even if humanity globally comes, and all seven billion are in unison and come to an agreement, and wholeheartedly proclaim in one accord that there is no God. If Science, Philosophy, politics, the entertainment industry and every other sphere in life support one another in the 'no God quest', 'He is'. Let us move up one notch with a hypothetical statement. Even if the global church goes public and confesses that they are sorry but they made a mistake in believing there is a God, and that now they have come to the understanding there is none; 'God is'. Listen carefully to me, friend, even if all the above happens; it will not change one iota of the historical, current and futuristic aspect that GOD IS! The popular 'no God' voice, which rejects the truth of the existence of God, has no validity whatsoever. God is also not in need of a majority popularity vote to acknowledge Him.

## JESUS' PERSPECTIVE

The premise from which we have to work here is the understanding that the church is not a building made out of bricks, stones and cement. In fact, it has less than zero to do with a physical building. I will define this for clarity's sake:

❖ **I Corinthians 6:15 KJV** "Know ye not that your bodies are the members of Christ?" (spirit, soul and body)

Dr. Adolf Jonker Ph.D

- ❖ **1 Corinthians 6:17 KJV** "But he that is joined unto the Lord is one spirit."
- ❖ **1 Corinthians 6:19 KJV** ". . . know ye not that your body is a temple of the Holy Ghost which is in you, which you have of God, and ye are not your own?"
- ❖ **Ephesians 5:23 KJV** "For the husband is the head of the wife, even as Christ is the head of the church . . ."
- ❖ **Ephesians 1:22 KJV** "And hath put all things under his feet, and gave him to be the head over all things to the church . . ."
- ❖ **1 Corinthians 11:3 KJV** ". . . the head of every man is Christ; . . . and the head of Christ is God."

We cannot argue against the scriptures above. They are an unmistakable indication, illuminating our minds with the knowledge that the global church is made up of born-again believers, human beings by nature. The real head of the church is not the Pope, Priests, or even any number of Pastors, but Jesus the Anointed One, the Son of God, is the real head, as well as the only one. In the economy of God, Holy Spirit comes and baptizes every believer into the body of Jesus the Anointed One; (Church) at rebirth. Take note that I am not referring to baptism in water in the Name of Jesus at all. This is adding another member to the spiritual body (church) of Jesus the Anointed One. This does not indicate adding to the Catholic Church, or the Pentecostal Church, the Reformed or even the Charismatic and any other Renewal denomination. I will quote something so profound and encourage you to keep coming back to this scripture again and again.

> **Ephesians 4:4-6 KJV** *"There is one body, and one Spirit, even as ye are called in one hope of your calling; One Lord, one faith, one baptism, One God and Father of all, who is above all, and through all, and in you all."*

It is so evident that we can add to the above 'one church' and not for movements claiming the 'church title'. God is not divided; neither does He imply divisive strategies. The above scripture is indicative of a synoptic godly oversight of the church.

With the utmost respect, in and towards God, I want to explore the divisiveness in the church and its intolerance towards another. The last statement is simply functional and evident that there is a lack of maturity, love, and the inevitable diabolic influence.

When anybody joins a particular church denomination or even independent group, they join what this particular group believe and stand for. These different groups each have doctrines formulated according to their belief and understanding. These doctrines define the individual groups' identities and modus operandi. In most cases people from the 'get going' adhere to the doctrinal statements of the group they join. These groups form their own individual identity and culture, mostly from a premise that they have sole ownership of Biblical truth. They will aggressively defend their doctrine, and quote scriptures to back them, quicker than lightning. Nobody dare query them, no matter what good intentions they have, and even present Scriptural backing to defy some untruths in their doctrine. They will simply expel such a person. Thus, my friend, my observation is that throughout history we have joined doctrines instead of the church, and in most cases, to many, the fastidious doctrine became nothing but an idol. They have not joined a church but a doctrine, and there are those who are willing to die in order to protect it. We have also seen many marketing their doctrine as if their very lives depended on it. These doctrinal differences and preferences became the very barriers raised between one Christian and another.

Why so divisive? I believe God gave us a clear example in the exodus of the Jews. He said that a cloud would direct them by day and a pillar of fire by night. When it moved, they were to move. God progressively reveals Himself. His revelation cannot be attached to one specific time or group. He reveals more and more from time to time. If only we can grasp this! Therefore there are certain people who will grasp what God is revealing spiritually. They will embrace it and move on with God. However, there are others who will choose to remain within the borders of the revelations, traditions and cultures of the yesterdays. They are not willing to move out of their current 'revelation comfort', to where God is taking them, which is out of their comfort zone. This is not uncommon to see and what is more saddening is that those who choose to stay in their comfort zones will many times automatically become the persecutors of those moving on. Regrettably, those who move on with God's revelation today, are also tempted to believe that it is the ultimate, and they do not completely understand that it is not the final revelation of God's guidance and strategy. Thus, the cycle continues . . . yesterday's persecuted ones become tomorrow's persecutors.

It is imperative to understand that the entire church is a divine constitution of human beings who are all imperfect by nature. (PSALM 51:3-4 KJV) No human being is angelic. (ROMANS 3:23; 6:23 KJV) It is therefore apparent that multiple mistakes, errors, weaknesses and regrettably so, sin, will emerge and be part of the body (the church). But this is WRONG and also totally unacceptable. We have to strive to live as Jesus the Anointed One did, and put all our effort into living blamelessly before Him. There are few things as precious as God's grace! In such situations this is what we can truly rely on. We know that we may err but we also know that we can immediately repent and confess and not let it get a foothold or become a bad testimony.

Multiple, self-ordained voices flourish in lavishly pointing to the mistakes of the church. Although most of what has been pointed against is true, I have to say, and it vary from sexual scandals to financial frauds; the unthinkable rape, and alcoholism; the list is endless. Isn't it amazing that this was the case from the beginning of time, and every time the hostility-promoters prophesied shipwreck, God miraculously kept the church going and moving forward? Throughout history many have predicted the end of the church; however, it is stronger today than ever before. If God is part of something and it is His design and order, no man will be able to stop it. (ACTS 5:39 KJV) The hostile attacks normally come from the political arena. However, through years of observation, it has been proven that there are very few politicians who are able to speak two consecutive sentences without lying about one. The media is worse. One will very quickly see that the journalism, which is supposed to inform the general public, is filled with inconsistencies. It is also true that in the domain of the media, the breaking story is also told from different preferences and personal interpretations. War serves as a great example. Depending on the personal preference and interpretation of the group, we will be provided with two sides of the story. Those who are not in favour of the nation being attacked will report great devastation and a 100% death rate, and hospitals in the specific area will promote an influx of unimaginable proportions of casualties, whereas those in favour of the nation who attacked, will report no serious injuries or casualties. Different reporters will have different stories. Whenever children and women are involved during a specific attack, one can already doubt the validity and truth of the report. Women and children's deaths became a propaganda tool, playing with the emotions of the people in this subsequent age. This spills over into every aspect of life. Everybody is playing on everybody's emotions, with the main aim to succeed in lobbying for support, and ultimately sales. News is surely profitable. The vehement attack against the church then is nothing but people using the mistakes of other people, hoping to discredit the work of God. Let me call into remembrance: "all have sinned . . ." (ROMANS 3:23 KJV)

All of the above-mentioned are a direct result of the Fall in the Garden of Eden. The proof of the depravity of man can be traced from the ethnic tribes in the Amazon, with their barbaric apparel and lifestyle, through to the wealthy businessmen, politicians and even ministers dressed in western modern regalia, living their high-profile lives and enjoying celebrity status.

The deviation from God's plan in the church domain came when we replaced Jesus the Anointed One with our doctrines. The current elected Pope, Francis, made a profound statement during his election. He clearly told the Catholic Church that if they do not turn back and preach the pivotal message of Jesus the Anointed One they will eventually become an NGO (Non-governmental organization). I would like to erase the 'eventually' and say that most churches are already NGO's. You see, friend, in God's divine constitution He never asked us to follow in the way of humanity, or to follow doctrines and interpretations. He understands our fallen nature and its inclination towards evil. He specified, with unambiguous clarity: "Follow My Son! Have faith in My Son! If YOU (humanity) do not do this, you have already judged yourself as guilty."

Everything about God is faith-related. You prove Him by faith, or shall I say, discover Him. Scientists want to use microscopes, carbon dating etc. Picture the following with me. Let's argue that scientists want to prove the influence of telomeres on your DNA and to do this they apply financial economic principles. This is absurd, isn't it? It is a truly ridiculous and outrageous concept. This statement is indicative of a lack of intelligence of whatever kind. Should we not rather say the statement points to the absence of any form of intelligence? My question to you is this: are we not doing similar things in our walk with God? God says you will discover Him by faith, analogously, in accordance to the above; people want to apply their own adopted methodology, contrary to 'faith'.

We may disagree on the above statement, but what do we do when God says "You will discover Me by faith?" Do we attempt to apply so-called scientific methodologies, investigating cause and effect, design and so forth?

## PERSPECTIVE REGARDING RESISTANCE

Resisting the devil postulates divine understanding and insight. A curse is nothing outside of some form of calamity, disguised in diverse forms, and it unsettles your life in every, and in any sphere. You can compare it to a fire. The New Living Translation Bible states in Ezekiel 15:6-7, "Since they are useless, I have thrown them into the fire to be burned and I will see to it that if they escape from one fire they will fall into another." In other words, here we see fire upon fire. May I say that they will discover suffering upon suffering, curse upon curse and calamity upon calamity! The one thing will not yet be dealt with then you'll discover something new. Have a look at your local news stations; anytime you wish. If it is not the Tsunami today, it is an earthquake tomorrow, and the next day an aeroplane that falls and kills many; or a drought here or there. You are familiar with the endless negative facts that are being presented day after day, bulletin after bulletin. Many Christians experience things like that in their lives; destructive, disruptive, uncomfortable and ultimately it is simply the manifestation of a functioning curse.

Resisting the devil is to close all open doors or, differently said, setting out the fires of killing, stealing and destroying.

Dr. Adolf Jonker Ph.D

# **Part 3** BLESSINGS AND CURSES

## SUBJECT RULE 3: GENERATIONAL CURSES

**KEY SCRIPTURE:** Proverbs 22:6 KJV

"Train up a child in the way he should go: and when he is old, he will not depart from it."

**KEYWORDS:**

**Inheritance**

**Transferable**

**Participation**

**Similitude**

**KEY CONCEPT:** Understanding the origin, functionality and advancement of blessings and curses; a look into generational inheritance.

# SEED POSTULATES GENEALOGY

It is fascinating to note in the Bible how much time and energy went into formulizing detail of the genealogy of so many people. The Books of Chronicles, for example, go to extreme analysis in laying out the ancestral lines of the Jews. Matthew introduces the New Testament with a generation by generation account of Jesus' family tree. In the first book of the Bible, God introduced us to the mandate of humanity, and one of the things mankind was blessed to do was to multiply, in other words, have children, increase in number, in the concept of family. Can we agree that in order to multiply with the context of a family, we need a male and a female, the cornerstone of a family.

We have to infer from the above that family is important to God.

> **Jeremiah 32:39 KJV** *"And I will give them one heart, and one way, that they may fear me for ever, for the good of them, and of their children after them . . ."*

> **Acts 2:39 KJV** *"For the promises is unto you, and to your children, and to all that are afar off . . ."*

In following God, He is not only concerned about the present generation but even about those to come. Therefore we can say that He is a generational God, or differently said, concerned about all. So when Deuteronomy 30:19 speaks of 'thy seed'; (STRONGS, H2233) the word 'zera' is used, and translated as posterity.

Our key scripture calls our attention back to the relation between children and parents, with unambiguous godly guidelines. Train, educate, instruct, prepare and teach your children about God. He places the responsibility of the next generation solely on the parents of the children. This is an extremely important point to remember. Drill His ways into them. (EPHESIANS 6:4 KJV) Model it to them, because when they grow up they will adhere to and follow the path laid out before them. Your conduct and your lifestyle as a parent will influence

Dr. Adolf Jonker Ph.D

your child's life. Your behaviour, in response to God's Word and call, will show your children the way they should go.

Adam and Eve became the parents of the human race. The result of the Fall in the Garden of Eden still affects their posterity up until today. We were present in Adam's loins, and his judgment became our judgment, whether we want to know it or not. Genesis chapter three gives us an account of the Fall. Note that God cursed all parties involved and that the cursing part did not come from satan. Prior to the incident, Adam and Eve were walking in the glory of God. I doubt if the word 'curse' ever occurred to them. The first two human beings on planet earth were cursed by God because of their rejection of His Word. God did not ask their permission, test their knowledge, or ask them to debate on public television, about blessings and curses, according to their knowledge and understanding.

It is of paramount importance to note that was not God's perfect plan A for them. On the contrary! God did not activate the curse; it was ushered in by humanity's choice and poor decision-making. In cursing them, God expelled them from the Garden, which in essence meant they were being expelled from the immediate glory of God. Thus a curse is a sign of the absence of God, in either a specific facet of a person's life, or an area, or even altogether. (ROMANS 6:23 KJV) The importance of this statement is substantive. Make a mental note of this.

> **Romans 5:12 KJV** *"Wherefore, as by one man sin entered into the world, and death by sin; and so death was passed upon all men, for that all have sinned . . ."*

> **Romans 5:17 KJV** *". . . by one man's offense death reigned . . ."*

> **Romans 5:18 KJV** *"by the offense of one judgment came upon all men . . ."*

> **Romans 5:19 KJV** *"by one man's disobedience many were made sinners . . ."*

Well, it is clear that this 'man' in the scriptures above refers to Adam. You will agree with me that you and I were not physically present in the Garden of Eden. However, in God's divine wisdom, He judged all of humanity, as the posterity of Adam, guilty. Name it in any way you want, and what your linguistic abilities allow; but what we see here is a sure generational curse at work, even now as you are reading this book. Today, as we speak, if people do not accept Jesus as Lord and Saviour and confess and believe He is the son of God, that particular person, if faced with death, will end in hell. How is this then possible? The simple answer is that it will be the direct result of the sin of the first father: Adam. Irrespective of that person's belief in or against curses it will not alter the end result. Whether we choose to believe in the relevancy and function of curses or not, it will affect you one way or the other.

Digging a little deeper we look at another father, Abraham, called the father of faith. God called him out of his homeland. He went to Egypt, and as he entered he realised that the beauty of his wife could cost him his life. What did he do? He lied about her identity and told all who were interested that she was his sister. (GENESIS 12:10-13 KJV) Years later, his son Isaac dwelled in Gerar with his wife Rebecca, and when he was asked questions about her he did exactly the same thing his father did. He lied about her identity and the fact that she was his wife. (GENESIS 26:7 KJV) This can be argued in two ways. The first is to argue that he inherited it from his father; in other words, indicating that what happened was generationally familial to do. The other option is to say that Abraham had a very confidential father / son discussion about the truths of life, and that Abraham had told him exactly what to do whenever he was in a similar situation. Which do you think it was? Did he really sit down with Isaac for a man to man chat? How is it even possible that Isaac could replicate Abraham's action to the tee? I am prone to say that the truth leans toward the first logical conclusion.

I have laid a foundation through all I discussed in the above paragraphs to draw your attention to the reality of curses, but most definitely also blessings. However, for the moment we wil concentrate on the curses before we deal with the subject of blessings.

Dr. Adolf Jonker Ph.D

# DERIVATION OF CURSES

Curses do not fly in midair, seeking a place to land! They have a definite origin and a place where they have been initiated or proposed to function. The story of Adam and Eve explicitly shows that where the Word of God is rejected, and replaced with a different response to that of God's original intent; that it opens up a door for the manifestation of a curse. We can boldly say that sin allows the possible entrance of a curse.

> **DEUTERONOMY 28:15 KJV** *"But it shall come to pass, if thou wilt not hearken unto the voice of the LORD thy God, to observe to do all his commandments and his statutes which I command thee this day; that all these curses shall come upon thee, and overtake thee . . ."*

> **ISAIAH 3:11 KJV** *"Woe unto the wicked! It shall be ill with him: for the rewards of his hands shall be given him."*

Isaiah gives a well-illustrated explanation when he says: "You will be rewarded," thus the evil workings and sinful occurrences reward humanity with curses. It also overt to see that the intent of the curse is simply there to overtake you! Allow me to use a stronger word and say that it wants to overpower you. It seems so appropriate. Be reminded of the scripture I quoted earlier, where it speaks of one fire upon another fire.

# WHY THE NECESSITY OF CURSES

The inevitable question remains: "Why the necessity of curses? What makes them relevant? What makes them even remotely part of the equation of a God of love?" We have to look back at what happened with the pronouncement of the very first curse, to be able to shed light on the above questions. However, regardless of these comments and suggestions we should revisit the foundation laid.

An inevitable fact is that we should be reminded of the previous chapters which laid a solid foundation for the reader. In these chapters we established that God is Creator and also owner, and therefore He has juridical rights, which supersede any other. After digesting the previous chapters, the reader should understand that God is sovereign and in His sovereignty He has freedom of decision on how to run His universe. Let me then make this bold statement—that humanity has no valid premise to question God and His functioning. Such behaviour borders within the same structure as satan's attempt, which was verbal at best, to ascend to God's holy throne, in an attempt to replace the Almighty. (ISAIAH 14:13-14 KJV) Questioning God exhibits the depravity of humanity in the illogical conquest of a finite mind, with limited knowledge, to challenge the infinite, transcendental God of all knowledge. This is something that Eli, the priest understood. God spoke a prophetic word over him and his sons through Samuel, and although Samuel was reluctant to break the news, Eli insisted. He received a most devastating prophecy; surely not anything anyone would ever want to anticipate! However, his response towards this was noteworthy: "It is the LORD: let Him do what seemeth good." (1 SAMUEL 3:18 KJV)

In response to the above, I would also like to comment on the following and emphasize that it is the author's opinion that the plan of the enemy, throughout the ages, was and still is to seduce the church realm into believing the picture he painted of God. He wants us to believe that God Himself is somebody who does not adhere to His own truths. He proceeds in attempting to seduce us to believe that God, in the essence of His being, is on similar levels as humanity and that He is comparable to mankind. My comment to the last statement is acrimonious! Such conduct and cogitating in regards to God, is in direct contrast with the core of the transcendental God (ISAIAH 55: 9+11 KJV) Regrettably, the overwhelming evidence is that this is exactly what we have done with God in general—we have degraded

Him to the level of humanity. Suffice to say, we unintentionally did so, but will not acknowledge that the overwhelming majority of the church's views and the secular worldview of God do not differ all that much. Take note that we are a fallen race, and only God knows all we lost that one fatal day in the Garden of Eden. God cannot be defined on our human levels—at all!

The same race, us, who have a horrible past, arrogantly and adamantly earned ourselves the right to think that we can bring God to justice and then demand questions directly related to His supremacy and sovereignty! I see no need to even illustrate this. From the above understanding, with a similar spirit and attitude of Eli, I will endeavour to answer what triggered the establishment of curses.

## INVENTION OF THE CURSE

Looking, then, at that dreaded day in the Garden of Eden, my first explanation will be that that day wasn't the trigger of the creation of curses. God, in His foreknowledge, knew what would happen and He was not caught off guard, but He was ready to instil His justice, thus the introduction of the curse. His original plan, notwithstanding the above, was to bless His people, and it is still the same today. Man sinned and activated the eventual initiation of the curse. The above rejection initiated the curse.

## WHAT HAVE THEY DONE

God gave Adam and Eve clear commands regarding their conduct, participation and lifestyle pertaining to the Garden, and defined their role and consequent contribution with elucidated detail. He gave them the pros and cons of the Edenic habitation. Within the borders of beauty perfected and beautified beyond human understanding, the most outrageous act of humanity ever took place. It was grossly offensive towards God and His Word. It was a hideous and extreme act of narcissism, dressed in diabolic seduction, enabling the unthinkable to take place. In the borders of divine glory, serenity and an indescribable dimension of perfection, mankind still found it in their hearts to reject God and His Word. What am I emphasizing? Rejection of the Word of God triggered the commencement of the first curse. Can you see that God's creative consequences encompass the inevitability of curses? Where the Word of God is rejected, God is rejected. These two concepts are inseparable in nature. The above rejection initiates the curse.

## MAN IS A CREATIVE BEING

The Bible explicitly states that man was created by God. However, God did not re-create in the same manner to ensure the increase of mankind. He encoded man with His divine creational encryption and equipped and gifted the human race with reproductive abilities. He planned that man and woman would come together, and have intercourse, using the reproductive creative abilities with which God made them, in order to recreate after man's own kind. This makes man a divine institution and also the biological product of parents. Differently said: Adam had the potentiality, and the coherent capacity, to produce the human family. Therefore, God remains Creator of every single soul. Added to the above, posterity lies incessantly within the seed of man. Therefore without further reasoning, or whatever contradiction; man is a generational being and posterity is the product of the seed. This generational biological reproductive ability was transferred from Adam to his sons, to their sons, and even up to today mankind continues to function within the framework of the transferable productivity.

Dr. Adolf Jonker Ph.D

# RESPONSIBILITY

In the unfolding of the drama in the Garden of Eden we clearly see the Creator rightfully place man within the borders of His perfect will. He thus commands them certain things under the umbrella of His mandate for them which is to be fruitful, multiply, fill the earth, subdue and rule the earth.<sup>(GENESIS 1:28-29 KJV)</sup> The commands were released: firstly leaving mankind with a choice and secondly accompanying His commands were the consequences. These consequences related to whether man adhered to God's will as presented in His Word. Arguably, nobody can object or disagree to the fact that our creative purposes imply decision-making (choices) and consequences related to each decision taken. The consequences will have either positive or negative outcomes depending on what was decided and acted on. Hence the conclusive evidence that we are created to be responsible for our own choices and consequences. Mankind's responsibility rests in direct relation to God's perfect will, accompanied with God's forewarning.

> **Deuteronomy 28:15 KJV** *"But it shall come to pass, if thou wilt not hearken unto the voice of the LORD thy God, to observe to do all his commandments and statutes which I command thee this day; that all these curses shall come upon thee, and overtake thee . . ."*

We see in both cases related to blessings and curses, the inescapable responsibility. In both the above scenarios, blessings and curses, it boils down to a key factor in our execution. The key factor I am referring to is responsibility. We have the choice to either be responsible or not. The question in this is whether we are going to embrace God's Word or reject it. Therefore, responsibility is always found in the context of the Word.

# RESPONSIBILITY – THE PLOT THICKENS

The Word of God states our current personal state of affairs is as a direct result of the implementation of faith in Him, the practical application of His Word or the rejection thereof! Differently said we are at the exact place in our lives due to a combination of both our own choices and actions.

However, the plot thickens. God increases the responsibility levels by adding the repercussions of our choices. Exodus 34:7 KJV "Keeping mercy for thousands, forgiving iniquity and transgression and sin, and that will by no means clear the guilty; visiting the iniquity of the fathers upon the children, and upon the children's children, unto the third and fourth generation." Numbers 14:18 and Deuteronomy 5:9 reiterate the above. Deuteronomy 23:2 goes on to extend the curse to the 10th generation.

We see that where personal choices are related to God it becomes a familial affair. It goes beyond the individual and affects the individual's children and their children and the list continues. Your responsibility proceeds beyond the borders of self and your posterity is inescapably drawn into the equation and affected by your decision-making. Differently said; the aftermath of your choices are that it has transferable properties. Listen to God's remarks: ". . . as I thought to punish you, when your fathers provoked me to wrath . . ."(ZECHARIAH 8:14 KJV)

Let me dissect as follows: Firstly, I am God and I make the rules. Secondly; You execute your decision and thirdly: your action contrary to My Word, My will and ways provokes Me. Hence, My statement that God always wants to bless us and fourthly provocation results in a counteract of God. The fifth is extremely important and it is that as a result of your ancestral line, their doings, you inherit the punishment (or a curse, if you wish!)

Dr. Adolf Jonker Ph.D

Look at the following schematic explanation of genealogy:

Figure 1:

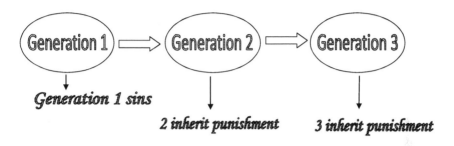

Figure 2:

What if Generation 3 does exactly what Generation 1 has done? We see this occurring over and over in the families of the Jewish Kings.

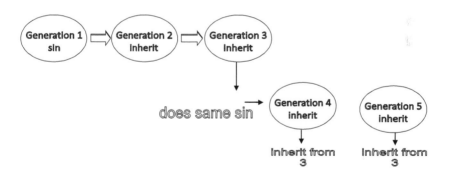

Your stance with God directly influences your bloodline. This generational phenomenon with its transmissible manner and the effects and outcome go beyond families to geographical areas, nations and territories. The short and sweet of it all friend is that through the genealogy of our bloodline we inherit either blessings or curses and both are transferrable. In view of the above I urge you to review Part 3; Subject Rule 1 from pg. 153-166 again. Allow me to share the review of my personal conviction of what we see happening globally;

historically through to the current, in our own lives, families and even in different nations. Every situation whether with the individual, families, corporately, nationally or geographically can be traced back to this profound concept: blessings and curses. What am I suggesting? Blessings and curses influence our lives' spheres.

Jesus' own words back my exclamatory emphasizing of the previous stance:

> **John 10:10 KJV** *"The thief cometh not, but to steal, and to kill, and to destroy: I am come that they might have life, and that they might have it more abundantly."*

Let me rephrase the above scripture. The diabolic wants to force curses down our throats but Jesus wants us to be blessed in abundance. I accentuate the above with Jeremiah 29:11 KJV "For I know the thoughts that I think toward you, saith the LORD, thoughts of peace, and not of evil, to give you an expected end."

God forcefully stressed the above in Isaiah 55:9 KJV "For as the heavens are higher than the earth, so are my ways higher than your ways, and my thoughts than your thoughts."

His plan was, is and will always be filled with uncountable promises of blessing His people. Should we walk contrary to the Biblical constitution the unavoidable curses will be evident in our lives.

## HUMANITIES MANDATE

In looking at the mandate God has given man, we see that five main points complete it.

> **Genesis 1:28 KJV** *". . . Be fruitful, and multiply, and replenish the earth, and subdue it: and have dominion . . ."*

Dr. Adolf Jonker Ph.D

God placed us in the Garden of Eden which extends to the border of the four corners of the earth. We became the CEO's of God's planet with the instructions vividly laid out in the manual of godly life: the Bible.

Allow me to synoptically define the Bible and say that "the Bible" is a term we use for a compilation of books which we refer to as God's Word. It constitutes two covenants and is introduced to us by God, referring to Himself as YHWH, and adjudged to be Creator thus owner of the universe. It is a historical narrative of the fall and redemption of mankind and was written by authors chosen by God and inspired by Holy Spirit in different linguistic styles; law, historical, poetic, prophetic, allegorical and apocalyptic. The focal point is Jesus the Anointed Son of God and the sole interpreter and a must-constant in all interpretation is Holy Spirit. Variable tools exist in aiding our understanding and it consists of a variety of debateable models, of which most are non-agreeable. This is a short summation of the context of the Bible.

Thus God created, encoded and then gave us the operating handbook. In handing the earth over to us, he mandated us in running the earth according to His wishes. Let me divert from the above to clarify. Joshua became leader of the Israelites as they entered and started possessing the Land of Canaan. In Joshua chapter 9 we see how a group called the Gibeonites came to Joshua and deceived him about who they were and where they came from. Joshua made a covenant with them contrary to God's initial instructions. However, God honoured the covenant they made. Why would He if it was done against His instructions? Simply because God appointed Joshua as leader and he was now managing on God's behalf. We see later in the history of Israel that when Saul disrespected the oath of Joshua that God punished 'generationally' and the next generation of King David experienced severe drought. Why? God honoured Joshua's position as God's steward on earth acting on God's behalf. He had a mandate. (JOSHUA 9:152 SAMUEL 1:21 KJV)

Hold on, I am taking you somewhere. Without going into too much detail we know that satan became prince of this world as a direct outflow of the Edenic tragedy. So, instead of the whole earth be fruitful (successful and prosperous in God); multiply (increase in number); fill the earth (with godly people); subdue (bring under godly justice); rule (govern with godly principles) the aftermath is that instead of having a global godly community, we have a mixture of godly and idolatrous people of which the latter is the majority. The fall, spelled out in no uncertain terms, that humanity was set for devastation. Thank God that He sent Jesus to rectify all that had gone wrong!

## VALIDITY AND INFLUENCES OF CURSES

As a result of a detailed study in all the whys and wherefores; I want to point out that curses and blessings are spoken out by two entities:

- ✓ God
- ✓ Humanity

Let me give some examples. God speaks to believers (born-again children of God) saying "bless and curse not". (ROMANS 12:14 KJV) Thus, even we as believers have the capability to curse. If this is proved to be wrong according to our doctrine and understanding, then God made a false incompetent statement. God is not bound to human doctrines and He knows our abilities. Let me rather change capability with authority and say that we have the ability to bless or to curse and it will have resultant effects. If this was not true then God's statement was unnecessary and out of place.

James clearly understood and said "Therewith bless we God, even the Father; and therewith curse we men . . ." (JAMES 3:9 KJV) Matthew says the same however he adds another dimension to it; ". . . bless them that curse you." (MATT. 5:44 KJV) The 'you' addressed in the scripture is

Dr. Adolf Jonker Ph.D

the believer. We see that human beings, believers and non-believers curse one another and that if it had no effect or value why bother mentioning it at all? Noah cursed his grandson Canaan (GENESIS 9:25 KJV) and that curse affected his entire posterity and again it wasn't just empty words but had real significance as well as consequence.

The spectrum expands as Deuteronomy 11:29 states and commands Israelites to put the blessing upon Mount Gerizim and the curse upon Mount Ebal. The book of Ezekiel is flooded with examples where God told the prophet to speak to the rivers, the hills, the valleys and the mountains. This was certainly not a religious ideology to train the prophet how to execute proper prophecy! In the story of Jericho we see yet another example of a place that has a curse on it. God said that anyone who would dare to rebuild it will pay a price (1 KINGS 16:34 ASV) because the place is cursed (JOSHUA 6:26 NLT) also see that certain 'things' have curses that were placed on them and an excellent example is to look at what happened with Achan. We read the story of Achan in Joshua 6:18 and see how one man who rejected God and His Word, brought a whole nation under God's wrath. And he only touched an accursed thing. Isaiah 34:5 KJV related to curses on people groups *"For my sword shall be bathed in heaven: behold, it shall come down upon Idumea (most probably referring to the Edomites), and upon the people of my curse, to judgment."* We see flood wave upon flood wave of God prophesying doom over specific regions and nations. We should not forget about God cursing the snake and when we look at the detail as described in the Bible we still see evidence that this curse is still relevant today. May it be said that God primarily created the snake in perfection. God cursing the snake indicates the probability of curses even on animals. I'm reminded of the group of pigs in whom Jesus drove the demons into and again this is not a blessing I would say. (MARK 5:13 KJV) Have you ever thought about what happened to those demons after those pigs rotted away? In talking about being created and created in perfection by nobody else than God, we think of the angels. However, some in their perfect beauty and splendour rejected God and His Word and thus invoked the punishment of God. What was the result of this punishment? They were cast out from their original domain and position. Their initial flawlessness of God's creation was reversed into them being denied, and they became completely depraved and disgraced from all former glory. Their action adulterated God's initial creative purpose. Simply said, friend, their actions corrupted their creative purity.

## YOU SHALL SURELY DIE

The ignorance concerning blessings and curses relate to a misunderstanding as to what happened in the Garden of Eden. The event is mostly academically referred to as historical fact suggesting the disobedience of humanity, represented by Adam and Eve. However, the depth of this occurrence sheds so much light on who we are and what truly happened beyond the simplicity of the mere vocabulary utilization of the word disobedience.

> **Genesis 3:2-3 KJV** *"And the woman said unto the serpent, We may eat of the fruit of the trees of the garden: But of the fruit of the tree which is in the midst of the garden, God hath said, Ye shall not eat of it, neither shall ye touch it, lest ye die".*

> **Genesis 2:17 KJV** *". . . for in the day that thou eatest thereof thou shallt surely die."*

I would like to point out to the reader the inescapable truth of God's command; eat and you shall surely die.

We know they rejected God's Word, succumbed to demonic, seductive and deceptive encouragement from satan and ate from the particular tree. Notwithstanding is the clarity of God's statement when He addressed them again. He asked them where they were! (GENESIS 3:9 KJV) Did He ask them because He, God, did not know where they were? No, certainly not! The question is what happened to the promise of death? It wasn't a meaningless threat because God re-emphasised this 'promise of death' with the word choice of: "You shall surely die!"

We need clarity! If we want to clarify the above we need to elucidate the makeup of a man.

## MAKEUP OF MAN

To understand the makeup of a man we need scriptural indicators. Firstly we look at Genesis 1:27 KJV "So God created man in his own image, in the image of God created he him; male and female created he them". In addition Genesis 1:26 speaks of His likeness. So, man was created by the Triune God; the Father, the Son and the Holy Spirit; in his likeness and image. Our makeup is elucidated by 1 Thessalonians 5:23 KJV "And the very God of peace sanctify you wholly; and I pray God your whole spirit and soul and body be preserved blameless unto the coming of our Lord Jesus Christ." Paul could have substituted the word 'wholly' with holistically and with that have said that the whole makeup of who you are consists of a spirit, soul and body. Again, he could also have said that we, you and I, are triune beings.

Christians, we are allowed by God to think! If we do not allow ourselves to think; let's read then: spirit equates one part of our makeup; soul another and body yet another part! 1 Corinthians 2:11 KJV refers to man's spirit (pneuma) in the same manner as the Spirit (Pneuma) of God. Soul is referred to as breath (psuché) and body as soma. (STRONGS G4151, G5590, G4983) Hebrews 4:12 KJV refers with divine distinctiveness to the difference between soul and spirit: "For the Word of God is quick, and powerful, and sharper than any two-edged sword, piercing even to the dividing asunder of soul and spirit . . ."

Spirit represents the part of man that is God-conscious and can communicate with God. The soulish realm refers to the personality of man and the seat of self or self-consciousness. It is also referred to as heart and mind or the inner man. Hebrews 12:3 speaks of 'minds' and refers to the Greek word 'psuché'.(STRONGS; G5590) The other reference heart (kardia) is also used in the context of the soul but dear friend it is metaphoric in reference to your emotions and feelings. Your heart has one function: pumping blood. Mind then refers to humanities volitional capability and certainly has no bearing on your brain capacity. Your body is the part of you that is conscious of the natural and with the five senses of a human contact is made with the natural realm. Enough of the technicalities; I trust the makeup of man is clear now.

Let us return to the Garden of Eden. "You shall surely die!" Did Adam and Eve die? No, because they were still around the next day. What happened then? If we understand that man is a triune being; spirit-conscious, self-conscious and natural body-conscious, it gives us an indication to what happened. Adam and Eve saw their nakedness after they have sinned and made a decision to clothe themselves. Their volitional ability which relates to their soul; their inner man: heart, mind and seat of self was active thus this part of them was still alive. They were still in their physical bodies because that was what they were trying to cover. Can we conclude that something happened to their spirit? Their spirit, the God-conscious part, died. Isaiah 59: 2 says that your sin has separated you from God, God asking them "where are you" is God's emphatic statement that they, who had constant communication with Him, were now cut off. The moment the sin occurred their spirits immediately and automatically died as a result of God's Word. We can also say that it happened as a result of their encoded system. They were immediately severed from their God-consiousness and for this reason God asked but Adam and Eve: "Where are you?" Their communication with God was cut-off and they lost God's life that was within them.

Look at this: Let us argue hypothetically and say it was Monday and they walked with God, in the cool of the day and everything was ok and they were alive and well. Tuesday morning they gave in to the temptation and sinned. On Wednesday the very same people continue to function in the soulish and natural realms. The difference in this is that on Monday, before the sin, they were gloriously exalted beings in intimate contact with God. Tuesday they were different because although they were still functioning and walking around however they were spiritually dead. In Amos 5:4 ISV God says: "Seek Me and live!" God did not address dead bodies or people but people with spirits that have died. Thus, real life is a life connected to God. Functioning in only two parts of what should be a triune being is at best a life depraved from the ultimate blessing in God.

Do we understand now that we have died spiritually that fatal day when Adam and Eve sinned in the Garden of Eden? We changed from glorious to being different people? Death separated us from God and its definition is just that: separation from God. How was God going to rectify this gruesome situation? With nothing less than a glorious event! He promised and prophesied and then produced by sending His only Son, Jesus the Anointed One to come and regenerate the mess. The crucifixion, resurrection, ascension took place and this ultimate price was paid to bring everlasting reconciliation between God and man. No other way, no higher price and no better reward and inheritance can a human being have than this. And the best of it all is we did nothing to deserve it . . .

> **2 Corinthians 5:17 KJV** *"Therefore if any man be in Christ, he is a new creature: old things are passed away; behold, all things are become new."*

What happened? The once glorious person was being turned into a different being separated from God. The person referred to in the above scripture speaks of 'the old things' or 'old man'. I suggest that through Jesus the Anointed One the old man has become a new creature and the characteristics of this new creature is someone reconnected to God. In other words this person's spirit is reborn and he becomes God-conscious once again and now true godly life is restored.

Let's look at another hypothetical example.

**Monday:** Tom is a sinner and disconnected from God. He strives for success with all his abilities and puts a lot of effort into all he is doing

Tuesday: Tom attends a business meeting. A born-again child of God, shares the Word of God and the theme is about success. He explains that true life and success can only be found in God. Tom is touched and decides to embrace truth and accept Jesus the Anointed One as his Lord and Saviour. His spirit is now born-again and alive.

Wednesday: Tom is back at work. Will his colleagues now call him John because he is a new being? No. Does anything change in his physical appearance like his hair suddenly turns black from blonde or the other way around? He will still be recognised as Tom, the person they knew the day, week and year before. Did Tom change then? Oh yes! His spirit man is renewed and reborn making him a completely new being. His soul and body will stay the same as the day before. His reborn spirit will change and influence his soulish realm over a period of time. This is a lifelong transformation for the soulish man. If Tom was known to be quite depressed there would now be a joy in him and it will show on his outward appearance.

Let me continue now to connect everything in this chapter with perspective and show you the relevancy of it all.

## RELEVANCY

The time to think has arrived, dear reader! I will propose certain statements and you need to pray and allow Holy Spirit to guide you and judge the relevancy of the statements by the Spirit of God.

**Galatians 3:13 KJV** *"Christ hath redeemed us from the curse of the law, being made a curse for us: for it is written, Cursed is every one that hangeth on a tree . . ."*

First we have to understand that the primary purpose in becoming the curse for us is found in

**Galatians 4:5 KJV** *"To redeem them that were under the law, that we might receive the adoption of sons."*

The first and foremost purpose for breaking the curse was to redeem us from the law, to become children of God the way He intended from before the beginning of time. It is vital to understand this statement! Meditate on it and embrace it completely, because everything else, every other outcome, is secondary to this one. He removed the law from us as Anointed One fulfilled and completed the law.

Let us now take scripture and interpret certain things that happened on the cross and that are verified by the Bible. The Word says: ". . . and that He died for all, that they which live, should not henceforth live unto themselves, but unto Him which died for them, and rose again."

2 Corinthians 5:15 and Hebrews 7:27 are scriptures that alternate 'all' with the whole world. I said earlier that it is time for us to think, so let's put it to good use with question time! The Bible said that Jesus died for all. Correct? Is everybody on planet earth saved, redeemed and a born-again child of God? Were all adopted as sons yesteryear? No, not in the least. Does this make the Bible statements incorrect? Certainly not. Isn't it obvious that we must question our interpretation thereof? God placed us in the Garden of Eden, provided us with uncountable wealth and blessings, and together with this He gave us instructions as to how we were to proceed and also conduct ourselves. We received a huge responsibility, and this responsibility was also preceded by decision. The outcome of the decision would lead to practical application. He died for all, but not 'all' accepted Him as

Lord and Saviour. Thus the scripture is true. However, it needs to be aligned with the whole context of the Bible. Some just simply didn't or do not apply the potentiality to their personal lives.

2 Corinthians 5:17 analyzes and says we are all new creatures; all the old things have gone. The interpretation of this scripture simply says that the day you are saved or born-again every old thing can be classified as historical by nature and extinct and according to God there is no trace of your yesterday's wrongs. Isn't this a little confusing then? Romans 12:1-2 encourages us to renew our minds, but why? The old has gone and been stripped away. Colossians 3:9-10 says that we should strip ourselves of the old man, with his deeds and clothe ourselves with the new man! Why do you need to strip yourself? What do you need to strip yourself from? Are you and I not classified as new beings, according to scripture? Didn't our old already pass away? According to theological persuasions 'strip off' appears inconsistent with scripture. It can only be understood by godly revelation, and the truth is that it is not inconsistent with scripture; not at all. Let me explain in laymen's terms why this is not. Your spirit is renewed (born-again), your soul and body are the same right after conversion, and only because of rebirth can you now start changing to align with the Word of God. Therefore, the scripture is talking about the soul and body that need 'stripping from the old things', with the renewing of the mind. Said in other words, it simply means that now you adopt the will and ways of God in your heart and mind. God says in Ephesians 4:23 KJV *"And be renewed in the spirit of your mind . . ."* Hence my statement: God tells Joshua that He has given Abraham the land of Canaan; he was to go in and possess it, and his strategy would be that to either embrace God's Word or not. When God speaks, it requires action from us. We decide whether we will apply the potential that is already ours, or whether we will hide from it in a passive corner.

The key in understanding is that humanity also has a role to play, and what happens in and to our lives does not solely depend on God but on how we decide to take responsibility and act. We have to decide: application of the Word of God, or rejection thereof. The potential for us is unlimited, and the responsibility lies in decision time. Our application is the precursor to the ultimate outcome. Yes, Jesus surely died for all. However, the choice, responsibility and the actual application lies with us. Yes, He became a curse for us, but the application belongs to us. Yes, Yes, He died for all our sins, iniquities and transgressions but it is up to us to confess and repent. Yes, He paid a price for us to be healed, but the application lies with us. Yes, He became all for us but we need to believe and apply. Yes, He blessed us and multitudes upon multitudes upon multitudes of Christians walk outside the manifestation of His blessings. You, as reader, should be able to work out the answer to the why question by now! It is in the application—faith in action.

## BIBLICAL INDICATORS

Please walk with me through the corridors of Deuteronomy 28 from verse 15 and onwards. This is a never-ending list of curses. Let's stop, in this journey, at certain indicators, to establish for ourselves the relevancy of curses in present day Christianity.

**Deuteronomy 28:18 KJV** *"Cursed shall be the fruit of thy body . . ."* Fruit refers to children. May I suggest that miscarriage is one of the signs of the curse of this fruit? Dare to ask any woman who ever lost an unborn child whether it was a blessing or severe heartache (curse) to them. I have met and also know various Christian ladies who had to endure this unfortunate happening, some even more than once.

**Verse 21**: "The pestilence shall cleave unto thee." Do you know of any pestilences? Do you know that pestilence is any epidemic disease, with a very high death rate? Would you say that we can classify heart disease, cancer or even HIV Aids as candidates? We surely can.

**Verse 22**: "The Lord shall smite thee with a consumption, and with a fever, and with an inflammation . . ." This may be from the Old Testament, but it is definitely a curse, and still functioning in modern days. Do you know how many Christians, born-again believers, battle at times with fever and inflammation? I have a question despite how ridiculous it may sound. Did this curse of the Old Testament turn into a blessing in the New Testament? I doubt it! In fact, we know it did not. Or are we ignorant enough to claim that Christians do not suffer from any type of inflammation whatsoever? Our own reasoning, in matters like these causes us to be in trouble, or we have a complete erroneous interpretation of Galatians 3:10-13.

**Verse 28**: "The Lord shall smite thee with madness, and blindness . . ." So, according to some interpretations of 2 Corinthians 5:17 and Galatians 3:10-13; the moment that a blind man turns to God, he becomes a new man and the curse is broken, suggesting he will not be blind any longer but will immediately see. Please forgive me for elaborating in this manner. I am not in the least trying to be insensitive or disrespectful to all involved in these horrific situations. However, friend, the Bible is not a multiple-choice book, where we can look at the options and then select what we believe on the basis of our own assumptions. There is a real world, with real people, who have real problems. It is about time we say it like it is, so that all real people with real problems will get to understand that there is a real God who wants to bless us with all His heart. Our interpretations, based on our own assumptions, need to be compatible with the whole truth and not only the parts we take out of context.

**Verse 29**: "And thou shalt not prosper . . ." I do not know about you but I know of multitudes of born-again children of God who love Him with all their hearts and follow Him, yet they are still not prosperous, no matter how much effort or how many resources they put in.

Dr. Adolf Jonker Ph.D

**Verse 38**: "Thou shalt carry much seed out in the field, and shalt gather but little in; for the locust shall consume it." I know of many born-again farmers who continuously experience the above. I was one of them many years ago, and whether we want to blame it on poor weather conditions, too much or too little rain, it does not change what the Bible says about it. God says that it is a curse. There are church folk and theologians who boldly proclaim that Christians cannot experience curses. I do not know about other people, but I choose to believe God and what He says about it.

**Verse 44**: "He shall lend to thee, and thou shall not lend to him: he shall be the head, and thou shalt be the tail." I guarantee you that there are multiple millions of Christians who are in debt way over their heads. Irrespective of your theological persuasion, I absolutely guarantee you that they daily live with the experience of being 'the tail'. This means they are not in complete control and others make decisions on their behalf. Did Jesus break the curse on the cross? Amen and hallelujah and amen He did! Does it still affect born-again believers today? Yes and regrettably so. We need to review our interpretation for the sake of allowing the truth to set us free. Some will argue and say that these people are in debt as a result of poor financial decisions that they made. It doesn't matter how they got there, God still calls such a curse. Whatever input is made, whether little or intense, positive or negative, the result will always align with the accompanied curse (or blessing). The outcome always defines itself as either curse or blessing! When the root of the curse is addressed in God, the input will differ and it will have a positive blessing outcome as a result!

**Verse 46**: "And they shall be upon thee for a sign and for a wonder, and upon thy seed forever." Dear Christian, a curse is not a sign indicating that we are evil Christians with poor characters, or not even Christians at all. It is a sign that is indicative of us, or our forefathers, or us and them combined who rejected God and his

Word. This sign can serve as a notice to us as to what went wrong and what we should correct.

**Verse 61**: "Also every sickness, and every plague, which is not written in the book of this law, them will the LORD bring upon thee, until thou be destroyed." Let us just spend some time here and camp in God's guidance. 1 Peter 2:24 KJV says, *"by whose stripes ye were healed."* I suggest to you that it refers to physical healing. Isaiah 53 refers to it as well. Thus, if we interpret it according to the way we do Galatians 3:10-13, we will have to be consistent and adamantly say that Christians cannot be sick, because the Word says we are healed by His stripes. James clarifies the incorrect, erroneous interpretation of Galatians 3, as described, by saying in James 5:14 KJV *"Is any sick among you?"* He acknowledges that Christians are also vulnerable to sickness. He continues to give instruction in how to bring about healing. We have a dilemma, because Deuteronomy defines sickness, diseases and plagues as curses. Once again the question: did it become a blessing in the New Testament? It is absurd to even want to reason in such a way. Therefore the same curses in the Old Testament manifested in the New Testament. However, there is a sure difference in how they are and should be dealt with today.

One Sunday morning, years ago, people brought, or let me rather say dragged, a thirty year old, man to church. When I saw him my immediate observation and thought was that this guy was dying, and would do so before the service was halfway through. I asked the people who brought him to please carry him to the front, so that we could pray for him. They informed me that this young man had Aids, could not speak anymore, and was hardly able to breathe by himself. As I began to pray, Holy Spirit immediately switched me over to prophesy. This was awkward, but I knew God had a word for him. The Lord said to this young man that within 18 months from that day he would have his own flourishing business, that he would be married, and that they would have two children. To cut a long story short . . . Two years later a young man walked into the service with

Dr. Adolf Jonker Ph.D

a wife and two children. He seemed somewhat familiar, but I just couldn't place him. He came up to me and told me that God was so faithful, and that he just had to come and tell me that God gave him a flourishing business, and that he fell in love and married a young widow with two children. If those people had not brought him to church that day he would have died that day or week. If we had not applied God's Word and prayed over him, we would have conducted a funeral service with our theological persuasions, saying that the Lord giveth and the Lord taketh. The practical application of the finished work that Jesus had victoriously and successfully done on the cross moved this man into the glory realm of God. Was his sickness a blessing? Absurd! God, not television preachers or theologians, says that it was a curse. The blessing of healing and recuperation was ushered in as the curse was reversed.

As this portion of scripture was primarily given to the Jews, we can go through it, verse by verse, and find historical evidence of the manifestations of these curses. The purpose of these curses, as set out by God, was absolutely destructive by definition. The outcome was supposed to bring people to repentance.

Since the unfortunate event in the Garden of Eden, we see how humanity has been paying the price for the rejection of God and His Word, in particular when they replace the true and only God for false gods that are no more than demons. (1 CORINTHIANS 10:19-20 KJV) Throughout the history of Israel, and even Modern day Christianity, we see the manifestations of both blessings and curses.

I have experienced these personally. My forefathers fled Europe and left for South Africa, as they were being persecuted for their faith in God. They landed at the Cape of Good Hope and, because of a family feud they split into two groups. My lineage started travelling the length and breadth of South Africa. They moved north, then back south, then west and next were east. They lost all their money, went insolvent and struggled for survival. My grandfather was born, and he became the personification of poverty. Yet they were still travelling all over, never settling down. My father followed in the exact same pattern of moving all around, and also went insolvent. Guess what? I was next in line, and what did I do? The exact same happened with me. I moved from one place to another and even experienced times where I had to move to another place, even before I was able to unpack at my new abode. There I was, just arrived, not even unpacked and yet again loading another truck to move to yet another place. My children went to so many schools. Before their new-found friends had time to get to know them, they had to say goodbye and re-introduce themselves elsewhere. To top it all, I went insolvent at the age of 30, and now I was real competition to my grandfather's status of being the most impoverished. Interesting enough, my grandfather, my father and I were all blessed with extreme musical abilities and were able to play different instruments. All three of us competed nationally and internationally in a variety of sports, and were also extremely well-educated. Please, friends, can you see the evidence of curses in the above examples? Can you see the manifold and evident pattern and the cyclic nature of generational inheritance: both curses and blessings?

I prayed, I fasted, the church elders anointed me; I was counselled by a variety of outstanding counsellors. I sought the face of God regarding the above the debt I owed, and for years and years nothing changed. Then one day I was reading the Bible and came across the story of Cain, and the curse God placed on him in Genesis 4:12-16. I read about how this curse caused Cain to become a wanderer and a vagabond.(GENESIS 4:16 KJV) The Hebrew word 'Nud' (STRONGS, H5110) refers to a wanderer, someone to flee, to disappear and make to move. It struck a nerve with me, because all of a sudden the mystery of my family unfolded. Be reminded that we are not Jews.

Reading the Word of Almighty God shook the core of my foundations because what I saw in my life (and that of my family) was the historical manifestation of this curse. I burst out in tears and just wept before God, cries of desperation and of bold faith in a living God. I stood before God in the simplicity of a child and I shouted: "I break the curse of Nod, of being a wandering spirit," and I confessed all that came to mind. I confessed the sins of my forefathers, of my family and of myself. Words of confession and repentance trumpeted from deep within my being; stripped from any self-awareness, left my mouth loudly! I bound the demonic forces relating to the strongmen of particularly debt and poverty. During this intense time of prayer, I knew I was not alone, I knew it was not me praying but God using my voice to establish His truth in my life. He was there with me. All along He knew what He had planned, and at the appointed time He suddenly came and set me free.

This prayer that I told you about happened 18 years ago. I have not moved once in the past eighteen years. I still had years of incredible financial lack and desperation. However, in many situations God miraculously provided. At the beginning of 2012 a lady prophesied over me that God would pay off my home loan during 2012. I was baffled, because in the natural it was totally impossible. She came back later that day and prophesied that God said the final payment would be made before the 30th of September 2012. True to Himself, God did it! At the end of September 2012 the final payment on the bond was made and it was paid in full, seven years before the end of the initial contractual termination. Apart from not moving again after that prayer, apart from the home loan on the small holding I own, I have been debt free for the past eight years. Currently, I owe nobody anything and poverty is a mere historical nightmare! Isn't it also interesting that now none of my three children and their families, experience any trouble with poverty, debt or a wandering spirit. Some might say that it is just coincidence! You are absolutely right. The moment I dethroned my doctrinal demons; the moment I replaced my denominational persuasions with the truth of what God says; that exact moment when I applied God's Word to my situation it coincided with the manifestation of God's power and the finished work of the Cross.

Let me jump back and end this chapter with Joshua. God said to Joshua: "Son, there is the Promised Land in front of you. If you do not go in and possess it, I, God am doing nothing as well. However, Joshua, if you go and take what I have given you; I will go before you and accomplish in the spirit (the impossible) and it will manifest in the natural (the possible).

Dr. Adolf Jonker Ph.D

## **art 3** | BLESSINGS AND CURSES

## SUBJECT RULE 4: DYNAMIC OF CURSES

KEY SCRIPTURE: **Revelations 3:20 KJV** "If any man hears My voice, and opens the door, I will come in to him, and will sup with him, and he with Me."

KEYWORDS: **Supernatural Powers**

**Evil devices**

**Interactive**

**Investment**

KEY CONCEPT: Portraying the interaction between the spirit and the natural relating to curses.

# INTRODUCTION

Daily and constantly there is a table set before us, a table set by God representing blessings and curses. The variables are believers, and what we choose to eat. Will we feast on blessings at the table of God, or will we be satisfied with eating from curses that satan keeps on the table? These are effectuated by the evil forces. Will we embrace or reject God and His Word? Or will we succumb to the status quo multiple-choice phenomenon, and choose only to embrace that part of God's Word that fits into our comfort zone or, even closer to home, our interpretation and beliefs?

My grandson, Jadon, illustrated the above concept perfectly one day during mealtime. He was presented with a plate that had peas and corn pits on. He studied the plate and then started picking out all the corn pits and throwing them on the ground. He was warned not to do it again, but he did so, and was tapped on the fingers as a last warning. Jadon, however had already made his personal choice and preference of what he wanted, and did not want to eat, and thus continued in the same manner, irrespective of the punishment. Don't we, as God's children, find ourselves in similar scenarios at times? We have all of God's Word at our disposal but somehow we decide to eat only some of it, and then at times even from another table; we claim for ourselves the right to pick and choose.

I realised that we have been expelled from the splendour of the Garden of Eden, but every day we as Christians stand in front of a 'Garden of Eden choice' . . . what we will or won't have. We can eat freely from the tree of life and there are no boundaries to it. However, we should refrain from eating from the tree of knowledge of good and evil. This tree is quite frankly advertised wherever we go. It is done in a way which is symbolic of the system of this world and it functions in opposition to God and His Word, and can only lead to death.

Dr. Adolf Jonker Ph.D

I have witnessed it, over and over; again and again. God calls somebody in a specific realm and anoints that person according to the mandate of God, in order to accomplish God's purposes. The person becomes established in the call and is extremely blessed by God in that particular area. As other people start to recognise the call, anointing and authority; they also establish a platform to become a voice for God. However, in this process there are times and situations where the person called loses track of the specific redemptive and geographical keys with which God has entrusted to him or her specifically. Let us illustrate this with a simpler example, and make use of a name for more clarity. God calls Adolf prophetically. God anoints Adolf, and he is extremely blessed in the accuracy of prophecy and regarded as a true prophet. He has crowds attending prophetical meetings, but then one day Adolf speaks to his leaders and announces that he has been invited to hold evangelistic outreaches. The anointing of God is not on Adolf evangelistically, and although it may sound and seem like a good opportunity, Adolf will be doing a lot of damage with his proclamations, outside of his anointing and call.

Follow me now; I have seen blessed servants, leaders of God, interviewed and asked certain questions on topics that are not their expertise. I have seen how these anointed people blabber erroneous assumptions, simply because they have no anointing or redemptive key from God to speak on those particular areas. However, because of pressure and, many times, honest zeal to impact the world for God, they simply step out of line and get involved in something that was not on God's agenda for them. There are so many examples of this happening throughout the church of God. People anointed by God and functioning in His anointing and blessing as marital counsellors will be asked about inner healing and deliverance, and because this is not their area of expertise (being anointed by God to do it) they will be prone to make outrageous remarks and even comments that will be incompatible with God's Word, and also out of touch with what is happening daily in the lives of people. Can you start to see where it all goes wrong? There are people who are absolutely anointed in the area of inner healing, yet their experience and knowledge about deliverance may be zero. If they encounter situations where deliverance is discussed, and even worst case scenarios, where it is needed, they will make the silliest comments and also fail to be of any help. They are even prone to say that there is no such a thing as deliverance according to the Bible.

The problem lies in the fact that we are told by God that He reveals His secrets to His prophets. (AMOS 3:7 KJV) Take note that 'prophets' speaks of the plural noun. In other words, God uses different people with different callings, gifts and skills to establish His church. What He reveals and allows the one to function in may very well not be what He gives the other to do. Does that mean that one of them is in the wrong? No. It simply suggests that there is no-one out there in current society, or ever has been and never will be, who has all the answers to all the questions. Please take note! This is of paramount importance. We are all called by God, and we as His children are all part of the ministry team of Jesus. The same goes for you as reader. You are a part of the ministry team of Jesus and what He calls you to do; that which He reveals to you will be unique. However, it will always be compatible with His Word. The problem with those people out there, who make the ridiculous statements in areas where God has not called them to function, is that because of the anointing and authority of God on their lives, there are men and women who respect them and the call of God. Sadly, these people therefore err in believing erroneous statements, because of someone who wasn't sensitive to the boundaries God set for his / her life.

People will always be people and in the same way they looked up to anointed men and women of God in the Bible, they look up to anointed people today. This is a rude awakening because whatever you say and do will influence the lives of all those who respect, love and follow you. They incline their ears to hear God's Word through your life, and therefore the responsibility is far higher than we want to make it out to be. This does not exclude you and me. Every child of God is anointed, appointed and authorised by God with a specific call. What you do and say, the way you choose to live, will influence other lives for eternity.

Dr. Adolf Jonker Ph.D

At one time I listened to a very anointed man of God whom I respected a great deal, and still do. During the years I've learnt so much from him, but on this specific day he made a comment stating that Inner-healing is not part of nor is it a ministry of God. That same day I had an appointment with a young man who came to see me for counselling. We've had been counselling him for a couple of months, and gave him lots of advice. However, it seemed as if no good came of it. This day he started off by telling me that he believed that he was in need of inner-healing. That caught me off guard, also because the words of this man I respected were still fresh in my mind. My listening to what that man of God said that morning made me doubt about the subject. However, I did not have much time to reason about it.

I prayed with the young man, and he told me that God had showed him a vision of a young boy on the back of his mother, and the parents continuously shouting curse words at him. In African culture, it is a norm for the mothers to carry their babies wrapped in a blanket on their backs. He felt that God said that he was that boy, and he needed to be healed inwardly. We prayed, and asked the Lord, to silence those voices and completely remove its intentions. We asked Holy Spirit to walk back in history with this young man to those particular events, and to heal and restore his inner man, removing all fear and trauma. Today, it is almost three years later and all I can say is that I witnessed the healing and restoration he received and his transformation after the healing prayers, was one of the most radical and remarkable changes I have ever seen in my life, and in countless counselling situations.

The question remains: from which table do you eat? What do you choose to eat? Do you choose the table of man's opinion, or the table of God's truth? The saying goes that the proof lies in the pudding. Needless to say, that day I learnt a valuable and lifelong lesson. If I allowed the interpretation of the understanding of God's Word, of this man of God to whom I'd listened, I would have been instrumental in the continuation of the destructive life that this young man was living. However, by God's grace and Holy Spirit's intense involvement, He taught me a lesson at the same time brought massive change to a young life; one that once headed for destruction but is now on a path of glory, for the honour of God and His Kingdom.

## WHAT DO YOU EAT?

The problem in the Garden of Eden was initiated by man's choice as to which tree he would eat from. God encourages us, in the key scripture for this chapter, as to where we should eat, and its message runs through from the beginning in the Garden of Eden, way down to the end of the era of grace, as described in the Book of Revelation.

In having said the above, I want to introduce the reader to the dynamics of curses. Analogously, I will refer to the table of blessings and curses; a table of choices. The choices made have ramifications, resultant from which is executed. It all depends on your choice and execution.

I will expand on the content in a schematic illustration, in order to provide a clear understanding of what blessings and curses entail.

God sets before us blessings and curses. He properly expounded on what this encompassed, and strongly advised us to settle for blessings.

Dr. Adolf Jonker Ph.D

The table of choices is set clearly before us every day, in all spheres of our lives.

Ezekiel 20:9 KJV "But I wrought for my name's sake, that it should not be polluted . . ." Other translations refer to the honour of His name. In verse 14 and 22 He continues in the same line. Thus blessings are as a result of honouring God's name and curses related to pollution and dishonour. The next diagram will speak for itself.

| Blessings | Curses |
|---|---|
| Live by God's Word | Reject God and His Word or play multiple-choice in what to believe and what not. |

Nothing has changed since we were in the Garden of Eden. It is still all about choice. Therefore the last diagram refers to what happened in the Garden, what happened with the Jews; and what is still happening with humanity in its broader spectrum today.

| Blessings | Curses |
|-----------|--------|
| Favour | Judgement |

Blessings and curses are like the two sides of a coin. The coin can be representative of God's Word. On its sides it has either favour, or God's judgment.

| Blessings | Curses |
|-----------|--------|
| Life | Death |
| Honour | Dishonour |
| Live God's Word | Reject God's Word |
| Favour | Judgment |
| Personal choice | Personal choice |

## DEFINING CURSES

In defining curses we look once again at the first implementation in Genesis. We can clearly observe God's judgment here: "A curse is the expulsion of the original blessing and it is a direct result of God's judgment." It is extremely important that we grasp the true nature of a curse:

a. Spirit,

b. With a natural manifestation,

c. Opposing blessing. Blessing represents the life (truth) of God, thus the manifestation of a curse is not only that of opposing the blessing, but it certainly is not reflective of God's original intent.

d. The manifestation of the lie.

As a result of the above, we can clarify it as follows: the blessing is indicative of God's truth, whereas the curse is the unfolding of a lie. Let us re-emphasize

**John 10:10 KJV** *"The thief cometh not, but for to steal, and to kill, and to destroy: I am come that they might have life, and that they might have it more abundantly."*

What is God saying with this scripture? He wants His abundance to be expressed in every area of our lives—spirit, soul and body. He warns us that, in fact, the curse is simply reflective of the absence of the abundant life He desires us to live. Let me put it differently: wherever there is an absence of the abundant life of God, a curse manifests in one way or another.

## THREE POINTS OF IDENTIFICATION

I suggest to you, as reader, three vital points in identifying a curse. Hence, my theory that a curse is exhibited by:

❖ Struggles
❖ Suffering
❖ Lies

# STRUGGLES

Struggles are the evidence of a clash taking place between blessings and curses. Due to several influences inspiring the above, the one will always oppose the other. When you think about the word 'struggle', does it excite you or remind you of something pleasant? No, it doesn't, because a struggle is where you are engaged in a fight. The primary reason for this fight is that a party involved in the struggle is fighting to gain control. Remember what Paul says: 'we wrestle'? Wrestle indicates a fight that is taking place. But who is wrestling then? We are because we have to resist the enemy, who wants to abuse situations and circumstances in our lives to gain control therein. So, we can also say that curses are, at times, the manifestation of the one who is having control over your life. This is scary but true. The current make-up of satan is one of wanting control. The struggle is then a battle field for regaining your freedom. Curses enslave you, and blessings give you freedom to subdue and rule in God's favour, power and anointing.

The diabolic purpose of the struggle is to get you to reject God's Word. The demonic methodology is to seduce you in the arena of the "lust of the flesh, the lust of the eyes, and the pride of life." (1 JOHN 2:16 KJV) This scripture is a perfect description of the spirit of this world, whose objective is to get you to doubt, and then reject God and His Word, so that he (satan) can kill, steal and destroy. I am of the opinion that the last three words are the ingredients of a curse manifesting.

# SUFFERING

Suffering is similar to the scripture in Deuteronomy 28:44 KJV, which refers to a person being the tail instead of the head. Differently said, you are subject to what? You are subject to whatever you experience and undergo in your life that is unpleasant; for example, poverty, sickness, death, destructive relationships, or even enslavement to drugs (to mention but a few examples). The list mentioned controls your life and you live with something that is unpleasant. Unpleasant is to be defined within the borders of the intensity of the effect it has on you.

## LIES

Lies are defined as falsehood; a deviation from truth leading to a particular state or condition. A curse, then, is a lie manifesting with a measure of deviation, establishing a falsified state or condition. Many curses appear as a lie, within the context of this definition. For example some Christians believe that it is God's will for them to be poor. This belief only manifest because of the lie believed. Most people who believe something like, "God's will to be poor," will take a robot-like appearance on the subject, because they believe what they have heard from their peers, leaders and denominations, who unfortunately emphasise certain scriptures out of context, only to strengthen their own stance. Such people will, without properly studying the overall message of God and gaining perspective within its context, only believe what they have heard and then stand by it. Most of the times the specific belief has also been transferred to them spiritually, from someone within the scope of their influence and authority, and such people allow it because of the respect and trust they have in those influencing them.

Some will even believe that God gives them a specific sickness in order that He can get their attention and talk to them. Hebrews 1:1-2 "God, who at sundry times and in divers manners spake in times past unto the fathers by the prophets, hath in these last days spoken unto us by his Son." Firstly the Bible refers to sickness as a curse, and secondly God's current and primary ways of speaking to us are through His Son and particularly His Word, by Holy Spirit. Nowhere in the Word of God will you see that He decided to speak through sickness over you. I am not denying that different situations of sickness can eventually portray messages from God at the time, but they cannot be seen as the channel God chooses and prefers to speak to us. The only good thing about sickness, disease and infirmity is when God uses them for His honour and glory through healing you from such. I am not saying that God doesn't speak to His people during times of their sickness. Many people have had great revelations, about specific things in their lives, in those times of sickness. This is as result of His immense goodness, kindness and grace toward them. But He will never cause you to be sick in order to talk to you.

However, although people never have to become sick in order for God to speak to them, the enemy comes like an angel of light, seducing people to sit back from the struggle and to be content with their situation. He camouflages the truth with one simple saying: "But . . . did God really say?" and many folks out there want to believe that they are sick as a result of God's doing. NEVER, in your entire life, is that remotely close to the truth. It is a curse manifesting in the context of believing the lie. Eve chose to believe satan instead of God. She wilfully rejected God and His Word and decided to eat what satan presented on the table. She was content to believe the lie. Today, looking back at the history, we know the truth. She was so wrong, that it affected every human being born on planet earth, from that day onwards.

I encourage you to ask God to show you where your own beliefs may be erroneous doctrines. Ask Him to reveal, by Holy Spirit, whether you have been content to believe a lie, and where such a lie might manifest as a curse in your life. Be bold. Boldness is not arrogance, but it is you allowing Him to strip you from whatever is contradictory to His Word and knowing that He is God, He is truth, and He will let His blessings flood your life. It means that you pray: "God, You alone have full control of my life, and I refuse to allow satan to have the slightest influence." It might be uncomfortable or even shocking at first, but trust God, and He who is the Creator of heaven and earth will restore your life to the place of walking in intimacy and glory with Him. Dare to ask Him. Dare to believe! He will never disappoint you!

## MAPPING CURSES

The medical world makes use of scans, x-rays and many other advanced methods in order to determine what is going on, inside the body. In this next session, I want to look at the complexity of mankind with regard to spirit, soul and body, in a manner that will help us discern the existence of curses in our lives and the relevancy thereof.

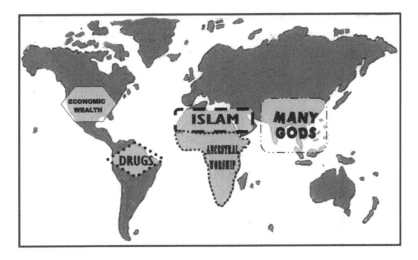

We can use the world map in order to define problematic areas, and also see that specific locations are indicative of specified manifestations. As much as things are happening everywhere in the world, specific things are overly emphasized in that particular area, geographically as well as territorially. Have a look at the above map. My directing to certain indicators is just for you to get an overall idea, and it is not a detailed and formulated outlay.

The local police in your specific location can point out to you certain areas that are vulnerable to violence, crime, burglary, murder or just petty theft, to mention but a few. The traffic department will be able to confirm certain areas that are known for speeding and accidents. The hospital will be able to tell you which sicknesses are predominant to the area, and also the types of emergencies. In this manner, you can go to the schools in the area and you will come to see that they too have particular things that dominate the same. If you take a roadmap and pin down these particular areas, you will get a clearer picture to understanding what is happening in the different areas you live. Mine will differ from yours, and it will be different with people living in unlike areas.

Similar to the above, I want you to look at your life as a roadmap. Start pinning down certain events that are re-occurring again and again. Some will be positive and blessings and others will be negative and curse-related. In South Africa, with our history of apartheid, you will still find Christians who are content to be racist, and this includes all skin colours: black, white, coloured and Indians. They still choose to live with the same form of bitterness, resentment, and prejudice, blatantly rejecting the truth. Praise God that the majority are delivered from this. Are those still functioning with the patterns of apartheid less Christian than the others? No. However, they are part of a group who sustain a curse. Some are content to continue living this way. If you seek God's deliverance, want to live in God's blessings, and want to be a blessing; have a look at your roadmap. Ask Holy Spirit to lead you and point out the re-occurrence of certain issues or situations in your life. Have a look at those things that just come back again and again, no matter what you do, and they keep on being a struggle for you.

Struggle is an indicator of a functioning curse. You have the opportunity now to map your own life and say: "God, in the Name of Jesus Your Son, the Anointed One with His anointing, empower me, by Holy Spirit, to eradicate every negative thing and every curse from my life. I submit to You Lord, spirit, soul and body, and declare

Dr. Adolf Jonker Ph.D

Your Lordship over my life. Thank you for every good gift in my life, Father, and for every blessing. You have come so that I may have life, and life in abundance, therefore I declare that every curse will be broken in Your name, Lord Jesus, and completely removed from my life. All glory to You alone." Remember that curses are always negative, and negativity in itself is also a curse. There has never been and will never be anything good coming from negativity. You can be guaranteed that only positivity will produce some or other form of good in your life. Positive people are always those who you can point out as ones who excel in life. People who are negative always struggle with being miserable, depressed, lack of vision, are discouraged, are disillusioned, and they will always want the company of similar-minded people, who are willing to be dragged along in negativity's depths of darkness.

## CONCLUSION

Curses then are evil devices, manifesting in the lives of people, and at times, have supernatural powers, supporting this interaction as an investment in the destruction of people. The indicative characteristics continue to be seemingly insurmountable struggles and sufferings, leaving those involved succumbing to being content with the manifestation of the lie.

Let me clarify the creational purpose and original intent of God for mankind. Remember that we, as humanity, thwarted the plans of God. God has not changed. The evidence is in Genesis. We do not play multiple-choice but have a factual presentation of God's creative power: Adam and Eve walked in God's glory! The choice of which tree (table) to eat from influenced the outcome of their lives. God wants the very same for us today. In Revelation 3:20 God invites you to eat from the table of life, which personifies His blessing. This was God's invitation yesteryear; it still is today, and will remain forever.

# art 3     BLESSINGS AND CURSES

## SUBJECT RULE 5: REVERSE THE CURSE

**KEY SCRIPTURE:** Joshua 24:5 KJV ". . . *I brought you out!*"

**KEYWORDS:**

    Alternating

    Respect

    Accolades

**KEY CONCEPT:**    Turn evil around and live in God's abundance.

# INTRODUCTION

I have clarified, at great lengths, the existence of curses. We have seen the portrayal of the tragic event in the Garden of Eden, which was the rejection of God and His Word; thus the initiation of the curse. The curse became the reversal of the purity of God's creation, and its intention was to destroy. Make no mistake: the fall was more destructive than we humans can comprehend. Man had walked in God's glory, and because of that one act of disobedience they were now expelled, became depraved and fell short of God's glory. Thus the curse, in actual fact, reversed God's glory to shame.

The devastation was cataclysmic by nature, and the reproduction of the above became generational. But, there is good news. We can reverse it. And we should not leave one stone unturned in doing just that! Jesus became the curse for us. He became what we need: healing, redemption, salvation, deliverance, righteousness and eternal justification. The truth is that what Jesus gained for us is a limitless package deal.

The Israelites were enslaved for four hundred long years. Then God brought them out of Egypt, with the purpose of taking them to Canaan. Let me rephrase the above: God took them out of the curse into the blessing. Differently said, He reversed the curse. To reverse the curse we need to understand why it was implemented in the first place. Revisit the previous chapter page pg. 219-220 and reacquaint yourself with what you have read.

In the Book of Judges, chapter 2, we are enlightened about the above.

> **Judges 2:11-12; 14 KJV** *"And the children of Israel did evil in the sight of the LORD, and serving Baalim, and they forsook the LORD God of their fathers, which brought them out of the land of Egypt, and followed other gods . . . and the anger of the LORD was hot against Israel, and he delivered them into the hands of spoilers . . ."*

The Book of Judges is interspersed with manifold scenarios such as the one above, and I would like to draw your attention to God's generational reference with one specific word; He made use of 'fathers'. Secondly, sin and other gods provoke God to release anger. Thus, without further unnecessary investigation, 'sin and idols (other gods)' will always be at the root of all curses. The basics of the provocation to judgment are established in the rejection of God and His Word.

## SIN

Allow me to divert for a while in order to highlight a few issues relating to sin. Permit me to make a profound statement regarding the above: God, and God alone, judges all sin. This is vitally important for you to settle in your heart and mind. Let me explain why I make this statement. There are many individual Christians, churches and leaders who, because of their own perceptions, declare certain things to be sin when this is just not true. History is deluded with manifold examples; therefore I will not enter into a discussion about it. Certain mannerisms and conduct, especially with regard to clothing (to mention but a few), are defined within the borders of specific people's perspective of the word as sinful.

The second main pronouncement proceeds from the first as fundamental. Sin is sin. All sin is sin. In a pre-modernistic society sin still remains sin. Sin defined by God was, is and will continue for eternity to be wrong, despicable and abhorrent in its entirety. In the modern day we see how certain church groups give in to the media pressure of society, celebrities and politicians or whichever 'peer-pressure-group' to which they are exposed. They compromise on the stand of sin to gain approval from the outside world. The controversy regarding homosexuality is one of the primary examples. According to God and His Word, it is despicable and wrong. The list continues.

The third critical point is that sin is the direct result of rejecting God and His Word. Thus rejection precedes the incessant sinful action and the consequences are death and curse. The upholding of God and His Word, on the contrary, has saving mercies, cleansing and redeeming you from an evil inherited nature. (PSALM 51 KJV)

The fourth important declaration is that sin is the pure manifestation of rejecting God and His Word, and this surely opens the door for worship of other gods (idolatry—religion). Again, certain celebrities, politicians and media groups are very keen to promote that 'all god routes' lead to and take us to the same place. Specific celebrities and especially those involved in talk shows; use their platform of popularity and abuse that position, where they are loved and respected by their followers for their skills, talents and entertainment. In doing so, they influence these people by making secular, humanistic and even demonic remarks. The promotion is that 'one glove fits all.' The purpose with their statements is to blur the line between God and demons; thus invoking a concept that all gods are the same. They use their success and achievements as some form of authority; as a platform to speak authoritatively on the subject. Their goal is that all must think as they think. Their knowledge of God's Word is depraved, perverted and depleted of any insight at all. The synopsis of the above is evident in my next statement. God says: "Jesus is the way, truth and life," and that He is the only way to the Father. (JOHN 14:6 KJV) People like those I described above are doing in similitude to what satan did in the Garden of Eden; questioning the above by saying: "Did God really say Jesus is?" Friend, no matter who you are, there is only one God and you can only be reconciled to Him by faith through Jesus.

In my final conclusion, I am addressing you as the reader. Your past sins, in their full, destructible and despicable magnitude, do not define who you are. No matter how vile, how reprehensible or how condemnable, they do not have the power to define your person! The only lesson that you can learn from the above is that what has happened in your past was indicative of the rejection of God and

His Word. Your identity as human being is hidden in God, and God alone. Hence my remark; truly biblical: "There is therefore no condemnation to them which are in Christ Jesus, who walk not after the flesh, but after the spirit." (ROMANS 8:1 KJV)

Let us dissect the above:

1. Flesh
2. Spirit

Friend, the above implies choice, potential, responsibility and consequences. It is evident that, according to scripture, Christians can walk in the flesh (sin) or by the spirit (in holiness). Flesh refers to dead works, not walking according to the Spirit and religiously applying only the letter of the Word of God following after the system of this world. (2 COR. 3:6 KJV) All of this equals dead works where the root is unbelief! The root of holiness and walking in holiness is faith. Walking in the spirit also implies confession and repentance, which initiate and promote sanctification by Holy Spirit. If we were perfect, why would Holy Spirit come to sanctify? If we were immune to any sin, why the intense need for an indwelling Holy Spirit?

> **2 Corinthians 3:18** *"But we all, with open face beholding as in a glass the glory of the Lord, are changed into the same image from glory to glory, even as by the Spirit of the Lord."*

The above scripture reiterates my point that we have factually and potentially received the full package from God, in Jesus. However, we have a part to play, which involves action, and thus involves being transformed. If it was a done deal, then why would we need transformation? Unless you activate God's gift, it will remain a dormant reality. Sin never defines who you are, but it is always indicative of walking in the flesh. Your identity is sealed in God by His grace, and sin has no relevance to this. Sanctification is a process by Holy Spirit, which transforms us into the image of Jesus, the Anointed One. The image that I am referring to is His righteousness, which was already imputed to you at rebirth. Thus, all Christians have

Dr. Adolf Jonker Ph.D

the potential within, to change from day to day. For clarity's sake, I will say that this transformation takes place in your soulish realm (mind, will and emotions). In other words, it is experienced as a personality alteration.

## REVERSAL PROCESS

In looking at the 'setting of the table', we see the following on the curse side: death, rejection, judgment and dishonour. We need to reverse the curse and establish God's blessings, thus instituting life, acceptance, favour and honour. All that I have said and done is about the honour of God. I have included a strategic step-by-step plan to reverse the curse at the end of this chapter.

Forgiveness proves to be the very first step in the process. Confession postulates acknowledgement and admission of guilt. It is also indicative of remorse, thus submitting to His Lordship and one vital, though ignorant perspective about confession is that it honours God.

**Joshua 7:19 KJV** *"And Joshua said unto Achan, My son, give, I pray thee, the glory to the LORD God of Israel, and make confession unto him; and tell me now what thou hast done; hide it not from me."*

Joshua made it clear to Achan that through confessing his sins, and what he had done wrong, he would honour God. There you have it. Confession is instrumental in honouring God. Don't postpone your confession; do it immediately and receive forgiveness from God and thereby honour Him.

Repentance is another form of confession. It is the action or conduct that validates your seriousness in confession. Repentance is faith in action; putting things right by reversing the previous incorrect behaviour. Repentance is the effluent ramification of true confession, and it can also be depicted as the inescapable branching-out of confession.

# CONFESSION

We have pointed out that curses can be inherited, self-inflicted (words and sins), come from other people (believer and non-believer) and also be upon territories and geographical locations; in other words, curses can be upon possessions, property and even animals. Thus, when we confess we normally start at the root of what took place to initiate the curse, hence asking God forgiveness for rejecting Him and His Word. This will always be the point of departure.

# IDENTIFICATION CONFESSION

Step two (after confession) in the reversal of a curse, I call identification confession. Some would know this term better, as identification repentance. However, repentance is the reversal of the previous wrong whereas confession is the admission of guilt. Daniel had an immaculate understanding with regard to identification confession:

> **Daniel 9:16 (KJV)** *". . . I beseech thee, let thine anger and fury be turned away from the city Jerusalem, thy holy mountain: because for our sins, and for the iniquities of our fathers . . ."*

Daniel firstly understood God's emphasis on families and nations (which are ultimately an expanded conglomerate of families) and therefore God's focus on generations. (DANIEL 4:31+34 KJV) In his confession he identifies with the sins and thus the condition of his forefathers, which includes himself, his family and his nation. He did this by:

a. Admitting guilt
b. Putting himself in their places as the guilty one thus identifying with them

Dr. Adolf Jonker Ph.D

c.  Taking responsibility for all
d.  Standing in the gap for all mentioned
e.  Acknowledging that everyone had sinned (rejecting God and His Word) and continued with their sin as outflow of the above
f.  Territorially included Jerusalem as guilty as well

The whole of chapter four is quite elaborative regarding identification confession. Sin then equals firstly, the rejection of God and His Word, sequentially the outpouring of diverse evil. Rejection of God and His Word is unbelief expressed in God and his authority.

## REPENTANCE

Repentance implies that you are taking responsibility on behalf of all mentioned, to turn from your wicked ways and do as God requires. You act on behalf of all others mentioned. In your repentance declaration, you renounce all sin and the demonic and declare your faith in God. I will not explain faith in this section, as the last chapter will cover the subject substantially and synoptically. In your renunciation you bind the strongmen, dethrone them from their position, never to return.

Subsequently, you break the particular curse in the name of Jesus, declare it null and void and ask God the Father, in Jesus name to send his holy angels to establish your request.

After breaking the curse, it hasn't stopped. The initial curse needs to be reversed. Consider the human genetic code in understanding our DNA. Your DNA is an encoded structure containing all the information of your biological make up. For clarity, allow me to make certain statements that you, as reader, can meditate and ponder upon. However, suffice to say, I won't go into the detail, although in part of the scope of this book we have to be selective in what should be elaborated.

The above encoded structure is filled with countless fragments of information. Scientists have named everything in the human genome but still only have fragments of information. Thus the naming identifies every part of you found in the mitochondria and the chromosomes. The part that I want to lift out, as a matter of interest, relates to the word 'mutation'. Whenever this word is used, in relation to the genetic code, there is usually a negative connotation. Mutation is the alteration of the perfect code. This alteration is the formation of a different genetic characteristic. I want to suggest to the reader that the above, in simplistic terms, can be introduced as the manifestation of a curse. Differently said, a mutation defines the context or encoded structure of a curse.

In continuing, I want to remind the reader, that the DNA is the creative expression of God. DNA represents information, and it is information in continuous motion. Thus, in reversal of the curse, we ask God to restructure our holistic coding, thereby changing our current make-up with the promises of His Word to the original intent released in the Garden of Eden. My purpose is not to release too much technical information, but to release enough to create a better understanding of a curse. With the DNA, one can see that a curse is a structured, encoded system influencing you. Therefore the reversal needs restructuring. The restructuring takes on the information of God's blessings. Can you still remember God saying in Deuteronomy 30 that it is in the seed? To what am I referring? The encoding of who you are; spirit, soul and body which is within the seed.

## HONOUR OF GOD

In restructuring the coding system, nobody will get away from reordering everything but to honour God. I will now define my personal understanding of what it means to honour God.

Dr. Adolf Jonker Ph.D

First I wish to share with you the definition, and then I will break it up into smaller parts and wrap it all up. To honour God is to celebrate the sum total of God, by decorating Him with accolades of respect. Therefore, to honour God is the manifestation of your respect for Him. Respect is then, the reflection of you honouring God. Respect for God is similar to you winning all the gold, silver and bronze medals at the Olympic Games. The magnitude thereof is altogether indescribable.

**Celebration** is the jubilation of God, expressed through a joyous observance of His being, and it is an internalized festivity that might at times even manifest physically.

**Sum total of God** is the understanding of His complete make-up. He is eternal, transcendent (omniscient, omnipresent, omnipotent) sovereign, supreme and manifesting as YHWH, I am, the great I am, who was and will be at any point of time, a being unique by definition, a Triune God, Father, Son and Holy Spirit who is the Creator of all.

**Decorating:** My daughter is an interior decorator and I love it myself. It is the art of adorning a place with certain objects befitting the design. The art develops skill and insight through experience, as you visualize the end product and re-align yourself continuously in presenting a better design, in other words doing a better job. It is the art of the Christian in his personal walk, adorning Him.

**Accolades:** Talking about the Olympics, we know that the medal winners are awarded publically and called to a podium to portray a place of exaltation, thereby highlighting their excellent performance, where they are given concrete symbols (the medal) pronouncing the victory. The medal is an accolade, symbolically decorating them for their achieved performance. Our accolades for God are exhibited when we decorate Him with our respect. Respect is the verbal exuberance of Christianity, decorating God with our diverse acknowledgement of His being.

The honour of God is therefore a lifestyle, and it can never be depicted by just one event or a specific or special occasion, such as a Sunday morning or evening worship service, personal prayer time or even a special conference. Not one, or even all sporadic, can be regarded as the ultimate in honouring God. It is an all-inclusive pattern of a unique and individual lifestyle, surrendered unto God. Hence, my conclusion that it is the sum total of a man (spirit, soul and body) that honours the sum total of God, in an uninterrupted manner. (1 THESSALONIANS 3:10 ASV) Incessant worship of God, within the borders of the context of eternity, is what brings honour to God. It is an art that develops as the believer grows in his / her personal and corporate relationship with God. Honouring God is a growing experience.

Take note of this point, dear reader: please, no human being has the ability or the authority to define your personal walk with God. Neither do your past sins, errors and weaknesses define the genuineness thereof. Only God knows you! Only God matters! Worship Him with all your being!

## HYPOTHETICAL SCENARIO

I want to illustrate how to break a curse, and will present you, as the reader, with a fictional, yet brief, case study, thereby highlighting the negative pointers and the reversal of the curse.

John was a thirty-year old male, not married and living in an area where drugs are at the order of the day. He bought himself a property in a particular area that was affordable. However, he was in debt over his head and the bank threatened to repossess the property. John was a born-again believer, but as a result of his financial struggles he decided that he couldn't tithe and offer unto God. In attempting to solve his problems, he became involved in gambling, looking for a way out and a guide to remedy his problems. John's mother bet on race horses for years and years, so John was familiar with the gambling industry. John was extremely aggressive, and at a young age already he allowed his frustrations with problems to flow over into violent behaviour. John's father was a free mason and John was introduced to free masonry as a child because of his father's involvement.

Let us identify the key points:

| A. Territory | – drug infested | – | point to addiction |
|---|---|---|---|
| B. Finances | – debt | – | we know that one of the direct curses flowing from free masonry and the occult is debt, poverty and ultimately losing everything due to insolvency. This was because of John's father's involvement. (bloodline) |
| C. Gambling | – slavery | – | addiction (John himself was involved and so was his mother (bloodline) |
| D. Anger | – struggle | – | attempting to control by Improper emotions, with outbursts |

## SOLUTION

The point of departure towards a solution is to always identify the root. John's Mom and Dad (bloodline) rejected God and His Word, and thus sinned and served other gods. His problems were an outflow of the above, together with his own involvement and the contribution from territorial problems. The above summarize his life with conglomerate problems such as:

a. An inherited bloodline
b. Severe struggles

c.   Infested lies

d.   Suffering caused as a result of his situations

## PRAYER

1. **Honour:**
   a)   Bring exuberant honour to God. See my definition earlier.

2. **Confess:**
   a)   Forefathers' sins and their rejection of God and His Word. Name the sins you know about.
   b)   Ask God to reveal any hidden sin.
   c)   Your own sin and your rejection of God and His Word; gambling, anger, stealing from God by not giving your tithe and offering.
   d)   Ask forgiveness for the sins related to the area; similar to the above.

3. **Repent:**
   Verbally turnaround from all the above scenarios; renounce the demonic, their activity; the control and the curse.

4. **Binding:**
   Binding in the name of Jesus the strongman related, and his co-workers. Declaring their works of no effect, and prophesying God's judgment and wrath on all the demonic altars. Declaring in Jesus name these demonic powers never to return to their previous position. Destroying in Jesus name the contracts and covenants and sever yourself from any demonic allegiance.

5. **Reversal:**
   Declare in Jesus name the above curses null and void. Ask God the Father to command His holy angels to destroy the

encoded system relating to the curse. Ask God to reverse the curse back to Adam and Eve, and ten generations ahead.

6. **Coding:**

Proclaim the promises of God over your inheritance, your finances, your property, your area and over yourself. Continue to do the coding (prophesying) of the above, until you see the manifestation of God's promises (outcome).

7. **Faith:**

Release your faith in God to accomplish it all.

The above seven pointers are indicators of how to pray, and have no strict format to follow; thus the order and the actual prayer should always be led by Holy Spirit. What is important is that you submit to Him, pray in faith and prophesy His Word without fail, and you will certainly see a reversal of the curse and a godly outcome.

## POINTS OF ATTENTION

Throughout my career I have noticed that certain curses are broken after one prayer. You pray once, and it is a historical fact and not relevant anymore. Some, however, take time and are a continuation of a process. Generational curses are usually more dominant, and curses related to idolatry will be more intense and require frequent declaration, prayer and inquiring of the Lord.

If you focus on curses and the demonic you ARE already in deception. Listen to your language and your thought patterns to discern this. You will quickly pick up on your vocabulary. Your focus should always be Jesus the Anointed One, Son of God. If you spend most of your time on curses, looking for them and blame-shifting everything, labelling it as a curse, you ARE in deception. 'Greater is He that is in you than He that is in the world.' God has given us power over all the power of the enemy. He says: "Ask and I shall give unto thee." The overwhelming evidence is that the promises of God are more powerful than any negative force. Continually ask Holy Spirit to direct your every step. Stay focused on God; live a life of the victory of the cross, and deny the power of the evil one by breaking every curse.

Dr. Adolf Jonker Ph.D

**art 3** BLESSINGS AND CURSES

## SUBJECT RULE 6: THE BLESSING OF GOD IS FOR YOU

**KEY SCRIPTURE:** Hosea 6:11b TLB "*. . . I will prosper you again . . . !*"

**KEYWORDS:**
Abundance

Mandate

Restoration

**KEY CONCEPT:** God's intention is for His manifest blessing to be part of your daily life, a life of abundance holistically; the Christ life by Holy Spirit.

# THE HEART OF GOD

I have spent a lot of time on discussing the issue related to curses. However, the best is left for last. The best that I am referring to is symbolized in the manifestation of the blessing of God. I will refrain from using Greek or Hebrew words in translating the word 'blessing' and in my definition of blessing. I will also not bore you by involving vast explanations of dictionaries. The Lord impressed on me to abstain from defining blessings in such a way, and to rather move towards defining them within the borders of their godly definitions. Thus my definition reads as follows: Blessings are the manifestations of the goodwill of God, which are supernaturally poured out over you, to establish nothing less than the best, and a life of abundance for you. Thus blessings are the manifestation of God's heart in this equation, defined as the whole package deal of who He really is: 'YHWH, I am who I am!' The list is endless. He is provider, protector, deliverer, healer, saviour, care-provider, guider and who He is and what we use to describe Him and His awesome attributes continues incessantly. Therefore, blessings can be understood as follows:

a) Spiritual
b) Divine
c) Supernatural
d) Manifold dimension in context of spirit, soul and body
e) Invoke the honour of His Name
f) Abundant by nature.

That is why Jesus said in John 10:10 that He came so that we might have life; and also that we might have it more abundantly. (JOHN 10:10 KJV) To understand abundance I will look at the Greek translation 'perisos'. The meaning relates effectively to the concept of being superabundant. (STRONGS, G4053) Superabundant speaks of excessiveness, breaking the boundaries and limitations of the normal as understood and interpreted in its various manifestations of diverse perspectives.

Dr. Adolf Jonker Ph.D

As much as religion wants to unload their garbage belief of contentment with poverty, the Bible is flooded with evidence of excessive manifestations of God's abundant nature. Let's put it in context. King David explicitly declares: *"My cup runneth over"* (PSALM 23 KJV) I would have said that my cup was filled with the superabundance of God which would have been theologically correct: My cup is filled with the blessings of God. According to my definition then it would read: my cup is filled with God's heart. Hallelujah! This excites me immensely. God is pouring forth His heart over me. Be aware of the following. God has a unique corporate design for His church. However, as much as that is true, He has an individual and unique design for you! He defines the above clearly by assuring us that He is not a respecter of persons. (ROMANS 2:11 KJV) Thus He treats each individual the same, giving us all the same opportunity to literally have it all in Him.

Some ill-informed people will be content with an age-old lie and say but Jesus ". . . the Son of man hath not where to lay his head." (MATTHEW 8:20 KJV) Let's discover true assumptions related to Jesus. First of all, He was on a mission on earth. The purpose of His being here was not to gain wealth or to establish a home or family and so forth. He was focused on one purpose and that very purpose was the salvation plan of God. His goal and objective was to bring about the salvation plan of God and the fullness it encompassed. Second to the above is the truth that "the earth is the Lord's and the fullness thereof; the world and they that dwell therein." (PSALM 24:1 KJV) He surely wasn't in need of anything; everything (superabundantly) already belonged to Him! He wasn't interested in a few acres! The circumference of the universe was His. Was He in any need? He opened His mouth and expanded the universe.

Added to the previous paragraph, there is a generalized, unbiblical assumption that poor people fear God and are in God's will, and that rich people love the things of the world more than they love God. I know that this is an over-generalised statement baptized with religious hogwash. I can take you through Africa, India and many other places in the world where impoverished people do not even know about

God, much less fear Him! Then I also know many, many rich folk in this present day, who honestly love and fear God more than I've ever seen from any poor person! I also know a lot of people who are poor, yet greedy, and have a love for money, which is the core of all evil. (1 TIMOTHY 6:10 KJV)

Let me divert a little from the above and say that if we have this assumption that God's blessings entail only financial benefits, we are deceived. There are an abundance of blessings on anointing, on the life of God within us, love, servant-hood and the list continues. The financial side is just one minute part of the overall blessing of God. The blessing, by delineation, encompasses being fruitful, multiplying, increasing, subduing and ruling.(GENESIS 1:28 KJV) That is the foundation of our mandate, and God's blessing. It is confirmed and strengthened by 'go make disciples'. Secondly, and as important, we do not serve God to be blessed. We serve God for who He is: YWHW. Thirdly, as a result of our status of being children of God, we can walk in His blessing. Fourthly, should a curse manifest, we reverse it into a blessing, in His name and power.

Dear reader, I honour God for you! Christianity has been plagued for years and years with ungodly assumptions, perceptions and doctrines. I call it the manifestation of a spirit of religion. Christianity is not a religion, irrespective of theological persuasions or even the definition of a perverse society. Christianity is a relationship! Religion is a conglomerate of perverse, idolatrous ideas as diverse as imaginable. Religion symbolises the anti-christ spirit. This spirit cannot produce godly life at all, not even remotely close. Instead, it is filled with empty and vain rituals and rites, and these are as many as the stars in heaven. Christianity was defiled by religion as the nation of Israel was polluted by Canaanite idolatry. This is the same spirit behind the motive of Jesus being taken to the cross, in order to stop him from fulfilling His purposes. That same spirit wants to crucify Jesus in the lives of Christians every single day by defiling us with the same futility as described above.

You, as reader, can ask God to set you free from all that He decides is not worthy of being part of you, and to shake you loose according to His Word.

> **Hebrews 12:27 KJV** *"And this word, Yet once more, signifieth the removing of those things that are shaken, as of things that are made, that those things which cannot be shaken may remain, (verse 28) Wherefore we receiving a kingdom which cannot be moved . . ."*

I believe that all Christians are, to an extent, made up of shakeable and removable things, which are also part of their beings, conduct and lifestyle, but in the same breath, that which cannot be removed but is directly a part of God's divine investment in them. Friends, humanity unfortunately does not have the capacity to always discern, in totality, with immaculate godly discernment, and a complete divine objective. We are made up of some substance that we believe are truth, but are mere human assumptions and traditions. We need Holy Spirit to lead us in all truth. (JOHN 16:13 KJV)

The new covenant ushers in the most perfect of all God's plans. We inherited a fallen nature from Adam and Eve. God's faultless plan was to reverse our original bloodline and re-invent a speckless one in His Son, Saviour of this world, born by a virgin, no earthly father, as all earthly fathers were defiled. The work of God became flesh, and Jesus entered planet earth as the firstborn on planet earth: God amongst men. The plan was perfected, and we, as humanity were reconciled unto God only through the mediation of Jesus! Men adjudicate the validity by releasing faith in the sent one of God: Jesus.

As a result of the above, we as born again believers become heirs of God!

> **Romans 8:17 KJV** *"And if children, then heirs; heirs of God, and joint-heirs with Christ; if so be that we suffer with him, that we may be also glorified together."*

# BLESSINGS ARE GOD'S WORD MANIFESTED

I have laid intense emphasis on the ordeal of the Garden of Eden, summarised by the rejection of God and the Word of God. The reversal then will guarantee the manifestation of His blessing. Thus, the blessing of God, was in fact the initial intent of God. How, then, will the reversal be guaranteed? We need to once again, with all we are and have, return to God and accept Him and His Word.

The overall importance of the magnitude of the Word of God, in the lives of people, is critical to our understanding of God's blessings. There are millions of Christians who are completely ignorant about the status of the Word of God, specifically the irreversible, transformational life and power it gives. Many will be able to recite one, two or maybe three Old Testament stories. Some of the favourites that are easily remembered are Adam and Eve in the Garden, Jonah and the whale, and King David who sinned and looked at a beautiful woman—Bathsheba bathing and then he killed her husband. This is a generalised take on wherein people are familiar. Most are able to remember that because of what they have learnt as children, in Sunday school. However, John 3:16 sadly sums up the only Scriptural knowledge of most.

Then there are those Christians who have a deeper understanding, and their stories will include Mary and her child Jesus. They have an adequate understanding of Jesus being our Saviour. However, there are a smaller group who will truly allow Holy Spirit to use anybody as an instrument to teach them the deeper things of God. I merely portray a general idea of the levels of involvement of people in the Word of God.

Allow me, then, to first make a statement of momentous importance. The Word of God applied will usher in the magnitude of God's blessings. I can almost hear people querying the above statement, with counteracting statements of personal involvement in the

Dr. Adolf Jonker Ph.D

Word. Precisely for all the reasons above, the majority experience the minute blessings; small and little. The group who studies and applies the Word of God is in an entirely different category. Please allow me to address you as follows. Multitudes came to me stating their involvement in the Word and the apparent reverse effect. The blessings simply didn't occur. During my counselling I have observed many Christians who:

i.   Have an ignorant understanding of faith and by saying that they trust God they really mean that they believe in some magical manifestation, due to their statement and heart's intent.

ii.  Is part of a group who study the Bible, but the interpretation of certain Scriptural evidence is way out of line?

Mankind always had, and still have, the tendency to want to tell God to confirm that which they believe, regarding certain issues to be the truth, instead of laying them at His feet. In laying them at His feet, we should reveal to God our beliefs, distance ourselves from them and release them to God, asking Him to direct us in the truth and remove whatever is unbiblical from our personal belief system. This also includes denominational preferences, ethical persuasions, racial prejudice, national patriotism and any cultural dispositions that are biased misconceptions, ambushing the truth of God, and most definitely so-called scientific proof which is nothing but questions defined in a theoretical concept. Not everything said by Scientists is truly scientific, if at all. We are many times introduced to what they perceive with their prejudice, frantically soothing their rational gods or demons to be precise. This results in the truth evading people, and causing them to not experience God's promises corresponding to God's Word in their lives. The truth friend is that God's Word is truth. If you do not experience the blessing of the Word then you have filters causing God's truth to evade your life and you only experience a limited effect. You and I should find out what have we inherited that is contrary to the exactness of the Word of God.

Permit me to say that the church, through its leaders and theologians, has for years followed an alternative interpretation of scripture, other than what is prescribed by the Bible itself. We have introduced scriptural models that became idolatrous. Let me explain. Models that are either allegorical or literal interpretation, Greek and Hebrew models, are seen as the alpha and omega of interpretation. Secondary, to the above because of personal preference, other less specific important models were and are used.

I will not apologise for the following. We were wrong and inherited deceptive interpretations. Why? The Bible introduced us to a clear strategic biblical concept of interpretation, which the majority resisted throughout history.

> **1 Corinthians 2:10 KJV** *"But God hath revealed them unto us by his Spirit: for the Spirit searcheth all things, yea, the deep things of God."*

You can continue to read to the end of verse 16. The main fundamental principle of interpreting is found primarily in Holy Spirit, who is the main author of scripture. (2 PETER 1:21 KJV) Thus the focus is not found with the intellectual scholars, or in the aisles of the universities, but in deep reverence, in prayerful relationship with the residing Holy Spirit of God. Every other method should be applied as an aid, secondary to your already revealed understanding. Do we exclude other methods of interpretation? Do we disregard intellectual scholars? No, not in the least! I am also an intellectual scholar, but one who has come to the understanding that it is by grace and a living relationship and fellowship with Holy Spirit that one can gain true knowledge and revelation as many scholars have discovered. I do not suggest we exclude other methods; however, I do believe that it is time for us to strip them from their idolatrous positions.

It is important for us today to learn the truth from Holy Spirit. Thank God for so many who awoke to the revelation of Holy Spirit as the author and revealer of scripture. If you take two theologians and let them debate, they will differ in their interpretation. If you take two people from different nations, different race, culture, national

Dr. Adolf Jonker Ph.D

patriotism or ethnic background who allow Holy Spirit to lead them, they will both give exactly the same interpretation.

Bear the following in mind. Your denomination, race, ethnicity, nationality, patriotism and cultural values do not own God or His Word. He is supreme, transcendent and above ownership of man. He owns man.

The Bible is God's promise, God's guarantee to us of His blessing on us. The Bible is always true. If people have different opinions it doesn't matter or alter the truth of the Bible. The Bible, as the Word of God, is truth in itself.

> **Ephesians 1:3 KJV** *"Blessed be the God and the Father of our Lord Jesus Christ, who hath blessed us with all spiritual blessings in heavenly places in Christ."*

Let me close with understandable grammatical evidence. Maybe we do not understand Victorian English; so let me make it clear in simplicity and beyond any doubt. He has blessed all of us, past perfect! As you read this, it is not something that He still has to do for you; it has already been done! You just need to embrace it by faith, renew your mind, apply the Word and the blessing of God will follow you wherever you are and in whatever you do or plan. The truth is my friend, that in Adam, God blessed the whole human race presenting us with a decision to either receive Him and his fullness of reject it.

This concludes then, part three on blessings and curses. Amen and amen ☺

# Concept 9 · FUNCTIONAL

**KEY SCRIPTURE:** ROMANS 1:17 KJV

"... The just shall live by faith!"

**KEYWORDS:**

Indispensible

Semantic preference

Transmittal

Reciprocal

Maturation

Currency

Substance

Juridical

**KEY CONCEPT**  To encourage the reader, with practical guidance, to live a daily victorious life of faith!

# CONCLUSION

The introductory statement to this final chapter cannot be anything else but a summation of what faith is, and the most vital backbone scripture, in this statement, is: 'the just shall live by faith'. We have to understand faith and differentiate between cultural, religious ideas which mostly only mount to assumptions. Such assumptions are perceived as truth; however, mostly this is quite the contrary and end up being nothing but deceptive beliefs which cannot and will not ever help anyone. The challenge for us all is to discern, in God, which are deceptive assumptions. We need to lay it all down before Him; completely surrendering what we believe, and ask and allow Him to transform us and ultimately enable us to walk in more truth.

There is not a single person on planet earth who has never formed or believed in a type of false or erroneous assumption. It happens to all of us at some time or another in our lives. We cannot be ignorant about the fact that although all God's children love Him and desire to walk in His perfect truth, we are still exposed to the fallen nature and its consequences: mixed seed. However, God supplies us with such an amazing encouragement: "the just shall live by faith." I do not think 'live by' suggests one single incident or event. This is surely indicative of a lifelong journey; a journey that presents interaction between the natural and supernatural realms. To understand this is to secure a fundamental foundation in your walk with the Almighty God, Creator of heaven and earth and the supreme owner and author of all. Therefore He is sovereign in all He does. Why would His sovereignty be excluded from our individual lives? It wouldn't!

# DISCOVERING THE TRUTH OF FAITH

The purpose in discovering the truth of faith is a long and may even be a controversial journey at times. However challenging it is, it will always be topped by encouragement, because God's guarantee to us is that His truth will set us free. True deliverance and freedom will always allow us to experience true godly encouragement. Truth will always be controversial, and sometimes contradictory to what we may believe, and will for this reason also be offensive. However, the seed of God, his Word has a unique way of unveiling and retrieving truth. This is not a 'one size fits all' scenario. Every reader and disciple of Jesus our Anointed Lord, will have a different journey, with different experiences. However, the fruit will always be eternal, and all the glory will be the Lord's! Always!!! All glory belongs to Him. I understand that some might have a different perspective about the journey than what I have and that is perfectly fine. Whether most concur with me or not, I know that those who wholeheartedly put their trust in God, by living by faith will be transformed from glory to glory.

You, as reader, may have wondered why I have included the chapter on the First Principles. I have also agonised about it in the writing process, but God clearly confirmed that First Principles are foundational concepts He gives us, and in context of the bigger picture of the book they cannot be excluded at all. First Principles start off with repenting of dead works, which in well-known Christian terminology will translate to 'coming out of Egypt'. I want to take your hand in God, and help you to walk out of the Egypt of your past; walk with God into Canaan, the Promised Land, and figuratively speaking the abundance of what you can have in God. This land can only be discovered in the pages of the Word of God and you, dear reader, will be symbolic of the spies spying out the land. Only you can do this and the key is to inherit. You may wonder, "But what will I inherit?" FAITH in God. The baptisms are expressive of His will in how to enter His kingdom, and once initiated in your life, you qualify as a minister of God. 'Laying on of hands' is the practical application (ministry), of who we are in God, and who God is in us. God allows this to be a tool of transference. Whatever you do in this life will be judged by God in the life hereafter and the judgment will last for an eternity. Once you have died, none of what you have done can be altered or corrected. People may argue about why we should do what he wants us to do. We do it because He first loved us, and now we love Him back in and with all we do. (1 JOHN 4:17 KJV) Therefore, in believing Jesus is the Son of God—the Anointed One, we live in Him and He lives in us by Holy Spirit.

In our discussion about many different life situations, we have toured through the valley of the shadow of death and have discovered the ignorant, the opposed and also the controversial subject called 'blessings and curses'. I unambiguously and unapologetically confirm that the purpose of even touching this subject is to initiate freedom from generational and any other curses, and usher in and solidify the acquisition of and living in God's preordained blessings!

> *Blessing is the manifest goodwill of God that is poured over you to establish nothing less that the best and augmenting a life of abundance for you in God.*

Curses are the absence of the above and are detected by sufferings, struggles and lies. They result from dishonouring God and rejecting God and His Word. They are the manifestation of God's judgment and can only produce death. There will always be a clash and a contest for control, to determine who is the head and who the tail. A curse will try to overtake and overpower you, invoking a 'fire upon fire' situation (struggles and suffering). We are in an individual wrestling match with the abusing forces of evil, who have one purpose and that is to oppose God's heart for you.

The Bible expresses the importance of faith in quite an illustrious manner. To be quite frank with you: any debate around it is unnecessary! Faith is indispensible and foundational to the way we think, act, live and walk. It doesn't matter how you define faith or what rhetorical preference you exhibit, it all boils down to one and the same concept. It comes from God and we receive it as a gift. It transfers as the only currency acceptable to God between heaven and earth. Faith is transmittal and reciprocal by nature, and therefore it has movement, is interactive and transforms altogether. In faith's interaction there is an inevitable time of waiting, where patience and endurance will produce growth as dynamic. Faith is always functional in the now, 'TODAY'! It is a lifestyle, incorporating every single facet of your life. A lifestyle of faith postulates prominent focus on God, the heart of God and His ability. But what is His heart and ability? He has no limit whatsoever, and His heart is for you to ask so that He can show you that in Him there is endless potential and possibility. Is anything too hard for God? Just ask and believe. This is the very reason why doubt, unbelief and negativity are not part of the list of faith's vocabulary. These should never be part of or exercised by any child of God, because they simply result in death to the promises.

As co-heirs of Jesus, a lifestyle of faith is a continuance of the kind He promised us. It is not and should never be a hit and run or crisis management in times of distress and critical situations. The Bible is our legal document, enforced by God, where He obligates Himself to this New Testament covenant with us. Faith is then a statutory, binding entity, active in sealing the deal and unlocking God's miracle working power. You are the instrument in honouring and pleasing God. Please understand, then, that faith is functioning evidence.

## DISCOVER TRUE FAITH

<u>Defining faith</u>

We divided and phrased faith with divine concepts for you to have an elucidated understanding. It is backed with Scriptural quotations, Greek and Hebrew references, to denote a comprehensive overview and insight. With this said as backdrop in our minds, let us formulate faith, as clearly as possible, in practical ways.

Faith is spirit and spirit has substance. The substance of 'spirit' faith is then what we should define. It is a confidence, which is a conviction that serves as evidence. Let me explain it with a mathematical equation: Substance = confidence + conviction. The above defined substance (confidence and conviction), serves as evidence that the visual picture that you have formed in your mind will be answered and fulfilled by God. Let's simplify the visual picture as your request. Thus the above substance serves as definite evidence that God will answer.

What is vital now is to also understand that faith is reciprocal, which implies that God receives it from His children. We know that our faith is directed towards God, because we want to please and gratify Him. I appreciate the word 'gratify' because it sounds so complete in its meaning and purpose.

Follow me now; God is the object of our faith. What do we believe?

1. We believe that He is:
   ✓ YHWH encompasses who He is and is inclusive of all attributes as mentioned in previously on page 228.
   ✓ This being is representative of present tense; now, TODAY! And He is with us all the way.
   ✓ He is alive; He was, is and will always be the Creator,

2. Rewarder
   ✓ This is inseparable from God's integrity, His faithfulness and commitment.
   ✓ The juridical aspect of His Word.

The above implies that we believe God and His Word. I want to summarise this with a simplistic diagram:

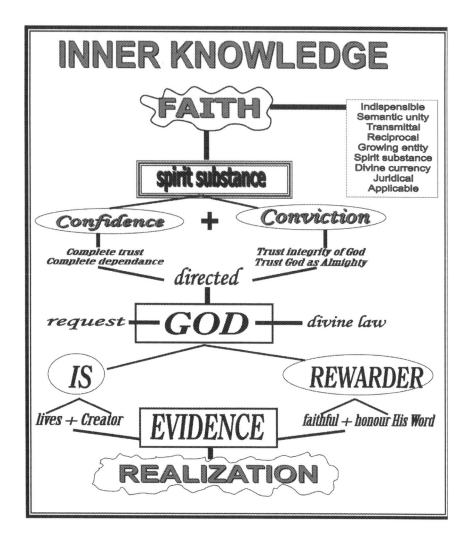

Thus you have an inner knowledge (spiritual) of confidence (spiritual) and conviction (spiritual) that you put in God:

- Who IS
- Who is a REWARDER.

The above is processed in your mind, will and emotions. Submit, believe and proclaim it with your mouth. (ROMANS 10:10 KJV) This serves as evidence that the visualized picture you expressed to God as a request, is something that cannot be seen, yet it is about to be

Dr. Adolf Jonker Ph.D

manufactured in the spirit by God. In His perfect and sovereign time, the realization of the request will manifest in the natural. Therefore, we can clearly see that the above faith is a creative force. Faith creates in the invisible realm that which you cannot see or experience, at that specific time, in the natural. It also defines the nature of faith! (Invisible creative force)

In synoptic terms, we now see that confidence and conviction in God and His existence, creative power and faithfulness equals what we call faith. Faith is the indispensible, transmitted, reciprocal currency with divine substance which is growing as you interact with God between the natural and supernatural realms.

Let's over-simplify it by saying that confidence and conviction in God equals faith. Without the defined confidence there can be no conviction. Therefore confidence in God (is—Rewarder), is of major importance. Please be reminded that confidence and conviction are spirit substance which is the make-up of faith, and therefore its trait is not mental by nature. To what am I referring? It is not a confidence that you have naturally in something. The title of the book is: 'Discover true faith!' True faith is divine confidence and conviction in God.

## PRACTICAL

In this section we will expand in a practical outline, on how to live by faith. Depending on where you are in your spiritual walk with God will determine the specific practical to follow and execute. I have compiled a guideline of a suggested strategy.

**FIRST PRINCIPLES:** If you have never studied and applied God's fundamental, First Principles, discussed in Part 2, then you need to ask God's forgiveness. The reason why you haven't done it previously is not important. What is important is that you acknowledge the wrong, but also the absolute lack of foundation it has caused in your relationship with God. Repentance means you turn around, thus, if you have never done it, you will have to spend time studying it and acquainting yourself with its truths. Then you will have to believe, embrace and finally apply it practically! Ask Holy Spirit to lead you in prayer as you also make a godly declaration that a solid foundation is laid in God.

**ASSUMPTIONS:** It is vital for you, on an ongoing basis, to ask God to remove, reveal, and replace erroneous assumptions you may have, their seed, the fruit and the reproduction. Cancel the above in Jesus' name and replace them with His truth.

**RELATIONSHIP:** The one thing that is undoubtedly of major importance is that you enter into a relationship with God, and not only have 'Sunday meeting times' with Him. Although I stress that this is of immeasurable importance, many folk come to me questioning this. I always ask them, and I ask you that same question now: "How will you define a relationship with God?" Do you have discussions with a friend, a mother, father, brother, sister and so forth? Everybody will concur. Will it be odd if you discuss something about your life with them and they answer 'yes' to every single question? Do you disagree with one another at times? Is your discussion always about the same thing, or does it vary depending on where you find yourself to be and what you experience? Do you make jokes? Do you have fun talk? Do you at times cry together? Or is whatever discussion you have serious and always the same? I do think that the answers are obvious. Look at the same scenario of discussing whatever with them, take their names out of the equation and replace them with God. If you do this, what do you have? A relationship! The only slight difference is that He is invisible to the naked eye. However, the biggest difference, I guarantee you, is that He is by far the better option and person with whom to have a relationship. This is basic, and the essence is indescribable. (2 COR. 13:13 KJV)

Dr. Adolf Jonker Ph.D

**EVALUATE YOUR FAITH:** Discuss your current state of faith with the Lord and ask Him to evaluate, teach and transform you. You do not want to be like somebody else, because you are special and unique as you are! Your main obligation is not to copycat others but to be true and be yourself! The Bible says that 'faith comes by hearing and that hearing comes by the Word of God.' (ROMANS 10:17 KJV) I am aware of the fact that there are many who promote listening to sermons. Let me unambiguously state my opinion. There is always a danger for anybody to just listen to somebody else's sermon. It might be that the person you are listening to has an interpretation of the Word of God, but some of what is preached is done out of humanistic presumptions. I want to advise you to rather listen to the Word of God only, in the beginning. First see to it that you leave no stone unturned in first and foremost establishing the Word of God in your life. The Word has the inbuilt ability and capacity to interpret itself to you through Holy Spirit. Secondly, if you are young in the Lord and you listen to the Word, do not form your own opinions based on what you have learnt culturally or doctrinally, but allow the Word of God to just be the Word in you. Allow God to feed you first, and trust Holy Spirit to teach you all truth in His time. You have eternity ahead of you.

**YOU NEED TO COMMIT TO A LOCAL CHURCH:** Pray and ask the Lord to lead you as to where you should worship. It is of paramount importance to pray, ask, and believe, that where you join is where God places you, and not where you fancy. Remember you are the 'church'! The truth is that when you commit to join a local church, you do not per se join the 'church'. You became a member of the global church the exact day and hour you were born again! Your commitment in this is simply becoming a partner of a local worship community of believers. They will call themselves by a specific name for example: River of Life Church. You become part of the vision and your involvement is to contribute and add value to corporate worship and gatherings of the saints in the establishing of the vision God gave them. You do this by making yourself, your time and your service unto God, available to them. Your commitment to a local church is evident in your submission to the leadership, representative of the office of God. You are not submitting to man, but to God! And in submitting to God you will honour those He placed to oversee you.

I do want to explain my previous statement on not listening to sermons but rather to establish the Word of God. God has placed you in a body, and He will surely allow specific people to impart to your life. What am I saying? You can listen to sermons and teachings or read books outside the Bible, but you have to be sure that whatever you 'eat spiritually' is what God allows you to have. Ask Him to show you clearly to whom you can listen and what books you can read, and when you do listen or read you pray and ask Holy Spirit to speak to you through this person, and declare that whatever might not be truth will not become part of you in any way! Whatever you listen to and it doesn't stir your spirit or faith, and motivate you to serve God in a better way; throw it away!

**PROCLAMATION:** I believe that proclamation is a hidden giant and a powerful tool that has been overlooked by so many children of God. I love to refer to proclamation as prophesying. Proverbs 18:13 KJV makes it very clear that humanity shall live by the fruit of their lips. Let's say that whatever leaves your mouth will return a harvest. Faith, in one of its execution forms, is proclaiming and prophesying God's Word into your life, your situation, your request, your family, your local church, your vision . . . and the list continues. Prophesy the Word of God over your life, and this very act will transform your entire life.

Many people are familiar with prophesying the Word of God and will also tell you that they are doing it. However, when you ask them when last they have prophesied, and how regularly, the answers will vary from "Ahhh, I can't really remember. Maybe a month ago?" However the general answer would be that they last prophesied God's Word into their situation a year ago, or even ten years ago, when their child was born. No, no, no! This is exactly what is meant by 'hit and run' kind of prophesying. Can a person then expect to see any other result? 'Hit and run' prophecies will have inconsistent and insufficient results and surely not the fullness of what you should be receiving. We need to prophesy daily: day and night! (1 THESS 3:5 KJV) This speaks of non-stop; every new morning is another 'TODAY'. Don't you ever stop!

Make yourself little cards and put them up everywhere in your home, car, office or place where you study. Place them there where you are spending most of your time during the day. The cards are proclamations. Some of the examples of my proclamations cards are:

> Never, never, never give up!
> I will think, act, walk and live by faith!
> God is my only source and provider!

You know who you are and what you want and need to establish in your life. Do the same as I have done. There are times where I will write letters about what I trust for, from God. I write the letter, but interweave His Word with my request. What is the purpose, you might wonder? Every single time that I speak out God's Word and hear it, my faith rises. Why? Because faith comes by hearing, and as you hear your faith grows and God is pleased.

This is most important! Millions of Christians will find this childish, too silly, too charismatic, or even too much of an effort. Many are baptized in complacency. Some complain about time; during the week they work, weekends they socialize, and for many who participate in sports for example cycling can only do it on a Sunday. If you go to them and have a closer look at their lives you will see that they do not experience or live in the abundance of God. Their complaint is: "Where are you God when I need You?" Why is this you may ask? Simply because we want a microwave solution where we tell God once what we want, then wait on Him to produce it as soon as possible. And if we had it our way it should already have happened yesterday. Surprise, surprise! He is supreme and sovereign in every way. Go to people who do the above, and who prophesy daily and analyze their lives. They are faith people, excelling in all they do, leaders of God par excellence!

My grandson cannot speak yet. Every Sunday, before we go to church, I lay my hands on him and prophesy over him. I am telling you the truth in God; after every single sentence he nods his head and says 'Yeah!' Let us rather become like children again and take the Kingdom of God violently. <sup>(MATT. 11:12KJV)</sup>

**TITHE AND OFFER:** Friends, I have observed throughout my life, that people who tithe and offer at their local churches, where God places them are faith people. Please let go of all ideas that you 'pay' your tithe and offering! And you certainly do not pay your church. Whatever you give, you give unto God. Stealing from God, through unbelief and erroneous doctrines, pathetic sermons, and human assumptions, will surely shoot you in the foot. If you resist this truth it will ALWAYS remain a stumbling block in your walk with God. Remember that it is not that God needs or wants your money. This blessing test to give ungrudgingly is for you. Through your giving you express your commitment, worship and faith in God. You are the sole benefactor! Give, and you shall receive and be blessed in Jesus name. If you do not give, you curse yourself; if your ancestors did not give to God, then you have to deal with a generational curse. Break all curses. Follow my guidelines. If you need someone to help you pray, then let them pray with you. Be careful never to place too much focus on the devil, the wrong, the sin, or the curse because the blessings of Jesus will run away as quickly as possible and in the end you will only harm yourself even more. If those who help you do likewise and overemphasize the demonic, politely thank them, and end your involvement with them. Learn to discern curses, and only do it in Jesus by Holy Spirit, then your success is guaranteed. 'Map' yourself prayerfully and accordingly. Resist the devil and do not ever, ever be content with his demonic devices and diabolic interference.

**NEGATIVITY:** This is nothing but a monstrous killer and destroyer of life in itself. Faith and negativity are two irreconcilable, incompatible concepts. Negativity must be avoided at all times and at all costs. During your time of faith in trusting God to accomplish something for you, many factors are inclined to oppose you negatively in all your faith endeavours. These factors relate to circumstances and situations that physically appear to oppose the outcome of your faith. During this time, remember to be extremely careful with your words. I am talking about words of people around you: family, friends and others. When Jesus was crucified it appeared to His disciples that everything, all previous prophecies and proclamations have been nullified, erased and were over and done with. However, in their apparent despair and loss of vision, Jesus was in the process of attaining the greatest victory in all of history. When you look at God to still answer you, everything will appear as if you walk through the valley of the shadow of death. (PSALM 23 KJV) Remember, it is only a shadow and temporary of nature. Do not allow words and curses of people and negative situations to alter your walk of faith in any way.

**MIND:** Stand firm! In the midst of whatever apparent opposing situation, stand on God's Word. God's Word has more inbuilt power than any resistance life can ever think to concoct. You have all the power in you to overcome whatever opposition. Fix your eyes on Him, He can and will change it all for you. No matter what amount of time it takes, or whatever effort is needed, He can! You, on the other hand, can't.

Stick to your confidence and conviction in God. Visualise the outcome of your request already materialized. Perfect the above as concrete, and a done deal in your mind. Rebuke and bind all opposing matters and declare it as naught and void. Fix your eyes on Jesus, and not the physical day-to-day occurrences. Be reminded that God specializes in accomplishing the impossible. The above is comparable to you possessing your 'Promised Land' in your mind. Make it your own. Embrace it, and never let go of it.

**WORD:** Human language can never express the importance of God's Word, because it exceeds our human comprehension. Understand firstly, that the Bible is not a scientific concept or instructional manual. Its purpose is not to enhance your intellectual knowledge, but to enable you to apply it by faith and act it out. It is a manual and constitution for divine life in God. Faith without the Word of God is mental, pragmatic, soulish or demonic. Do not even argue. The Word of God without the application of faith is a meaningless concept, and no different from reading any type of magazine or newspaper. Neither is the Bible a textbook that should be used as students do at school or university. God's Word is spirit based and has revelation powers. The Word of God applied by faith is a creative, transformational power beyond human definition. If you have a sporadic 'now and then' look at the Word, it cannot be efficacious. It compares equally with physical food which is a daily necessity.

Your success in life will be measured by your own study and application of the Word of God by faith. The above is expressive of your commitment and dedication to God, and displays your seriousness in order to effectuate the outcome of your life. Therefore, by acting on the Word, you will modify your own metamorphosis.

**HONOUR GOD:** Nothing that I have mentioned up to now will take place, or be effective unless your make-up as Christian embraces the above phenomenon. Honour God! To honour God is to celebrate the sum total of God by decorating Him with accolades of respect. During your day, you are involved in a variety of happenings; you eat, you work and you do all kinds of things. The importance is to honour God in everything you do. Modify your life in such a manner that you are constantly aware

Dr. Adolf Jonker Ph.D

of God. In whatever you think, feel, touch, do and experience, honour Him. The sum total of who you are will perpetually honour the sum total of who He is.

I prophesy over you that you will become a powerful faith warrior in God! God will immerse you in unwavering, unstoppable, all-powerful, overcoming and enduring faith for all eternity. Your life will be translated into someone being associated with the five virgins. You will be a Christian who functions daily in true godly faith, who will impact the lives of whomever you touch, and come into contact with. Your influence in His kingdom, as His disciple, will bear eternal value. I bless you spirit, soul and body in Jesus name!

# FAITH WORKS LIKE THIS

## PROCESS

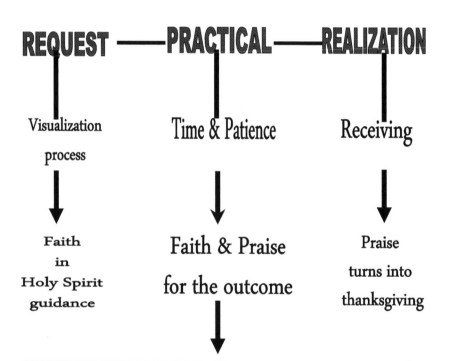

| REQUEST | PRACTICAL | REALIZATION |
|---|---|---|
| Visualization process | Time & Patience | Receiving |
| Faith in Holy Spirit guidance | Faith & Praise for the outcome | Praise turns into thanksgiving |

The time of faith in action: think, act, walk, live faith!

Dr. Adolf Jonker Ph.D

# bibliography

E-Sword 9.9.0, 2013, Rick Meyers. Strong's Concordance,

Wordweb 6, Copyright © 2013. WordWeb Software.

# glossary

| | |
|---|---|
| **Absolution** | *Complete forgiveness and remission of sins* |
| **Accolades** | *Tangible symbol signifying honour of approval or distinction* |
| **Acrimonious** | *Marked by strong resentment and cynicism (scepticism, pessimism)* |
| **Actualization** | *Marking real of giving the appearance of reality* |
| **Aesthetic** | *Concerning or characterized by an appreciation of beauty or good taste* |
| **Affinity** | *A natural attraction or feeling of kinship or an inherent resemblance between people or things* |
| **Albeit** | *Even though* |
| **Analogy** | *Drawing a comparison in order to show a similarity in some respect* |
| **Analogously** | *Similar or equivalent in some respects though otherwise dissimilar* |
| **Anglicize** | *Make English in appearance* |
| **Apocalyptic** | *Prophetic of devastation or ultimate doom* |
| **Augmented** | *Added to or made greater in amount or number or strength* |
| **Authentication** | *A mark on an article of trade to validate and indicate its origin and authenticity* |
| **Calamities** | *Events resulting in great loss and misfortune* |
| **Chastisement** | *Verbal punishment; A rebuke and correction for making a mistake* |

| | |
|---|---|
| **Cogitating** | *Use or exercise the mind or one's power of reason in order to make inferences, decisions, or arrive at a solution or judgments, consider carefully and deeply; reflect upon; turn over in one's mind* |
| **Constitution** | *The act of forming or establishing something such as the law determining the fundamental political principles of a government* |
| **Convolute** | *Practice sophistry (Practice sophistry; change the meaning of or be vague about in order to mislead or deceive); change the meaning of or be vague about in order to mislead or deceive* |
| **Cul-de-Sac** | *A passage with access only at one end* |
| **Cussing** | *Utter obscenities or profanities, cursing* |
| **Delineation** | *A graphic or vivid verbal description, drawing of the outlines of forms or objects,* |
| **Deluged** | *Filled beyond capacity; as with a liquid* |
| **Depravity** | *Moral perversion; impairment of virtue and moral principles* |
| **Despicable** | *Morally deserving severe rebuke or censure* |
| **Dispensation** | *An exemption from some rule or obligation* |
| **Divination** | *Successful conjecture by demonic powers and forces to have unusual insight, or good luck* |
| **Diabolic** | *Showing the cunning, ingenuity or wickedness typical of a devil, Extremely evil or cruel; expressive of cruelty or befitting hell* |
| **Effluent** | *The process of flowing outward* |
| **Equation** | *A state of being essentially equal or equivalent; equally balanced, The act of regarding as equal* |
| **Efficacy** | *Capacity or power to produce a desired effect* |

| | |
|---|---|
| Elucidate | *Make clear and (more) comprehensible, free from confusion, ambiguity* |
| Encapsulate | *Put in a short or concise form; reduce in volume* |
| Encompass | *Include in scope; include as part of something broader; have as one's sphere or territory* |
| Equivalence | *A state of being essentially equal or equivalent; equally balanced, Qualities that are comparable* |
| Exerting | *Put to use, have and exercise* |
| Exuberant | *Unrestrained, especially with regard to feelings such as joyously* |
| Familial | *Relating to or having the characteristics of a family, Occurring among members of a family usually by heredity* |
| Fastidious | *Giving careful attention to detail; hard to please; excessively concerned with cleanliness* |
| Gruesomely | *In a shockingly repellent; inspiring horrific manner* |
| Humdrum | *Not challenging; dull and lacking excitement, Tediously repetitious or lacking in variety* |
| Hideous | *Grossly offensive to decency or morality; causing horror, So extremely ugly as to be terrifying* |
| Illuminated | *Make lighter or brighter, Make free from confusion or ambiguity; make clear* |
| Inadequacies | *A lack of competence, Unsatisfactoriness (The quality of being inadequate or unsuitable) by virtue of being inadequate* |
| Inaugurating | *Be a precursor of, Commence officially, dedicate formally* |
| Inexplicable | *Incapable of being explained or accounted for* |

| | |
|---|---|
| **Incessant** | *Continuing forever, or for an indefinitely long time* |
| **Indicative** | *(usually followed by 'of') pointing out or revealing clearly* |
| **Indispensible** | *Absolutely necessary; vitally necessary, Unavoidable* |
| **Invoke** | *Summon into action or bring into existence; Cite as an authority; resort to; Request earnestly (something from somebody); ask for aid or protection* |
| **Irrefutable** | *Impossible to deny or disprove* |
| **Juridical** | *Relating to the administration of justice or the function of having to judge* |
| **Linguistic** | *Consisting of or related to language; relating to the scientific study of language* |
| **Longanimity** | *Good-natured tolerance of delay or incompetence* |
| **Misconstrue** | *Interpret in the wrong way* |
| **Modus operandi** | *An unvarying, lacking variety, habitual method or procedure* |
| **Mutation** | *genetics) any event that changes genetic structure; any alteration in the inherited nucleic acid sequence of the genotype of an organism* |
| **Myriad** | *Too numerous to be counted* |
| **Mystical** | *Having an import not apparent to the senses nor obvious to the intelligence; beyond ordinary understanding* |
| **Narcissism** | *An exceptional interest in and admiration for yourself* |
| **Oblivious** | *Failing to keep in mind; (followed by 'to' or 'of') lacking conscious awareness of* |

| | |
|---|---|
| **Parameters** | *Any factor that defines a system and determines (or limits) its performance* |
| **Permeate** | *Spread or diffuse through; Penetrate mutually or be interlocked* |
| **Perturbing** | *Causing distress, worry or anxiety* |
| **Pious** | *Having, showing or expressing reverence for a deity* |
| **Pivotal** | *Being of crucial importance* |
| **Polarised** | *Cause to concentrate about two conflicting or contrasting positions* |
| **Polarity** | *A relation between two opposite attributes or tendencies* |
| **Postulate** | *(logic) a proposition that is accepted as true in order to provide a basis for logical reasoning, demands, calls for, maintain or assert* |
| **Pragmatic** | *Guided by practical experience and observation rather than theory; Concerned with practical matters* |
| **Presumptuous** | *Excessively forward; Used of temperament or behaviour; lacking restraint or modesty* |
| **Prerequisites** | *Something that is required in advance* |
| **Prognosis** | *A prediction about how something (as the weather) will develop* |
| **Profound** | *Showing intellectual penetration or emotional depth; Far-reaching and thoroughgoing in effect especially on the nature of something* |
| **Proximity** | *The property of being close together; The region close around a person or thing* |

| | |
|---|---|
| **Ramifications** | *The act of branching out or dividing into branches; A development that complicates a situation* |
| **Reciprocal** | *Concerning each of two or more persons or things; especially given or done in return* |
| **Renunciation** | *Rejecting, disowning or disclaiming as invalid; The state of having rejected your religious beliefs for your political party or a cause (often in favour of opposing beliefs or causes)* |
| **Replicate** | *Bend or turn backward, Make, do or perform again, copy, duplicate* |
| **Rhetoric** | *Using language effectively to please or persuade* |
| **Salsa** | *A dance to Latin American style of music, influenced by jazz* |
| **Semantics** | *The study of the meaning of language: a word, phrase, sentence or text* |
| **Scenarios** | *Situation treated as an observable object* |
| **Statutory** | *Prescribed or authorized by or punishable under a statute* |
| **Sublime** | *Inspiring awe, Worthy of adoration or reverence, Of high moral or intellectual value; elevated in nature or style* |
| **Succumb** | *Consent reluctantly (not eager, unwilling) and be fatally overwhelmed* |
| **Suffice** | *Be sufficient; be adequate, either in quality or quantity* |
| **Synoptic** | *Presenting a summary or general view of a whole for example: Presenting or taking the same point of view; used especially with regard to the first three gospels of the New Testament* |

| | |
|---|---|
| **Theocratic** | *Relating to being governed by a deity (or by officials thought to be divinely guided)* |
| **Thwarted** | *Hinder or prevent (the efforts, plans, or desires) and disappointingly unsuccessful* |
| **Transcendent** | *Beyond and outside the ordinary range of human experience or understanding, exceeding or surpassing usual limits especially in excellence* |
| **Transference** | *the process whereby spirit emotions and other are passed on or displaced from one person to another* |
| **Transmittal** | *The act of sending a message; causing a message to be transmitted* |
| **Unambiguously** | *So as to be unique in specific manner* |
| **Vantage** | *The quality of having a superior or more favourable position, lace or situation affording some advantage (especially a comprehensive view or commanding perspective)* |
| **Vehement** | *Marked by extreme intensity of emotions or convictions; inclined to react violently; fervid, Characterized by great force or energy* |
| **Verdict** | *An opinion formed by judging something* |
| **Verification** | *Additional proof that something that was believed (some fact, hypothesis or theory) is correct* |

*River of Life Church (ROL) is the unveiling (foundation and transformation) first fruit of the vision corresponding to the New Jerusalem in Revelation. Jesus Anointed Ministries International (JAMI), is the seed of the vision, hence the apostolic arm portraying the 'sending' of all involved. The purpose of Revelation 22 Global church is to go, make and train disciples by being true Disciples of Jesus the Anointed One and not of doctrines, churches or ministries per se. Therefore Revelation 22 is the manifestation of the vision of God and the focus is not on a specific individual, group or church but those who are seeking and living to be part of the five wise virgins (set apart). This can then include any of these mentioned, and our ministry is to those God pre-ordained to be part of the vision and ministry He initiated.*

## RIVER OF LIFE CHURCH

- Vision: *To follow Jesus*
  *To know Jesus*
  *To become like Jesus and*
  *To give God all the glory*

- Purpose: *Building a spiritual lighthouse where God's River of Life will flow in extreme abundance*

## JESUS ANOINTED MINISTRIES INTERNATIONAL

- o Vision: *Building a spiritual house for God worldwide*
- o Purpose: *Equipping and preparing the Bride*

*Jesus Anointed Ministries International, is part of River of Life Church, Kroonstad, Free State, South Africa.*

# REVELATION 22 GLOBAL CHURCH

- o    Vision:    *Globally making disciples of Jesus by Holy Spirit*
- o    Purpose:    *Being the spiritual house of God, manifesting godly fruit*

## *Please visit or contact us on:*

Website: www.jami912.com    *Jesus Anointed Ministries International* Twitter: @jami912

 jamint33@gmail.com You can also find us on  and God Tube

P O Box 2425
Kroonstad
9500
RSA